FROM THEM TO US

'Inclusive education' has become a phrase with international currency shaping the content of conferences and national education policies around the world. But what does it mean? Is it about including a special group of disabled learners or students seen to have 'special needs' (them), or is it concerned with making educational institutions inclusive, responsive to the diversity of all their students (us)?

In this unique comparative study, the editors have brought together an international team of researchers from eight countries to develop case-studies which explore the processes of inclusion and exclusion within a school or group of schools set in its local and national context. The study includes classroom observation, the experience of the school day of students, and interviews with staff, students, parents and school governors. Through an innovative juxtaposition of the case-studies and commentaries on them, differences of perspective within and between countries are revealed and analysed.

The study arose from a dissatisfaction with previous research, which presents 'national perspectives' or seeks findings that have global significance. This book avoids such simplification and draws attention to the problems of translation of practice across cultures. The editors start from an assumption of diversity of perspective which, like the diversity of students within schools, can be viewed as problematic or as a resource to be recognised and celebrated.

Tony Booth is a Senior Lecturer in Education at the Open University. **Mel Ainscow** is Professor of Education at Manchester University. They have had a longstanding involvement in the development of theory, policy and practice concerning school improvement and inclusion in education, in the UK and internationally.

FROM THEM TO US

An international study of inclusion in education

Edited by Tony Booth and Mel Ainscow

London and New York

First published 1998
by Routledge
11 New Fetter Lane, London EC4P 4EE

Selection and editorial matter © 1998 Tony Booth and Mel Ainscow;
individual chapters © their authors

Typeset in Times by
M Rules
Printed and bound in Great Britain by
Creative Print and Design (Wales), Ebbw Vale

British Library Cataloguing in Publication Data
A catalogue record for this book is available from the British Library

Library of Congress Cataloguing in Publication Data
From them to us: an international study of inclusion in education /
edited by Tony Booth and Mel Ainscow.
p. cm.
Includes bibliographical references and index.
1. Inclusive education—Case-studies. 2. Inclusive education—Cross-cultural studies.
I. Booth, Tony. II. Ainscow, Mel.
LC1200.I53 1998   97-43154
371.9′046—dc21   CIP

ISBN 0–415–13979–1 (Pbk)
ISBN 0–415–18739–7 (Hbk)

CONTENTS

CONTRIBUTORS

Mel Ainscow, School of Education, University of Manchester, England.

Julie Allan, Department of Education, University of Stirling, Scotland.

Jeff Bailey, Faculty of Education, University of Western Sydney, Australia.

Keith Ballard, Department of Education, University of Otago, New Zealand.

Jim Bennet, Headteacher, St Colmcille's Boys National School, County Dublin, Ireland.

Tony Booth, School of Education, Open University, England.

Alan Dyson, Department of Education, University of Newcastle, England.

Hugh Gash, St. Patrick's College, Dublin, Ireland.

Trevor MacDonald, Department of Education, University of Otago, New Zealand.

Kari Nes Mordal, Department of Education, Hedmark College, Norway.

Mark O'Reilly, Department of Education, University College, Dublin.

Sip Jan Pijl, Groningen Institute for Educational Research, University of Groningen, The Netherlands.

Gerry J. Reezigt, Groningen Institute for Educational Research, University of Groningen, The Netherlands.

Marit Strømstad, Department of Education, Hedmark College, Norway.

Linda Ware, Department of Special Education, University of New Mexico, USA.

ACKNOWLEDGEMENTS

We would like to acknowledge the financial support for this study given by the Open University and the University of Cambridge. We are grateful, too, for the helpful editorial suggestions from Nandita Bardhanray on behalf of Routledge.

1

FROM THEM TO US:
SETTING UP THE STUDY

Introduction

This book documents and analyses the perspectives on inclusion and exclusion revealed by researchers in eight countries in their studies of a school set in its national and local context. In this chapter we provide a background to our concerns and describe the process of creating the individual studies and our analyses of them.

The study arose from a dissatisfaction with much of the existing comparative education research. International studies, which seek findings that have global significance, indulge in oversimplification of educational processes and practices, and ignore problems of interpretation and translation. Alternatively, studies may assume the existence of a single national perspective, constructing an official version of events rather than reporting the conflicts of interest and points of view that arise in all countries. In these ways important differences between and within countries are omitted from study and debate.

We intend that the book should enhance an interest in the shaping effect of national and local policies and cultural and linguistic histories on educational practice. It extends existing comparative reviews of inclusion by making their viewpoints explicit through the illustration of practice in all its messiness (such reviews include OECD 1995, O'Hanlon 1993 and 1995; Meijer, Pijl and Hegarty 1994; Pijl, Meijer and Hegarty 1997; Wade and Moore 1992, as well as the regular 'country briefings' in the *European Journal of Special Needs Education*). It goes beyond them, too, by challenging the way notions of inclusion, exclusion and 'inclusive education' are interpreted through the lens of traditional special education.

Our interest in inclusion and exclusion is part of a long-standing involvement in understanding and attempting to resolve the barriers to learning experienced by students. We link these concerns to a commitment to increase the participation of students in, and reduce their exclusion from mainstream schools. Both of us have been critical of any narrow conception of the field of 'special education', concerning ourselves with the development of schools

1

that are more responsive to the diversity of all learners rather than concentrating on a group of students categorised as having special needs or disabilities (e.g. Ainscow 1991 and 1995a; Booth 1983; Booth, Potts and Swann 1987). On this broader view, inclusion or exclusion are as much about participation and marginalisation in relation to race, class, gender, sexuality, poverty and unemployment as they are about traditional special education concerns with students categorised as low in attainment, disabled or deviant in behaviour. This book can be read as an exploration of the possibilities for redefining traditional special education around the notions of inclusion and exclusion, thereby providing a viable and productive area for further research.

The view that a concern with inclusion is primarily about the location of students assigned to a special education category can lead to the presentation of misleading statistics that imply that educational difficulties are to do with the numbers and placement of disabled students or others seen to have difficulties in learning (e.g. Csapo 1986 and 1987; Mittler 1993; Okyere 1994; Wiesinger 1986). This in turn leads to an assumption that solutions must focus on prevention, cure, or steps to make these students fit into an unreconstructed educational normality. Such statistics distract our attention from the ways in which attitudes, policies and institutions exclude or marginalise groups of children and young people (Stubbs 1995).

We do not attempt to identify 'good practice' and would stress the limitations of such a quest, particularly in a comparative study. Readers may use this book as a source of principles and practices to encourage and avoid but neither the researchers nor their schools were selected with the development of teaching and learning practice principally in mind. In any case, good practice is in the eye of the beholder. Even if we make explicit the world view in which our definition of good practice resides, the quest to represent it may encourage a distortion of reality, an avoidance of reports of the messiness and inconsistencies of real schools and real lives, and the swirling contradictions of particular cultures and minds. However, we regard the task of uncovering the nature of perspectives and the way they are culturally and politically constrained as an essential step in learning from the practice of others.

Our perspective and the perspectives of others

Our view of inclusion, then, which we repeat in chapter 16, the English case-study, involves the processes of increasing the participation of students in, and reducing their exclusion from, mainstream curricula, cultures and communities. We link the notions of inclusion and exclusion together because the process of increasing the participation of students entails the reduction of pressures to exclusion. Further, the link encourages us to look at the various sources and types of pressure acting on different groups of students. We are also aware of a 'comedy' played out in some schools whereby some students, previously excluded and in special schools, are welcomed in through the front door while others are ushered out at the back. Others may have 'a revolving door' that allows students to come into a school with one label, such as 'learning difficulty', only to be relabelled and excluded with another such as 'emotional and behavioural difficulty'.

A concern with overcoming barriers to the participation of all in education is captured, for some, by the notion of 'inclusive education'. This term has acquired increasing international currency, which poses the danger that wishful thinking about the way it is used or applied may distract people from exploring the realities of practice. As we will discuss in detail in the study that we wrote with Alan Dyson, in England the concept of 'inclusive education' – that is, increasing the participation of all students in a neighbourhood in their local school – cannot sensibly be separated from ideas of community 'comprehensive' education.

The idea of inclusive education was given impetus by two conferences set up under the auspices of the United Nations. The first of these, held in Jomtien, Thailand in 1990, promoted the idea of 'education for all'; this was followed in 1994 by a UNESCO conference in Salamanca, Spain, which led to a Statement that is being used in many countries to review their education policies. The Salamanca Statement proposes that the development of schools with an 'inclusive' orientation is the most effective means of improving the efficiency and ultimately the cost-effectiveness of the entire education system.

However, there is a long way to go if the rhetoric of 'education for all' is to be made real. In poor countries, millions of children are still denied their right to basic education. Considerable concern has also been expressed about the quality of teaching offered to children in some of these countries (Lockheed and Levin 1993). Meanwhile, in richer nations, where sufficient school places are usually available, the participation of many students may be limited by the way schools and classrooms are organised.

The *International Journal of Inclusive Education*, established in 1997, encourages the same broad conception of 'inclusive education' as ourselves, involving an examination of all the processes of inclusion and exclusion in education. However, some people continue to think of 'inclusive education' as a new name for 'special education' and limit their concern to students who are categorised as having 'special educational needs' because they are identified as low in attainment, deviant in behaviour or as disabled.

Most contributors to this book have a professional background in 'special education' but they differ considerably in the extent to which they derive their notions of inclusion and exclusion in a traditional way from this field. The book reflects the difficulties of redefining a field from within, the professional interests that stand in the way, and hence, our own ambivalence about making substantial realignments. Perhaps we should see this as 'a coming of age' book. In such a project a transition to adulthood requires us to define concepts and pursue studies according to their academic fertility rather than their institutional kinship.

It might seem that the assumptions we brought to the study would have created a circular process; that we would have communicated them to other researchers and that the case-studies produced would be neat reflections of our views. As we describe below, we made considerable efforts to avoid such circularity, stressing that we wanted to understand the perspectives of others. As will become apparent, far from managing to draw views together, the perspectives of research teams differed far more than we had anticipated.

Our title for the book, *From Them to Us*, alludes to some of the contrasts in perspective between and within chapters. Most clearly, it is related to the extent to which the chapters concentrate on a group of students identified as 'abnormal' or 'deviant': as 'them'. It is also linked in a slightly less transparent way to the significance we give to recognising and valuing difference, not as a contrast to a normal, right way of being and thinking but as a resource for our learning. 'From them to us', therefore, indicates the careful unravelling of the gifts we create for ourselves when we acknowledge the separateness of other people and other worlds. It is about an approach to comparative research that retains this exchange.

Approaching comparative study

Even if we did not step outside the borders of our own country, we already possess extensive knowledge of the existence of differences in perspective on issues of inclusion and exclusion between and within schools, between parents and professionals, between disabled people and the creators of legislation about disability, amongst disabled people themselves, within and between a variety of cultural groups and amongst academics and researchers (for example, in England see Armstrong 1995; Armstrong and Galloway 1992; Booth 1995; Corbett 1996; Debenham and Trotter 1992; Goody 1992; Morris 1992; Oliver 1990; Rieser and Mason 1990). This knowledge of differences in view should ensure that we avoid two pitfalls of comparative research: the idea that there is a single national perspective on inclusion or exclusion, and the notion that practice can be generalised across countries without attention to local contexts and meanings.

Yet some writers present reports of their own or other countries as if they were monocultures (e.g. Mazurek and Winzer 1994; Mittler *et al.* 1993). What is called a national perspective is often an official view. In the case of the UK this can be particularly problematic, given the divergence of the education systems and their basis in legislation of Scotland, Northern Ireland and England and Wales (see, for example, Allan 1994; Booth 1996). We hope that this book will contribute to an end to attempts to treat countries as having a uniform approach.

The tendency to present single national perspectives is often matched by a failure to describe the way practice is to be understood in its local and national context (e.g. Ward 1993; Alban-Metcalfe 1996). This lack is part of a positivistic view of social science in which research in one country can be amalgamated and summed with that of another. Given the volume of research published in the USA this may have the effect of treating all people in the world as if the largest part of their make-up is American. The problem is compounded by differences of meaning of concepts, which is of particular significance in relation to categories of inability and disability. Yet, for example, in the special issue of the *European Journal of Special Needs Education* the review of European research on 'integration' is conducted as if all countries share the use of a category system used in England and Wales (Evans 1993).

All of this is in marked contrast to studies where there is a deliberate attempt to draw out nuances of the meaning of practice (e.g. Armstrong 1995). An important contribution here is provided by the work of Susan Peters (1993 and 1995). Speaking as both a disabled person and a professional, she argues that concepts such as disability and education are culturally and context bound. Similarly, Miles and Miles (1993) draw on their experiences in Pakistan to outline how concepts such as childhood differ substantially between cultures, a view reinforced by Stubbs (1995) who reports accounts that indicate 'childhood' does not exist under Lesotho law. Rather, the population is divided into 'majors and minors', the latter being unmarried males and females who are not heads of families. As a result, in Lesothan primary schools pupils may be in their late teens or even early twenties, having spent their younger years herding animals.

Such careful analyses of differences in perspective, context and meaning enhance rather than reduce the contribution that an examination of unfamiliar contexts can make to local practice, though it invalidates any attempt at simple imitation (Fuller and Clarke 1994). The power of comparison for the development of practice involves using the stimulus of more exotic environments to reconsider thinking and practice in familiar settings (Delamont 1992). It is about making what is strange familiar and what is familiar strange, like seeing your own town in a new light when showing a visitor around. Features that are normally ignored become clearer, possibilities that have been overlooked are reconsidered, and things that have been taken for granted are subject to new scrutiny.

If written accounts of other countries provide sufficient information to make practice transparent they can present some of the opportunities afforded to travellers. But being there is no guarantee of learning. Without an understanding of the rules of particular educational, cultural and political systems it is very difficult to make sense of what is in front of one's eyes. Visiting classrooms can be a disappointing experience in the most favourable circumstances since most of what is interesting about what is going on is locked away in the heads of teachers and students.

Classroom encounters

Some brief observations may help to make clearer some of the dilemmas of comparative research. First of all, picture a primary school classroom in Inner Mongolia, China. There are approximately seventy-five children, sitting in rows of desks packed into a long, rather bleak room. The teacher stands at one end of the room on a narrow stage in front of a blackboard. In the back row of the classroom there are some students who look older than the rest. These turn out to be children who started school late, or are repeating a failed grade. Lessons are forty minutes long and although each subject is taught by a different teacher, there is a common pattern: the teacher controls the lesson, talking or reading, and frequently questioning the students to stimulate choral or individual responses from the class. Throughout the lesson the pace is fast and the engagement of students seems intense. Afterwards, the teacher explains how she tries to help those who experience difficulties by directing many more questions to them and by encouraging their classmates to go over the lesson content with them during the break-times.

What does a foreign observer make of such an experience? Does it suggest patterns of practice that might be relevant to teachers in their country? In England for example, despite much smaller class sizes, it is not uncommon to encounter students in classes whose participation is marginal, to say the least. Why are these Chinese students so quiet and obedient through a day of lessons that to an outsider can seem repetitive? It would be easy to jump to simple conclusions that might appear to offer strategies that could be exported. Yet many influences help to shape the events observed in the classroom. We are told that teachers are held in high esteem in Chinese society but that this is changing as economic reforms disrupt status patterns (Bond 1991). There is great pressure for success at school in families. These and other factors that require a detailed knowledge of local circumstances need to be examined before the practice can be understood or conclusions drawn.

A second example comes from Ghana, West Africa. In a primary school in a rural district, class sizes are much more manageable than those observed in the Chinese school. Typically there are fifty or so children in each class. On the other hand the physical resources are noticeably poorer. Many of the children arrive in the morning carrying a stool on their heads. It seems that this is the equivalent, in richer countries, of bringing a pen and a ruler from home. Each evening the stools are returned home for domestic use, or in some cases there may be a reluctance to leave them at school where they might be stolen, since the classrooms have few walls. One of the teachers explains that the biggest problem is the lack of textbooks. For most lessons he only has one copy of the book and frequently copies text onto the black-board. There are a number of disabled students present in classes. The headteacher explains that he has responsibility to admit all children in the district, asking 'where else would they go?'.

What sets of cultural or personal beliefs shape the views of the head-teacher in the school in Ghana? This inclusion, taken for granted, challenges the linking of participation to demands for resources, which is a feature of many richer countries as indicated in chapters 4, 6, 7, and 8. The idea that poorer nations may have a value system which sees exclusion as unnatural is discussed by Sue Stubbs (1995) in relation to Lesotho. Writing about the development of special education elsewhere in Africa, Kisanji (1993) discusses the way exclusion is influenced by cultural perceptions of disability, sometimes seen to be the result of witchcraft, curses, punishment from God or the anger of ancestral spirits. Sometimes children are hidden away by the family to avoid feelings of shame. The approach to inclusion of any group may be affected by economic circumstances but is always affected by particular personal and cultural beliefs.

A third example is from a primary school in Austria. Class sizes are smaller and resources luxurious by most standards. As in a number of other countries, increasing attention has been paid to including categorised groups of students in the mainstream (UNESCO 1995). As a result of legislation, the total number of non-categorised students in classes that include such students is limited to twenty and the numbers of categorised students to four. A wide range of support staff is made available.

The school in question is in a small town in the eastern part of the country. There is thick snow outside and the children wear slippers. There are seventeen children sitting mainly in pairs at tables, informally arranged, some facing the front, others the centre of the room. One boy sits alone at a desk towards the rear of the room. The lesson is about Christmas and all the children have a worksheet, prepared on a computer by the class teacher. After a short presentation by the teacher, the children carry out the tasks on the worksheet, chatting as they work.

The boy at the back of the room is being spoken to slowly and with simplified language by another teacher. She is there to provide support for two students, one of whom is absent. She has her own desk at the rear of the room. She has designed a separate, less demanding, worksheet for this student on the same topic as the other students and in giving him support places herself physically between this student and the rest of the class. A comparable practice is mentioned in several of the studies in this book. What is it that has led schools in several countries to resolve the challenge of inclusion by the relative isolation of students within mainstream classrooms? Is it seen as an apparently technical problem that requires a technical solution unrelated to pedagogical principles or explicit values? Does this apparently similar practice carry the same significance in different countries?

In this book we have placed issues of cultural and political context in the foreground, and in doing so hope to reshape the meaning of 'a national perspective'. The constraints on inclusion and exclusion that particular cultures and national policies provide always permit a plurality of perspectives, including challenges to an official view.

Developing the study: from conception to maturity

The study started with the recruitment of teams of up to three researchers, in each of eight countries, to conduct a study of one school in its local and national context. The membership of the teams reflected a continuation of the project that had started with a group of people meeting to discuss a common interest in inclusion and resulted in the book *Towards Inclusive Schools?* (Clark *et al.* 1995), although some people dropped out and new people and two new countries were added. The final list of countries comprises five countries of Western Europe – Norway, Holland, England, Ireland and Scotland – the USA, New Zealand and Australia. We are aware that different groups of countries might have contributed to a more fertile comparison of perspectives and we are concerned that our future comparative work should reflect more of the issues affecting poorer countries and our experience of them, as well as a greater political diversity.

We ended up with two teams of three, three teams of two and three studies conducted by a single researcher. The presence of teams enabled us to look at whether studies revealed differences of perspective between researchers within a single team.

The preliminary study

Each team was asked to prepare an initial study of 4,000 words for presentation at an extended seminar for representatives from each project, which would be revised in the light of detailed discussion. They were requested to prepare slides and other illustrative material that could be used during the seminar to make the school, the experience of students and the educational system, accessible to other participants.

We sent a set of guidelines intended to give the study coherence without imposing our perspective on everyone. The guidelines stated:

> The precise content of the case studies will depend on the interests of the researchers and the way inclusion is defined by them. However we feel that a productive basis for comparison may be best achieved if some key assumptions are shared and common information is obtained.
>
> We hope that the processes of inclusion and exclusion will be linked and explored, and that this will be a distinctive theoretical feature of this collection of studies. We assume that there are differences of perspective on inclusion and exclusion between researchers

in different countries, within a group of researchers in any one country and particularly between the members of a school community: students, parents, teachers, other school workers and bodies with a management function at the school. The study should explore the extent to which this is so.

Researchers were asked to select a primary or secondary school that 'in the eyes of the researchers . . . can be used to reflect productively on the processes of inclusion' and to discuss the reasons for its selection:

> We are not asking that the school should be chosen to reflect *good practice*. The reasons for selection will be made explicit and this will begin with the examination of the processes and practices of inclusion and exclusion to be analysed through this study.

Figure 1.1 displays the information we suggested might be gathered about the school. We encouraged researchers to look at the categorisation of students and the difficulties in learning they experience within an exploration of the participation of all students. In retrospect we can see that the range of issues mentioned may have contributed to a mindset that a concentration on categorised students was expected. There is no mention for example of the interaction between inclusion, participation and gender, race and class. However, we have to assume that other researchers are reflecting accurately aspects of their perspectives through their work, even though these may have been influenced by us, just as their approaches could lead us to challenge our own.

The final point on our list is deceptive. As we have indicated, the portrayal of the national and local background to the practices of inclusion and exclusion is a critical feature of this study. It is also an extensive task that can take up considerable time and space. We hoped that our seminar would help us to consider the question: 'what do we need to know about the local and national context in order to comprehend the processes of inclusion and exclusion in a single school?' Or to put it round the other way: 'what do we fail to understand about the processes of inclusion and exclusion at a particular school if we fail to set them in context?' In reading about schools in our own country we may even more frequently take the context for granted than we do in looking at education elsewhere. We argue that such practice also muddles our understanding of teaching and learning.

Researchers were free to pursue their study according to the methods that they found most appropriate to answer the questions which we were addressing. Their accounts were to include 'classroom observation, and interviews with staff, students, parents and others involved in the school'. It was suggested that students or groups of students might be shadowed in order to illuminate differing experiences of the school day. These requests pushed some researchers, who were more used to employing quantitative methods, towards more interviewing and description of observation than was their practice. Nevertheless, considerable methodological diversity remained, as will be seen

Figure 1.1 Suggested information about the school

School and community
- Number of students, age
- Selection criteria – who is included in, and excluded from the school, for example, in terms of attainment, behaviour and disability?
- What geographical area is covered by the school?
- How would the area and the communities of the school be characterised?
- What is the relationship between the school and its communities and how is this illustrated by formal and informal relationships with parents and others?

Categorisation policies and practices
- How are students grouped within the school by attainment within and between classes and what effect is this perceived to have?
- To what extent are some students more highly valued than others and how is this demonstrated?

Learning development and support policies
- What policies are in place to minimise the difficulties experienced by students or to support students who experience difficulties in learning or who have disabilities or are disaffected?
- How are students who experience difficulties identified?
- How are funds distributed to support differences in attainment or difficulties experienced by students?

Classroom practices
- How do teaching approaches adapt to differences between learners?

Participation
- What differences in academic participation are perceived in the school?
- What opportunities are there for social participation within the school and how does this differ between students?

Differences of perspective
- What differences of view about inclusion and exclusion are revealed by staff, students, parents and others involved in the school and between the researchers of the case-study?

Local and national contexts
- What local and national policies affect inclusion and exclusion within the school?

from the following chapters. It was up to each team to determine how far teachers and others would become collaborators in the production of the case-studies, and this itself was seen as a valuable area for later discussions.

The preliminary studies, at varying stages of completeness, were circulated to the other researchers prior to the seminar. At the seminar each group had a two-hour session in which to present their text and for others to seek clarification on the perspectives of the authors and request the further information needed about the school, local and national practices, policies and cultures to make the study comprehensible to those from other countries. In presenting their case-studies, researchers were asked to assume that other participants knew nothing about the education system and cultural circumstances of their country.

We assumed that a text had been read by each participant prior to the session in which it was presented. In a repeat of the process we would produce a more detailed rubric for reading the texts and build in critical reading time into the seminar. It is almost inevitable that some busy people will not have done all the careful reading that is required before a seminar starts and if they feel pressure to make a contribution then this may well be tangential to the text being examined.

Usually, one of us chaired the session while the other kept notes of the discussion that took place and summarised the key ideas at the end of the session. English was used as the medium of discussion and writing. We all made efforts to make ourselves understood across the language barriers. We were aware that more might be made in the future of the strength of having a linguistically diverse community and the exploration of different nuances of concepts that this might permit. However, the more we concentrated on making differences of perspective explicit, the more strongly differences appeared. Communication even between those most fluent in English often did not proceed smoothly.

The activity of interrogating text, drawing out the views of others, and absorbing education systems that were different from one's own, provoked impatience in some, keen to argue for their own view. We resisted such attempts in order to give the work of each presenter or group of presenters its fair share of attention and to avoid the repetition of positions that can be a feature of discussions of presentations on a similar theme. Sometimes we were conscious of a power struggle going on within the room about which views should predominate as we attempted to guide discussion back to the conceptualisations used within the paper under consideration. There was some wish to discuss the conclusions of the project at the end of the three days, whereas we saw the seminar as an intermediate stage in the development of the project and did not wish to congeal perspectives prematurely, hoping that they would be refined or transformed with the next draft of the case-studies. It should be said that a majority recognised and supported the idea that the final analysis of perspectives was our task.

The task of setting a school in its context is potentially vast for anyone. The initial word-limit was breached by several offerings, including our own. We were interested in the whole school and all students. Further, our attempt to retain the differences of voice and view between the three people working on the case-study in England created additional problems of length as well as continuity in writing. Studies that attempted to provide detailed stories about policies, schools, lessons or students, or the views of teachers and students rapidly increased in length. We came to see restrictions in length as exerting a restriction on the breadth of field of study pushing towards specialisation of content that, in the context of this study, would lead to concentration on particular categorised students.

At the end of the three days we had agreed how the case-studies should be developed in the light of discussions that had taken place. In several instances we asked for more detail of classroom practice, and in some we felt it was important that more reference to national policies should be added. The misunderstandings and attempts at clarification in each session were to be used to revise the study subsequently; in most cases this would require the gathering of further information. We hoped that the revisions would create greater coherence of issues without narrowing the development and explication of perspectives.

Participants were asked to comment on the seminar. Feedback was generally very positive though there was a reference to the Draconian chairing of one of us, zealously determined to keep to the task. People referred to how engaging with the unfamiliar had opened up opportunities for learning. One participant described how her 'cage was rattled' and she 'loved it'. Feelings of exhaustion as a result of the intensity of the interactions were also expressed, while there was frustration about things that had been left unsaid and concern that certain voices, unrepresented amongst the researchers, had not been heard.

Revising and editing

The case-studies went through several more stages. When revisions were received authors were sent very detailed comments on their chapters asking for clarification, pointing out omissions, asking about apparent inconsistencies of argument. By this stage clarity and structure were more important determinants of our editorial comments than the original guidelines and we accepted that there was a considerable degree of departure from them in some cases.

When this process was completed the case-studies were subjected to a careful and thorough re-edit, conducted according to the principles of further increasing clarity and accessibility of language, structure and presentation, while retaining the integrity of the voice, views, concepts and categories of the author or authors. We paid particular attention to the chapters from Norway and the Netherlands, not written in a first language, and tried carefully to increase readability without changing sense. The chapters ended up with a common format, with the national context towards the start of each chapter. Having completed the study we should report that even if we had vigorously tried to impose our view on the participants we would have failed. Our guidelines were resisted or partially ignored by several contributors and even the linking of inclusion and exclusion is only revealed in passing in some chapters. Individual perspectives proved remarkably resilient, even in those who vigorously challenge the significance of differences of view. This appeared to support our position that they reflect deeply-held beliefs and cherished identities.

Exploring perspectives

We have chosen to use the word 'perspective' to indicate the differences in ways of viewing inclusion and exclusion between and within countries, and the value systems that are connected to them. However, it is not possible to give 'perspective' a simple and precise definition. We include in the term the ideas of 'medical' and 'social' models, organisational and individual paradigms, professional and parental interests and ideologies. We share the choice of 'perspective' and our tentativeness about defining it with the report of Clark *et al.* on their study of innovative practice about what they call 'special needs' in schools:

> We found ourselves confronted by sets of views, practices and structures which had a degree of commonality. Each of these sets or constellations of views we regarded as constituting a 'perspective' on special needs. The term 'perspective' was not intended to convey a coherent and fully articulated set of beliefs and practices so much as broad and only partially articulated stances towards special needs within which some coherence could be inferred.
>
> Clark et al. 1995, pp. 82–83

Clark *et al.* explored the variations in 'dominant' and 'subordinate' perspective within schools and suggested that they were characterised by 'internal conflicts and contradictions' (p. 85). A contradiction, they argued, was illustrated by the expression by a headteacher that he valued all students equally alongside the 're-introduction of ability grouping and the re-establishment of a conventional special needs coordinator's post'. While it is a common human attribute to entertain sincerely and to espouse contradictory beliefs, simultaneously or successively, it is also common to mislead others and oneself about one's value system.

Perspectives, like minds, are complex. A hierarchy of dominant and subordinate perspectives may exist within one person, interwoven with aspects of personal identity that exert a control over action, depending on circumstance. A core set of beliefs may be surrounded with layers of rhetoric, perhaps in response to the group pressures of a symposium or the latest set of official guidelines. This may explain in part the observation of Roger Slee that 'new policy language is easily learned and accommodated, but it is more problematic for this to penetrate the fine-grain realities of organisation, curriculum and pedagogy' (Slee 1995, p. 31). This may not only be because the implications are poorly understood, but because, although grasped very well, they clash with more fundamental beliefs and values.

Further, perspectives are not neatly bounded nor are they found with a similar degree of integration or disintegration in different people. Understanding the way someone views their educational practice and the links they make with moral, spiritual and political beliefs is a task that is never definitively finished. It can be fleshed out in greater detail with a deepening knowledge of another person. Thus, apparently similar perspectives may be seen to diverge, and apparently different perspectives converge over time, with greater probing and observation.

As we illustrate in this book, the texts of researchers can be analysed to reveal the perspectives they contain in precisely the same way as interviews with teachers, students or parents. It is always possible to analyse the language, assertions and assumptions within texts, to reveal points of view.

When we started the study we expected there to be more agreement about perspectives than turned out to be the case. We had expected, for example, that given the amount of debate of the issues, all researchers would see inclusion and exclusion primarily as complex *processes* involving subtle, context dependent, variations of participation rather than as *states* of being, as implied in categorising schools as 'inclusive' or 'not inclusive', or students as 'fully included'. We also expected that local ways of categorising students would be carefully explained, given the amount of conversation we had had previously about the relativity of concepts and the particular needs in this book for the translation from other languages into English. Neither expectation was realised. In the latter case such a practice suggested that a belief in scientific precision of categories, explicit in one or two chapters, is nevertheless assumed implicitly in others.

As we read the chapters we added to our list of dimensions of difference in perspectives on inclusion and exclusion and produced the list shown in Figure 1.2. This list contains some of the dimensions along which perspectives on inclusion and exclusion may differ, the last two of which refer specifically to researcher perspectives. However, an understanding of the complexity of perspectives requires that the list should not be read as straightforward continua. Furthermore, some writers may adhere rationally to each end of a particular dimension, depending on the context. They are not meant to be read as simple dichotomies. We will not discuss the issues raised by the list here, leaving the sense of our distinctions to be revealed through the case-studies, our commentaries on them, and our discussion of perspectives in the final chapter. Any reader who wants clarification of the dimensions before reading the case-studies can find it in chapter 18, pages 233–243.

Figure 1.2   Dimensions of difference in perspectives on inclusion and exclusion

Definitions
1 Are inclusion and exclusion seen as unending processes or as states of being inside or outside the mainstream, or of being either 'fully' or not included?
2 Are some exclusions taken for granted and only some examined and contested?
3 Are inclusion and exclusion seen as separate processes, affecting different groups of students, or are they seen as necessarily linked?
4 Are inclusion and exclusion applied to a limited group of categorised students or are they applied to all students whose participation in mainstream cultures, curricula and communities might be enhanced?

Responses to diversity
5 Are some students seen as 'other', as 'them' rather than 'us'?
6 Are difficulties in learning or disabilities attributed to defects or impairments in students or seen as arising in relationships between students and their social and physical environments?
7 Is the response to difficulties experienced by students seen only as individual and technical or as also a matter of values and philosophies, policies, structures and curricula, affecting all students?
8 Is diversity celebrated as a resource to be valued or seen as a problem to be overcome?
9 Is participation within a local mainstream school seen as a right or as dependent on professional judgement?
10 Is there an emphasis on a common curriculum for all or on special curricula for some?

Recognising differences of perspective
11 Are inclusion and exclusion in school connected to wider social and political processes?
12 Are the concepts used to discuss inclusion and exclusion seen as universal or as embedded within a social and cultural context that makes translation complex and hazardous?
13 Are approaches to inclusion and exclusion seen as common within a country amounting to a national perspective or as reflecting particular perspectives, voices and interests?
14 Are differences in perspective on inclusion and exclusion among and between staff and students explored or ignored?
15 Are the differing voices within groups of researchers revealed or obscured?
16 Are forms of presentation and research methods seen as part of the approach to inclusion and exclusion or as distinct from it?

Writing a critical commentary

We have constructed a critical commentary examining the perspectives in each case-study which takes up a theme that is an alternative, or counterpoint, to that captured by the title of the original chapter. The title of each response is an attempt to encapsulate this reading. We have endeavoured to make our reactions to each chapter distinctive by emphasising different aspects of each case-study and by allowing an argument prompted by several studies to develop cumulatively.

After an introduction, we have structured our reflections on each study under the following main headings:

- How does the national context explain and constrain practice?
- Voices and perspectives on inclusion and exclusion.

Such a division corresponds to the way in which we have set out the case-studies and the relative significance we have given to the first question. However, we have included the way in which researchers have responded to the first question under 'recognising differences of perspective' in Figure 1.2.

We attempt to look dispassionately at the chapters in order to describe and analyse the perspectives they contain, but inevitably our comments are guided by our own perspectives. Perspectives include values and hence the critiques will contain some indications that we value some perspectives more than others, and we discuss this further in chapter 18. However, there is no suggestion that the texts can be interpreted in only one way. We do not expect your reactions to coincide with our own even if you are pursuing an agenda similar to ours. In addition, you may wish to analyse the texts for different purposes and choose to emphasise entirely different aspects of them.

In our critiques, we do not hold back from challenging the conceptions and consistency of our contributors. This may be an unfamiliar approach to putting together an edited text but is part of our attempt to make a distinctive contribution to the exploration of perspectives on inclusion and exclusion. We regard the close reading of the texts of our contributors as part of an appreciation of their work. But some people feel that academics should avoid such critical comment on the work of their peers. A colleague read a book review by one of us, thought by the author of the review to mainly express his enjoyment of the book, though it did contain some critical analysis. However, the critique was regarded disapprovingly and drew the comment 'I like to think that we are all toilers in the same vineyard.' This seemed to be an exhortation to recognise a *professional interest* shared with the writer of the book and other academics and to suppress academic debate. In this book we draw attention to those occasions where professional interests shape the perspectives revealed within the chapters.

We recognise the particular hazards of translation in commenting on the Dutch and Norwegian studies written in a language which is not the first language of their authors. We are in a different position, too, in commenting on the English study which we wrote with Alan Dyson. Nevertheless, we have tried to be self-critical, examining definitions, identifying the variety of voices and perspectives and searching out inconsistencies in our own work.

Although we asked researchers to look at differences in view between themselves this has happened in only two cases. It can be inconvenient in shared writing for authors to point out the differences in view between them. It creates the need for a novel but equally readable form of narrative and forbearance on the part of readers used to playing along with the deception of authorial consensus. In the main, we have chickened out of extensive revelation of our differences of view, though we emphasise their significance to this project and will need to explore this issue further in future.

In our responses we have explored all of the issues we have raised in relation to one or more case-studies though we have tried not to make our analysis too repetitive. We make some general observations on the *researcher* perspectives in all the case-studies in our concluding chapter (chapter 18). But we also have made cross-references in our comments where we feel that there is a particularly interesting point of comparison. We hope we have pulled off the complex task of writing the responses so that each section stands alone but also builds on those that precede it.

Reading the book

The eight case-studies interspersed with our much briefer critical commentaries follow this chapter. We do not expect the reactions of readers to the texts to coincide with our own but offer our interpretations as a further opportunity to think through the issues they raise. Finally, in the conclusion to the book we draw out some of the main lessons from the studies for future comparative research on inclusion and exclusion.

We have placed the chapters in an order which seems to us to provide a stimulating sequence. However they can be read in any order, over any period of time. We think that reading the book is most fertile when chapters are compared and contrasted. Readers very familiar with the national context for a particular chapter may wish to move straight on to the description and analysis of school practice in that chapter. However, we urge readers to recognise that there are an infinite number of stories that could be offered to contextualise schools and that the one they bring with them may bear little resemblance to the one offered, and that this may provide further points of comparison. Readers may wish to follow a chapter by comparing their analysis of it with the one we have given.

Introducing the chapters

In chapter 2, *USA: I kind of wonder if we're fooling ourselves*, Linda Ware considers inclusion in one classroom in Marge Piercy High School, in the Midwest. She concentrates on a theatre arts class that includes a student, Josh, who is severely disabled. He does not communicate through speech or sign-language and we do not know how much he understands of the communication of others. She explores the views of students and Josh's teacher about inclusion and exclusion and its value.

Chapter 3, *Liberating voices?* is our response to Linda's chapter. We emphasise the way she gives voice to the students, and the difference in perspectives that emerge within the first section of the chapter written in traditional 'academic' style and the second, imaginative, freer narrative.

In chapter 4, *Scotland: Mainstreaming at the margins*, Julie Allan focuses on two students within a Scottish mainstream secondary school: Graham, a 16 year old described as having 'moderate learning difficulties' and Fiona, a 15 year old with hearing impairment. Their academic and social experiences and the support they receive are explored in the context of local decision-making processes and the changing Scottish policy scene.

We have called chapter 5 *Professionals at the centre?* to complement Julie's exploration of the partial and conditional involvement of Graham and Fiona in the mainstream. We argue that the chapter illustrates the way in which the power and discourse of professionals provides an excluding pressure on these students, in contradiction to their avowed inclusionary aims. We examine the extent to which the author incorporates this discourse into her own narrative.

Chapter 6, *New Zealand: Inclusive school, inclusive philosophy?*, is by Keith Ballard and Trevor MacDonald. It is about Central School, a primary school for 160 students aged 5 to 12 years, which the authors describe as 'an inclusive school'. It portrays a diversity of voices – teachers, parents, students and the authors – but is characterised by a large degree of harmony of belief and purpose. The authors explore in depth classroom practices and the perspectives that sustain them.

In chapter 7, *One philosophy or two?*, we reflect on the conception of an inclusive school as a realisable possibility rather than an elusive ideal. We ask to what extent Central School is in tune with national policies and look at the consistency of such policies. Our main concern, however, is with drawing out the complexity of perspectives in the chapter and in particular the tension evident in the authors and teachers at the school, between a focus on disability and a concern with overcoming all barriers to learning.

Chapter 8, *Norway: Adapted education for all?*, is by Kari Nes Mordal and Marit Strømstad. They concentrate on the educational experiences of teachers and students in Berg school, a primary school in the Hedmark district of Norway. They pay particular attention to the inclusion of three students seen as having 'special educational needs' in a fifth-grade class. The chapter documents the effect of official moves away from whole-class teaching towards 'adaptive education' in the particular Norwegian context of small administrative areas or 'communes'.

In chapter 9, *Adapted education for some?,* we look at the way the extensive national framework, the emphasis on rights and the particular administrative structures reveal a distinctive Norwegian perspective. We ask whether the national guidelines on adapted education for all have been assimilated into traditional special educational practice by special educators who have interpreted 'adapted education' to be a new name for special education.

In chapter 10, *The Netherlands: A springboard for other initiatives,* Gerry Reezigt and Sip Jan Pijl explore the novel development for the Netherlands of a part-time special class in De Springplank primary school in Marum, near Groningen, and the way it has emerged from national attempts to change special education policy towards greater inclusion of categorised students in a system with a traditionally high proportion of excluded students.

In chapter 11, *Plunging into inclusion?,* we reflect on the particular focus of the chapter on reducing the large special school population in the Netherlands, while retaining a student deficit model to analyse educational difficulties. We ask whether the special class can lead to greater inclusion given the way it is conceived in the school.

In chapter 12, *Ireland: Integration as appropriate, segregation where necessary,* Jim Bennet, Hugh Gash and Mark O'Reilly discuss aspects of practice in three schools, two of which are linked 'junior' and 'senior' primary schools. They focus their accounts on students they categorise as having a 'mild mental handicap'. More than any other chapter, the authors reveal differences of view between themselves.

In chapter 13 we celebrate the revelation of differences of perspective between the three authors. We have called our response *Limited resources for inclusion?* to indicate the linking in the chapter of additional resources as a prerequisite for the development of inclusion, as well as the possible limiting of the development of inclusive practice by the perspective on inclusion revealed in the chapter.

In chapter 14, *Australia: Inclusion through categorisation?,* Jeff Bailey argues for the importance to their effective inclusion of applying a medical model to a group of students he categorises as having Attention Deficit Hyperactivity Disorder (ADHD). He reports on the experience of one student in a small Catholic school in Queensland and the views of his mother and teachers.

In chapter 15 we recognise the central significance of including within debates about inclusion students who are seen to pose challenges to classroom control. Our response, *Paying attention to disorder?,* however, is also a recognition of the way Jeff's study is furthest from our own perspective and how such difference challenges us and can be used productively. In turn, we question the evidence he uses to support his central contention that medical intervention is essential for the inclusion of the students he discusses, and the way this may deflect him from looking at school and classroom processes.

In chapter 16, *England: Inclusion and exclusion in a competitive system*, which we wrote with Alan Dyson, we explore the processes of inclusion and exclusion in education in Lovell Community High School, a mixed-sex school for 1,550 students aged 11 to 19, and a provider of day and evening courses and activities for adults in the surrounding area. We ask how the school responds to the diversity of all its students. We examine the contradictory pressures on schools that seek to include and value students in a competitive educational climate which creates social pressures to devalue and exclude students.

Chapter 17, *We wonder if we're fooling ourselves*, is our attempt to stand back from our chapter and look at it critically. In returning to the title of Linda Ware's study we acknowledge her reminder to be self-critical and, in particular, challenge our claim that we have an equally detailed concern with all exclusionary processes in the school.

In chapter 18, *Making comparisons: drawing conclusions*, we review what we have learnt about a critique of comparative studies of inclusion and exclusion, the nature of differences of perspective, and the possibilities for changing them so that 'special education' can be redefined in terms of inclusion and exclusion. We consider the contribution of our study to fertile directions for future research.

2

USA: I KIND OF WONDER IF WE'RE FOOLING OURSELVES

Linda Ware

Introduction

This chapter considers inclusion in one classroom, in a high school in the Midwest, a region of the United States that stands out as having only limited similarities to the rest of the country. An overview of the national and local contexts for inclusion are presented, and then a high school theater arts class is portrayed from data collected over a fifteen-week period. The chapter concludes with a synthesis of the issues raised by the case-study and their implications for continued progress toward the goal of inclusion in American society. The reader is advised that the formal voice utilised in the introduction to this chapter is intentional and contrasts with the personal voice used to tell the story at Marge Piercy High School.

The national context: history and politics

Inclusion should be viewed as a social movement connected to a history of social policy reform in the United States beginning in the mid-1950s. Included among these events are the 1954 Supreme Court decision on the racial desegregation of schools; the de-institutionalization of persons with mental illness during the late 1960s and 1970s; the 1975 passage of the Education for All Handicapped Children Act (EHA); the mid-1980s call for reform of this Act and "mainstreaming" in particular; the passage of the Americans with Disabilities Act in the early 1990s; and various school restructuring efforts over the past decade intended to overhaul American schools.

In the late 1970s and throughout the 1980s, mainstreaming was premised on the belief that students with disabilities should be separated from the regular class for special instruction. This instructional delivery approach followed the hard-won success of moving children with disabilities back into the public school setting. In the 1990s, in an inclusive program, the child is *presumed* to belong in the regular class that she would normally attend if she did not have a disability, in her neighborhood school. This underlying assumption is significant in that it invites exploration of the questions raised, but left unanswered, by mainstreaming.

However, despite the significance of social policy reforms and their sometimes cumulative impact on the inclusion movement, progress toward inclusion remains uneven in schools and communities across the United States. In the progression from mainstreaming to inclusion, the parallels are important to note, particularly when considering that mainstreaming ultimately failed to deliver on its promise. According to Skrtic (1995):

> What is so troubling today is that the inclusion debate is largely following the same pattern as the mainstreaming debate. It too is a form of naive pragmatism that criticizes current special education models, practices, and tools without explicitly criticizing the theories and assumptions that stand behind them.
>
> Skrtic 1995, p. 80

Skrtic's theoretical analysis of the field of special education aims for excellence, equity, and adhocracy through a deconstruction and reconstruction of both general and special education for a post-industrial economy in the twenty-first century. He maintains that an alternative paradigm, that of critical pragmatism, is necessary to reconstruct special education and disability. Without it, the current inclusion debate will not "resolve the special education problems of the twentieth century . . . [but] will simply reproduce them in the twenty-first century" (p. 80). He argues that critical pragmatism enables individuals to continually evaluate and reappraise the "political consequences of a profession's knowledge, practices, and discourses by critically assessing them and the assumptions, theories, and metatheories in which they are grounded" (p. 91). Although limitations of space prohibit a more extensive treatment of Skrtic's proposal in support of critical pragmatism, his analysis informs the case-study in this chapter and underscores the inspiration and motivation expressed by the drama teacher, reported in the conclusion.

Among those who anticipated the failure of mainstreaming during the 1980s, many challenged the institutional practice of special education, calling for widespread reform (see Reynolds, Wang, and Walberg 1987; Sarason and Doris 1982; Skrtic 1986; Will 1986). The radical restructuring of special education urged by Skrtic (1986; 1987; 1988) has yet to occur, although some states have attempted special education reform, often in concert with general education reform (Ferguson 1995; Thousand and Villa 1995). However, so-called "systemic reform" of special education is far from the norm in the United States (Beegle *et al.* 1995; Kozleski 1995; Roach 1995).

In their seminal work, "Public policy and the handicapped: the case of mainstreaming," Sarason and Doris (1982) identified mainstreaming with social reform, providing a critique that holds implications for inclusion.

> At its root, mainstreaming is a moral issue. It raises age-old questions: How do we want to live with each other? On what basis should

be given priority to one value or another? How far does the majority want to go in accommodating the needs of the minority?

Sarason and Doris 1982, p. 54–55

Their questions were largely ignored in the mainstreaming debate, although their predictions about how the endeavor would be framed were quite on the mark:

> The emergence of mainstreaming as an issue raises but does not directly confront these questions. To the extent that we put the discussion of mainstreaming in the context of education and schools, we are likely to find ourselves mired in controversies centering around law, procedures, administration, and funding. These are legitimate controversies because they deal with practical day-to-day matters that affect the lives of everyone. But the level of difficulty we encounter in dealing with these matters will ultimately be determined by the charity with which the moral issue is formulated. At the very least, it should make us more aware of two things: so-called practical matters or problems are always reflections of moral issues, and differences in moral stance have very practical consequences.

ibid.

The process of naming and defining the issues is central to sustaining change. Change occurs when its goals are seen to be personally relevant to individuals involved in developing and implementing policy, rather than through their concern to conform with mandate, predetermined policy, or reform by fiat (Ware 1994a; 1994b; 1994c; 1995a; 1995c).

For many involved in the current debate on inclusion, it is evident that the questions raised by Sarason and Doris over a decade ago remain unanswered, diluted by concerns that locate this endeavor within an educational rather than a societal discourse. The current literature on inclusion in the United States documents the way the practical realities (read fiscal concerns) related to inclusion continue to obscure the "charity" needed to frame the moral issue (Zigmond *et al.* 1995; Educational Leadership Special Issue Winter 94–95; and the Special Section on Inclusion in Phi Delta Kappan 1995). This literature, in combination with the concerns of Sarason and Doris and the warnings issued by Skrtic, challenge the success of inclusion. And yet, at this particular moment schools continue to grapple with inclusion: an ill-defined, and yet, ever-increasingly accepted and widely practiced reform.

In 1995, the US Department of Education reported an increase in the percentage of identified students receiving educational services in regular education classrooms, up from 28.88 percent in 1987–88 to 39.81 percent in 1992–93 (US Department of Education, 1995). Although it remains difficult to assess the quality of the programs reported as inclusive, it is suggested here

23

that two factors that determine success with inclusion be considered in addition to the training issue. First, the initial motivation for attempting inclusion, and second, the perception held by stakeholders relevant to its significance as a social movement, in particular, its evolution from mainstreaming.

The local context: community and school

Longview is a university community with a permanent population of 70,000, artificially inflated by the 28,000 students who attend two local universities, one public and the other, Hastings Indian Nations University. Longview has been ranked repeatedly among the top twenty-five cities in the United States for its ideal living conditions and overall community safety standards. Residents have identified the key strengths of the community and its families as appreciation of cultural diversity; commitment to community; pride in community; caring–giving community; appreciation of the local educational system; access to educational resources of two universities; availability of a wide range of human service providers; availability of parks, wilderness preserves, and recreation sites.

Longview school improvement and inclusion policies

Deputy Executive Director of the National Association of State Boards of Education (NASBE), Virgina Roach (1995) has identified four distinct approaches that characterize the implementation of inclusion at the level of district reform. These include:

1 **The evolutionary approach** – ad hoc, gradual, and generally inspired by individual parents or teachers on behalf of individual students.
2 **The pilot program approach** – a specially funded educational initiative, rather than a systemic reform effort, and generally inspired by the availability of targeted funding.
3 **The phase in approach** – establishes a deadline for comprehensive compliance district-wide, and generally inspired by the volition of individual administrators and teachers.
4 **The immediate conversion** approach – comprehensive compliance district-wide (usually in one to two years and often in small, or rural districts). This approach is generally inspired by community-wide willingness to attempt such large scale reform.

Longview, prior to the 1994–95 school year was best characterized by the "evolutionary" and "pilot program" approaches. Individual parents or teachers attempted unique and successful inclusion for some students; however, for the majority, mainstreaming in self-contained pull-out programs remained the norm. Both general and special education staff expressed concern that in

24

the absence of a district policy on inclusion, progress toward inclusion would be limited (Ware 1995b). Nonetheless, the Longview school district attempted to promote the development of inclusion policies and practices during the 1994–95 school year.

In the summer of 1994, the Longview Superintendent of Schools convened a retreat with all district principals and central administration administrators, numbering forty people in total, to determine goals for the district-wide improvement of schools. Although this effort was never heralded as district reform or restructuring, it was an approach similar to that of many other districts across the United States in the process of reform. By the conclusion of the retreat, the participants drafted the following goals:

1   We will continue to develop our resources from traditional and non-traditional sources.
2   We will continuously evaluate and improve our programs and services for all learners.
3   We will have facilities that meet the needs of all learners in the community.
4   We will improve our awareness of and access to relevant technology.
5   We will develop a stronger and more trusting sense of community.
6   We will have student-centered schools and inclusive schools.

Following the tenets of strategic action planning, twelve Action Teams, involving 130 people, were formed in the fall of 1994 to address these goals. Representation included teachers, administrators, school board members, and other interested representatives from the community. In a parallel activity, the district's special education advisory committee invited parents, students, staff, and other relevant stakeholders to provide input on the progress of educational services for students with disabilities. Three community meetings were convened and considerable information was solicited in the form of goal prioritization activities and questionnaires. This data was targeted for analysis during the summer of 1995 by members of the district special education advisory council. Although this effort was not intended to duplicate the work of the Action Teams, it represented a separate pursuit to address inclusion in the district.

Also during the 1994–95 school year, Longview hired an inclusion facilitator who was assigned to the high school. This position is a relatively new role in schools in the United States, often characterized as the liaison between regular and special education teachers. The role is defined by the demands of the local site, although in some instances the inclusion facilitator may serve more than one site. At M. Piercy, the inclusion facilitator was new to the community, and initially assigned to support two students with cognitive impairments who were included in general education classes and community-based job assignments at the insistence of their parents.

In addition, this research supported "evolutionary" inclusion efforts at four junior highs and the high school during the 1994–95, supported by the state department of education. It is a research approach that builds on previous work by me designed to shift the aim of inquiry from evaluation of the participants to empowerment of participants (Ware 1994a; Ware 1995a; Ware 1995b; Ware 1995c).

On the whole, 1994–1995 signalled an increase in activity specific to inclusion in Longview schools. For some, the potential emerged to consider general and special education issues simultaneously; for others, the inclusion conversation remained characterized by issues that historically divide general and special education teachers such as grading, curriculum accommodation and responsibility for students (Ware 1995b).

Although the abbreviated history of social policy reform reported earlier has not resulted in a seamless narrative that shapes the intentions and the actions of key stakeholders involved with inclusion, it nonetheless exerts a significant influence on the inclusion movement across the United States. Likewise, in Longview stakeholders were inspired by various historical events, although in the main they were prompted to action for reasons that were more local than historical. In this case-study the notion of "presumed membership" in society becomes the central theme explored as the means to 'enable those persons most responsible for creating change at its smallest unit (the classroom) to promote inclusion' (Ware 1995a, p. 143).

Longview's schools

M. Piercy High is a comprehensive high school with a student population of 2,000 students (Grades 10–12). It is the only high school in Longview, but during the course of 1995 Longview voters returned to the polls after three previously unsuccessful bids, and approved a bond issue to construct a second high school in the city. Although residents supported ten years of ongoing expansion to alleviate overcrowding at M. Piercy High, the district's efforts to build a second high school had been previously rejected because of concerns that a second high school would splinter the community and force unnecessary competition (e.g. athletics, scholarships, staffing) and thus impact the quality of services. In addition, there had been concern that migration to the West side of the city (where considerable growth of upper income families has occurred) would prompt further inequities, given that property taxes affect school financing formulas.

In Longview four junior high schools, each characterized by unique demographics, feed into the high school so, for many students, strong affiliations have been established prior to high school. Further, the notion that a homogenous community is preserved simply because the students are housed in a single structure is not congruent with the reality of schools, albeit a common misconstruction by those outside of schools. M. Piercy, like most comprehensive high schools in the United States, has structural features which perpetuate a culture of exclusion according to race, class, and levels of attainment (Apple 1982; Carnoy and Levin 1985; Giroux 1981). Moreover, the systematic tracking of all students through ability grouping is a common practice in most public high schools in the States, as students are assigned for instruction according to their purported learning strengths and assumed learning capacities. For some (National Education Association 1990; Wilson and Schmits 1978), this seems a sensible approach to academic diversity; however, others challenge this approach because it yields the "intergenerational transmission of social and economic positions" (Oakes and Guiton 1995, p. 30).

It is generally assumed in schools that success is attainable for all students, although careful analysis reveals contradictions that undermine the equitable distribution of advantage. When students are segregated by explicit academic criteria, they likewise tend to be segregated by social and economic characteristics (Oakes 1990; Rosenbaum 1976), and are placed in classes characterized by inferior instruction (Oakes 1985; Oakes, Gamaron, and Page 1992; Page 1991). For example, at M. Piercy graduation requirements include four years of mathematics, either basic consumer mathematics or advanced placement mathematics designed as college preparation coursework. Students are assigned to these courses prior to entry to senior high school, depending on their performance in junior high.

Identified special education students, that is those with Individual Education Plans (IEPs), are sometimes included in general education classrooms at M. Piercy on the advice of special education staff, and with the approval of the regular education teacher. Students receive support in the regular classroom from the special education department (teachers or paraprofessionals). As a result of support it is rare for a student to fail to meet the regular education course requirements and have to repeat the class. There are a number of other service delivery systems for those students who are not included in regular instruction. These comprise a mainstreaming, self-contained placement, supplemented by a gym, art, or music class; a community instructional skills class, or a vocational instruction class, the latter two placements taught by special education teachers for identified special education students.

The special education department consists of twenty-five staff, including ten para-professional support staff and teachers in the categories of gifted education, hearing impairment, learning disabilities, behavior disorders, cognitive impairment (severe mental handicaps, trainable mental handicaps, and educable mental handicaps), and one inclusion specialist. These categories are broadly similar across the United States. Students included in general education classrooms across the Longview district include those with behavioral disorders, and those with learning, physical, and other cognitive disabilities; although procedures to standardize inclusion district-wide have yet to be implemented.

27

Data collection and research methodology

This research was designed as a blend of participant observation and collaborative inquiry which simultaneously evaluated, supported and promoted inclusion efforts in Longview Public Schools. It was funded by a five year systems-change project awarded to the state department of education. The research elaborates methodological adaptations that cast the researcher as a "creative mediator" (Ware 1994a). In this project, mediation occurred within and across the five sites described below.

Data were collected during the 1994–95 school year in five schools (four junior high schools, and one high school) as they explored an evolutionary approach to inclusion. These included informal interviews, observations, video-taped performances and interviews, and analysis of a variety of relevant documents such as memos, lesson plans, meeting notes, scripts, and newspaper clippings. Observations were conducted in several classrooms during twelve weeks of the fall semester as classroom teachers, special education teachers, and para-professional staff worked in a variety of combinations to support inclusion. Teachers and students were interviewed at each site. The degree of participation with each site was determined by the participants, rather than the researcher, in keeping with the tenets of empowerment evaluation described by Fetterman (1994 and 1996).

Early conversations with Longview special education administrators yielded support for a research agenda that was more open-ended than generally afforded to traditional evaluation. The intention was to focus on inclusion activity underway in schools, and for the researcher to offer guidance and assistance with those activities rather than to generate new agendas outside the schools' activity. For example, at one junior high the researcher conducted fifteen interviews with teachers in both regular and special education to solicit and define their understanding of inclusion as it existed in their school, across the state, and nationally. The interviews were suggested by members of the school's site council (comprised of teachers, counselors, and administrators) with the hope that inclusion practices would be improved if an understanding of inclusion was articulated. Analysis of the interviews was considered by all the participants and the researcher, who collectively addressed common concerns. Although much more conversation on the topic was clearly needed, the participants outlined a number of steps to improve decision-making in the up-coming school year. In addition to the interviews, the researcher also observed in both academic and elective study classrooms in which IEP students were included.

The researcher, given her attendance at inclusion meetings across the district, was able to provide information from all sites as appropriate and pose questions that otherwise might not be raised. The researcher was also a member of the district's Special Education Advisory Council and the Superintendent's Inclusion Action Team. However, the bulk of time committed to this project was spent at M. Piercy High School in observations and interviews with students and teachers as they interpreted and implemented inclusion.

Reporting the study

Presented here is a case-study of theater arts activities at Marge Piercy High. The case-study is written as a narrative in three parts: the class, the parody, and the dialogue. It is a story about inclusion, involved with the creation of "dramatic or hermeneutic unity, and not merely with recording all the events that happened over a period of time" (Polkinghorne 1988, p. 145). Presenting the data in this manner captures a coherence of action that might otherwise elude the researcher and reader.

* * *

The theater arts class

Students saunter into the orchestra room in twos and threes, their attention fixed in conversations. It is as if their exchange alone rises above the din that suffuses the hallways during the change of classes. They navigate past metal chairs stacked on trolleys just inside the door. Past the once elegant grand piano which now appears exhausted, its surface dull and worn like workman's boots. The students wind their way to the half-circle of movable risers, to the stacks of plastic chairs they move one at a time creating the space where class will soon begin.

"Piano. Guys?" Janis calls as she sails into the room dumping her papers in a heap near the students. She is nonchalant as she steps between Chase and Joel who stretch out across the floor, self-pleased to create even more obstruction.

"Chase. Joel. Jake." Janis says, now more directive, although her inflection rises with each name as if to answer her own question. All three students move toward the piano that is awkwardly affixed to a dolly, ready to relinquish its position, center stage.

It is the last period of the school day at M. Piercy High, "sixth hour" and the orchestra room now serves as the setting for an experimental course: "Issues Theater". Janis Avers, the Theater Arts/English teacher, and her principal conceived of the class in an effort to draw minority students (Black, Hispanic, and Native American students) into elective courses in theater arts. Although pleased with the success of their overall drama program, students with more diverse backgrounds have been noticeably under-represented in her classes. Janis had a hunch that minority representation was low in theater classes because students may not have prior acting experience. Janis proposed the class as a combination of acting and theater exploration through the study of contemporary social issues.

There are no assigned readings in Issues Theater. No list of questions at the end of the chapter. No essay tests. Students write and perform their own skits bound only by the parameters of the theme for the semester: *inclusion*. By her own definition, inclusion means allowing every person in her class to participate as fully as possible. Although Janis drafted a list of instructional outcomes and student learning outcomes prior to gaining course approval, much that happens in this class cannot be predicted in advance. Using theater as a springboard for discussion and examination of social issues is something that Janis has attempted in a piecemeal fashion in her other classes, but never beyond the isolated incident nested in an instructional unit. Ironically, Issues Theater was not among the inclusion activities outlined by the district when the researcher conducted initial interviews with special education administrators. The class was, for all intents and purposes, an idea developed by a teacher and endorsed by the principal; it was merely a coincidence that it emerged alongside the inclusion trend in schools.

Richard leans at a 45-degree angle from behind Josh's chair. With one hand he pulls the door open and, in a slow rotation, inches Josh and himself inside the room. Their routine suggests struggle. In response, Chase abandons Joel, Jake, and the piano. He sprints across the room and pushes both doors open to their full extent as he boldly announces, "Hey Josh. Hey Richard."

Chase charms with his usual wide smile. Richard is at once pleased and amused by the attention they now command, remembering that in *this* class there is always the potential for antics, for a scene, for a script. He and Josh have safely escaped the crowded hallways, the glares, the rancor students are wont to effect *en masse*. The space that usually distances now draws closer as Janis's students increasingly display an uncommon kindness in their interactions with Josh and Richard. In the days that passed since Richard presented an overview lecture about students with disabilities, he has noticed that more students seek Josh out during the day, before and after school as well. Greetings are infectious among those familiar with Josh. Among the unfamiliar, there is silence and transparent discomfort as they look beyond Josh, or worse, avert their eyes.

"Ahhh. Ugggh. Jeeez." Joel and Jake echo in feigned struggle with the piano, hoping Chase will take his cue. As he leaps forward to help, all three students meet the disapproving glare of the orchestra teacher, who steps out from his office to caution, "That job is better done by three of you. Preferably, four."

The orchestra teacher turns, and closes his office door behind him, never glancing back to ensure his directive was honored. This is not his class. They are not his students. All is disruption in what promises to be a series of disruptions throughout the school year as construction of the new wing of the high school continues less than fifty yards away. The clank of heavy equipment, the loud voices of the construction workers, the reverberation of dump trucks that pass outside his office window persist: all uninfluenced by his comment. And now, relinquishing the orchestra room to Janis during his sixth hour planning period, so that she might better accommodate her Issues

Theater class, and in particular, Josh and his wheelchair, is yet another disruption uninfluenced by his comment.

Richard watches from behind Josh's chair. He wants to quiet his suspicion. He wants to believe this class will be different from the others. In the four years he has steered Josh into regular education classrooms in the name of inclusion, he has yet to feel included, yet to witness inclusion for Josh. In his most honest moments he names their roles: Josh the prop. Richard the appendage. They are ever *apart. Never a part.* Cooking, ceramics, woodworking, photography, interior design, weightlifting – who are we kidding? Josh doesn't cook. He isn't a photographer. The shop tools are impossible to use. And ceramics? Richard really disliked that class even though the teacher made a genuine effort to include both of them. Each class has left Richard perplexed about inclusion; less confident about its possibility, and less convinced that Josh can be known and valued in a non-disabled world.

By Richard's standards, Josh is alert, responsive, charming, and smart. He smiles a lot. And when he is pleased he makes sounds into the air, or softly whines in a high-pitched hum the way people sometimes do when they are wired to a Walkman. That he has spent most of his life in a wheelchair, has limited use of his hands, and no speech, fixes his identity to others: disability first, Josh second. This semester, they will tackle the thespian life: scripts, roles, lines, and cues. Richard laughs to himself recalling the words of the comedian, Lily Tomlin – "I am not an actor, I'm a real person."

* * *

"Everyone, everyone, everyone – over here." Janis insists as she completes the daily attendance slip. Her students are scattered around her on the risers, on the floor, several sit cross-legged on the floor near Josh and Richard. A few continue in conversation, although most shift their focus to her.

"I want to pull all this energy we have today together. Let's re-form ourselves into a world – a mechanical world. I want you to take a position over here," she says as she scurries across the room to their make-shift stage. Taking a deep breath she begins slow, almost elegant gyrations up and down in imitation of a machine: a single piston. As she demonstrates, she directs the students to consider machine action, machine sounds – the essence of a mechanical world.

"A world . . . where all . . . is machine," she drones and pauses before concluding, "and machine . . . is all." Her theatrics succeed as she holds the attention of her students. After a lengthy pause she adds, "think about a world like this and when you're ready, enter the machine world with me." With that, she becomes silent. Still. Until, slowly, her body once more stirs in syncopation, piston action accompanied by a deep groan, machine-like. Her eyes remain closed. One by one, the students join in: one in rigid deep knee bends; another stands arms akimbo and twists from the hip in slow motion;

another, posed with his legs wide apart, rigidly rocks from side-to-side against the sounds of a deep boom in echo to the groan from Janis. Richard and Josh enter and pace an invisible line in slow steps forward and then back. In a few short minutes, all the students have positioned themselves in this mechanical world, throbbing amid a cacophony of sound that competes with the real-time construction noise outside.

"Keep in focus." Janis calls out. "Keep in focus." For another two minutes the students' energy is collected *en masse*, in a mechanical world. With a clap of her hands, Janis yells, "BREAK! THAT WAS TERRIFIC!"

The students collapse in exhaustion and giddy self congratulation.

* * *

"Critique, critique," they yell.

"No, not yet. Let's do another one," Janis urges. "This time, an organic world."

"I want to start us off," Alyssa demands.

"Fine," Janis replies, "I'm going to sit with Linda and just watch this time. But don't forget what we just did. We'll come back to that action in our critique." Janis sits down as she fans the air around her to cool the warmth that swells color across her face.

"Does organic mean like a rain forest or something?" Jake asks.

"It doesn't have to. Just think opposite mechanical." Carmen answers.

* * *

Alyssa returns to their make-shift stage and begins sweeping flourishes outward with her arms – in and out – to suggest waves. Another student positions himself nearby and sways, slowly taking deep, loud breaths to create the sound of the ocean. Two others join hands and gently rock from side to side in an irregular rhythm. Another lies flat on the floor, followed by another who topples down as if to imitate fallen trees. Another shadows Alyssa's wave at the same moment a third student joins them, and soon all three move in sync. In no time, the majority of the students have positioned themselves in a more close space, although their movement does not appear restricted. Richard and Josh are the last to enter, they appear hesitant, pausing before they move in, and together, they trace a circumference to enclose the class in this, their organic world.

"Keep your focus. Keep your focus." Janis calls out as she moves to dim the lights. One switch at a time, the rigid spine of fluorescent lights yields to absolute darkness.

"Maintain the world." Janis whispers as the students continue in the total darkness.

"Main . . . tain!"

The class, has once again, reformed a world. Their energy contained until Janis flips on the lights and exclaims, "FANTASTIC!"

* * *

With a clap of her hands she hurries the students away from the make-believe stage and toward the risers where they convene as a class. Sitting down beside her students, Janis pulls her knees close to her body, leans into her palms that frame her face, and asks, "So, what did you think? Tell me about the two worlds." At once, the critique flows without interruption:

> The mechanical world was louder. We all did things by ourselves. It took up more space. Or maybe we just didn't get close to each other. Some sounds pushed other sounds out. Everyone seemed to know where they fit. But that's weird because, ok, we were in sync, but you know, in a way we weren't. I liked the second world better. Me too. Yeah, everyone was in tune there. It was cool when Cara imitated Alyssa. And Arden too. That was cool – turning out the lights. We got quieter after that. Did anyone pick up on how we kinda started making our own pulse as more people joined in? That's what I mean – we were more in sync.

Janis, interjects, "what do you think would have happened if I cut the lights on the mechanical world?"

Above all the others, Chase responds, "we'd probably just get louder."

* * *

The clarity of expression and the clarity of thought is remarkable among the students. They finish one another's comments and build from one another's points. I cannot take it all down fast enough, and I am certain that I have not taken it all in. My observations scattered over the past few days have left the impression that M. Piercy High is too big to implement inclusion successfully. Each classroom I observed was tolerant of the inclusion students, as they are sometimes referenced with apology, but interaction among the students was not evident. In many, but not all of these classes, students were supported by a special education teacher, or a classroom para-professional, with whom the student would, in most instances, exclusively interact. In effect, support separated the students with disabilities from the rest of the class. With the exception of Issues Theater, the classes were characterized by traditional instruction, traditional student expectations, and traditional classroom activity. Modifications were made for students with disabilities, but on the whole instruction was didactic and the content was static. By design, Janis's class departed from the norm: she sought diversity among the students, she kept the parameters for participation open-ended, and more importantly, she actively sought Josh's participation in her class. Issues Theater assumed that students would learn to exaggerate, to impersonate, to feign, to make-believe, to exploit, to perform. And through this raw expression of creativity and emotion Janis

33

hoped to tap into greater cognitive reasoning from her students about the concept of inclusion.

Several weeks into the semester, Janis and the class have all but created a catechism of sorts, a manual on inclusion in which their questions about inclusion led to answers, and answers back to questions. Creativity remains a constant, as has their enthusiasm, excitement, and willingness to stretch their thinking beyond a narrow, conventional analysis of inclusion.

The parody

"I gave them the task of doing a sketch on inclusion," Janis recalled as she described an assignment made early in the semester. "The class worked in small groups and almost everyone chose to define inclusion by going to its opposite – exclusion. They insisted inclusion applied to everybody and not just to people with disabilities." From that perspective, students explored how prejudice and injustice might feel, through their writing, thinking, and performance of skits.

One group of students risked even more, to conjecture how Josh might give voice to his experience with inclusion. According to Chase, "we wrote what we imagined Josh's response might be if he could talk." Chase gave voice to Josh's thoughts in the following skit, written and performed by eight students.

* * *

The skit opens in a crowded cafeteria where all the tables are occupied except the one where Josh sits surrounded by four empty chairs. Several students carrying lunch trays pass by, or stop in front of Josh and discuss where they should sit. All ultimately move on.

JUSTIN:	(*Avoiding eye contact with Josh*) Let's go sit . . .uhm . . . somewhere else, Joel. Oh, how about over there? (*Pointing across the cafeteria*)
CHASE FOR JOSH:	Here's some space . . . (*Interrupted.*)
ANDY:	Yeah, good idea. Over there.
CHASE FOR JOSH:	(*Impervious*) Well, another lunch all by myself. My manly persona must have scared them off. *[Three more students carrying lunch trays once again pause in front of Josh, and discuss where they will sit.]*
TANYA:	Do you see any place else to sit?
CHANTISE:	Well (*pausing to look around*), no, not really.
SARAH:	So do you see any place else? (*All look exasperated*).
TANYA:	So, maybe, well we could just sit . . . uhm . . . (*voice trails off*)

CHASE FOR JOSH:	I guess you guys could sit here, maybe?
SARAH:	Oh. Well. No, that's ok because . . . because, you see that window over there, it gives me a draft (*points to an open window several yards away*).
CHANTISE:	Yeah, me too.
SARAH:	(*Surveys the cafeteria again*) Why don't we uhm, well, we could . . .
TANYA:	Go outside?
CHANTISE and SARAH:	No, that *would* be cold.
TANYA:	(*Begrudgingly*) You guys, let's just sit here. Come on, I'm hungry.
CHASE FOR JOSH:	Wow guys! Gee thanks. Company!
TANYA:	Have you guys seen that new boy, Will?
CHANTISE:	Oh yeah, he's cute.
SARAH:	I think he's going to ask me to the dance on Friday night.
TANYA:	No he's not. He's going to ask me.
CHASE FOR JOSH:	No. He's not going to ask any of you. (*Glances directed to Josh, followed by nervous laughs. Prolonged silence.*)
TANYA:	Uhm, Chantise, maybe you should say something to him (*indicating Josh*).
CHASE FOR JOSH:	Yeah, Chantise, maybe you should say something to me.
CHANTISE:	No, I don't think so Tanya. You say something.
TANYA:	No, you. I mean, don't you know sign-language or something?
CHANTISE:	Uhm, well, I used to but I don't anymore. Besides you brought it up, so you say it.
TANYA:	(*Blasts loudly*). HI JOSH HOW ARE YOU? (*Chase flips backwards to indicate surprise.*)
SARAH:	Tanya! Not so loud. People are looking.
CHANTISE:	(*Embarrassed*). You didn't have to yell.
TANYA:	Well then you say something to him Sarah.
SARAH:	(Singing sweetly). HI-A-JOSH-HOW-ARE-YOU?
CHASE FOR JOSH:	(*Singing sassy*) Hiiiiiii. Hiiiiiii. I'm sevennnteeeen. I'm not a pup-peeee. (*Nervous laughs. Silence. Enter cute new guy Will.*)
TANYA:	Oh my gosh guys, here comes Will.
ALL IN UNISON:	Hi Will. (*Giddy laughs*)
WILL:	Hi girls, can I sit down? Hey Josh, what's up?
CHASE FOR JOSH:	Hi Will, what's up?
TANYA:	Oh, do you talk to him?

35

WILL:	Yeah, it's Josh, he's my friend (*smiles again at Josh and shrugs his shoulders in momentary confusion. Josh returns a smile.*)
TANYA:	How did you meet him?
WILL:	We have a class together.
CHASE FOR JOSH:	Yeah we cause a lot of trouble.
CHANTISE:	Are you guys friends?
WILL:	Yeah.
TANYA:	So how do you talk to him?
WILL:	The same way I talk to anyone else. You try.
TANYA:	*Once again, Tanya blasts*) HI-A-JOSH-HOW-ARE-YOU? (*Chase flips backwards again to indicate surprise.*)
WILL:	Whoa, Whoa. Not like that (*one hand over her mouth*). Just talk to him like you talk to Sarah or Chantise. In a normal tone of voice.
TANYA:	Josh are you going to the dance on Friday?
CHASE FOR JOSH:	Yeah, I already got a date. Do you?

* * *

In the final weeks that pass as the semester comes to an end, the students have written and performed a variety of skits, working in small groups and performing for one another. The majority of the class is working with Ron, Janis's husband, and an area playwright who has written a play for the district, entitled "Resolution". The play was initially commissioned for district teacher in-service training, as a vehicle to impact teacher attitudes on inclusion. Throughout the semester Ron submitted his rewrites to the students, and revised his work based on their input.

"Resolution" addressed inclusion by shifting its focus away from disability *per se*, to address the selfishness of its central character, a non-disabled student. Josh is one of several actors in the play, and although his role is an important one, his character is not the focus of the play. However, by his example and his presence in the Issues Theater class, the implicit analogy to Josh exists. According to Janis, "Who better to learn from than someone who hasn't learned to be selfish?" "Resolution" was performed for the public at the end of the semester, rewritten, and performed late in the summer for a national audience of theater educators. The entire cast traveled with Ron and Janis to perform the play in Minnesota, where "Resolution" received outstanding reviews and overwhelming approval for the subtle significance of its message. Ironically, the district has yet to utilize the play for district in-service.

At the end of the semester, the students agreed to a group interview with the researcher in which they reflected on inclusion, disability, and Issues Theater. As is evident in the candid exchange, the students were comfortable with the researcher in the dialogue that follows.

The dialogue

CHASE: Originally I'd never worked with anyone with a disability. I was really unsure – not really even that much of Josh – but more of myself. I didn't want to do anything that he would consider offensive. I wasn't sure how to act. I have to say that I had a lot of previous stereotypes. I guess I carried the stereotype that Josh was at least partially deaf and that he was very fragile (which aren't true at all), so when Richard talked to our class that day at the beginning of the year – that really helped out a lot.

CARA: And something I noticed throughout the semester was that at first, it just didn't occur to me that Josh was an actual Junior in high school. I mean, I know that he was, but it was a lot easier to talk to him like he was a 3 year old. Just like it's easier to talk to anybody I have a hard time communicating with – like in the same way that I talk to my 10 year old brother, and not someone who is really equal to me.

JOEL: Maybe I'm wrong, but I think that the big difference here was the communication barrier – in terms of him not being able to speak directly back. You know, you can speak to people with Down syndrome, and you can speak to people with cerebral palsy. I've had experiences with both of these disabilities before, but with Josh the thing that was most difficult for me was trying to communicate because of the condition that he's in, you know. He can't talk to you directly. Even someone who's deaf, but otherwise has everything else intact, can communicate. So that was hard for me. And I think it was hard for everyone. [*Pause*] You know, I would like to know what *is* going on in Josh's head. I think we would all love to, but unfortunately, as of yet, there is no way to know.

CHASE: But you know, after going through the whole semester together, you really can see his reactions. When he's smiling that's a pretty good sign that he agrees with what you're doing. When you spend a lot of time with him, you learn. Like, you can break smiling down even further and see when he's just kind of enjoying something and when he's *really* enjoying something. I think when he's real happy it's like a real quiet laughing. He stomps his feet and his eyes get really wide – that's how I know what he's thinking.

LINDA: That's a good point. It reminds me of some of our earlier interviews when I asked you all to think about how we might communicate in the absence of language. At the time, I hoped the question would provoke thinking much like you're describing now.

CARA: Oh, yeah. I remember that, you said it like it was our responsibility – I mean, well, that's how I felt anyway. I remember thinking, "hey that's right – if I can speak and I can know what I feel and think – and I *can* tell other people these things – why can't I try to understand when others can't?" Now I wished I had paid more attention in the beginning to Josh.

37

What was he telling me? Even while I interacted with him and I knew he had a smile on his face, I couldn't have told you the difference between one smile and another. I became more attuned to the subtle things by taking the time to pay attention and really observe what was inside his smile.

LINDA: In a few days you all start different classes, and so will Josh. I'm wondering how we could use your experiences to inform his new classmates in second semester?

ALYSSA: I don't think that would work – to tell our peers in different classes. Most classes aren't like Mrs Avers'. Our class *really* interacted with each other, but if it was a regular class where you just sit and listen, Josh would sit and listen just like anyone else and he wouldn't have that many interactions. Even if you did tell a classmate, it would be hard for them to understand if they hadn't gone through a whole semester like we did with Josh doing activities together. I'm sure in another class they would never do activities to get to know him and understand him like we did.

LINDA: Really? I remember we talked about how Mrs. Avers kept such a low profile throughout the semester, but you also raise the point that your class was, maybe, equally unique?

CARA: Oh, yeah, I think that a lot of the things that we did in class . . . I mean, a lot of us have acted before so it's not all entirely new, but for some people it was. We did things that I had never done before and all that – but I think that a lot of opening up and acting in weird ways made us realize that we could do the same thing with Josh. You know? It was like in this class it was okay to talk to him and that if we could do all these crazy things in front of our peers then we could also talk to and deal with Josh too.

CHASE: Yeah, because he was just like us. But as I think back, for the first week or so, everyone was kind of shut down and we didn't do a whole lot, with a couple of exceptions. Not everyone was real outgoing because we didn't know each other and we weren't comfortable. Neither was Josh, I don't think. But as time went on, we kind of opened up. We felt free to do more, and to act more fully, and to go crazy a little bit more often, you know?

LINDA: Sure, that's great. So does that narrow the possibilities for Josh here at M. Piercy High School? Will he only come to know and be known by actors? I don't feel so confident that Josh will experience the same degree of acceptance next semester. It's hard for me to say, "well, that's that, semester's done," and then next semester we just have to start all over.

JOEL: I see your point, but how else are we going to do it? To me, I think that curiosity is natural. It's one of those things that before you get to know someone like Josh, you're gonna have to confront that curiosity. You know? You're gonna want to look at him and maybe ask, "What happened?" And why is he the way he is and everything?

LINDA: That, or it's just ignore it all – pretend that Josh just isn't there.

JOEL: Well sure. When you see something you're uncomfortable with, what else do you do? Ignore it.

LINDA: So how can we break the pattern of things as they are – this isn't to say that you haven't done enough – but really, there's so much to change, isn't there?

CARA: You know, I've had classes with Josh before this one, and I guess I know what you mean: it's like he was there, but he wasn't.

CHASE: Me too. In Eighth Grade I noticed that a lot of the time it was his aide who the teachers talked to.

CARA: Yeah, I was in that class too, but you know I think that with a lot of people, the reason they react that way is because they don't know better. With my friends, the more I talk to them about Josh, the more they understand and the more willing they are to ask questions.

LINDA: Hm, so if people knew better they'd do better?

CHASE: I guess. But inclusion is a new idea. It's like with the civil rights movement – that was a long time ago and we still have racism. In Josh's life he's moved from a special school – separate from everyone else – to a school that still separated students with disabilities from everyone else. And now, to inclusion here where he has classes like I do. He has weightlifting, and then he has English class, a math class, and Issues Theater. To me, it's like there's a lot we don't know or understand about people that are disabled but I don't think we really know how to ask.

LINDA: Hm, we don't know how to ask, or we don't know if we want to ask?

JOEL: That's right, and that's what bothers me about all this – it's like how can we know anyway? We want to ask, but I mean, it's like what Alyssa said before about this class. Except for me, some of what we did in this class I had mixed feelings about. Sometimes to me it seemed like we were just using Josh as a prop, which I definitely think was wrong. You know? Because let's face it, he can't recite lines. Luckily, in his photography class he had his aide take the pictures. You know, he really didn't do anything. So from that standpoint, I kind of wonder if we're fooling ourselves.

CARA: OK, but, you know, I was there too, back in Eighth Grade when his aide took his pictures and stuff. And now, in all his classes . . . I'm sure Richard does a lot for him; but I hope it felt different to *Josh* in this class, more like *he* was taking the class and not Richard. It felt like that to me anyway. I hope he got a sense of it being something that *he* was doing. I got a new awareness of a lot of the issues we dealt with and I would hope that he got the same thing. I hope he now has an informed opinion about AIDS, or knows something more about it anyway, and about inclusion too – and that inclusion has to do with him. I hope he knows it was *him* in our class – not Richard.

JOEL: I would like to agree with you, of course, but you have to be realistic, he's never going to recite Shakespeare by heart. At least, I don't think so.

Maybe I'm wrong, but come on, Josh isn't an actor.

CHASE: Well, maybe I shouldn't say this, but hey, I'm not an actor either!

JOEL: That's not what I mean. Remember the scenes we did last year in Ms. Boneau's acting class – to me it felt a lot like an emperor's new-clothes-type-thing – or was I the only one who saw Josh just sitting up there, doing nothing, with . . with . . with just a taped voice to play on cue?

ALYSSA: I don't know about that class, but I think in our class he had a role. Sure, maybe his head was lowered a lot in the first part of the semester, but by the end, he was attentive and looking around. It was also interesting that at the beginning of the semester when he was in the skits, he played himself and the skits were all built around him being disabled. But towards the end of the year he always played . . . well, he wasn't always disabled. Like in the one skit he worked in a restaurant, in another, he played my son and he was part of a family.

JOEL: Yeah, so see he was acting then, but in the play that Ron wrote Josh is himself. I mean he actually had a real part in the play, an integral part in the sketches, and there I basically like inclusion—so, well, I don't know. I haven't figured all of this out yet. Does he play himself for us to use, or does he play a role we make up? I don't know.

LINDA: You've raised some excellent points Joel – I guess I just want you to keep returning to yourself for answers. I mean, reference yourself here – do *you* play yourself as an actor, or do we make up roles for you? You've heard the line, "All the world's a stage" – but whose lines do *you* get to read? Only those that are given to you? If I can stretch this a little more and ask about roles – if we have given Josh only one role to play, well, maybe that's all we can do right now. But it seems like Alyssa is saying she can accept Josh in the character of her child because she's in the character of the mother. It's all acting, right? And if Josh plays a character without lines it's not a problem for her, right, Alyssa?

ALYSSA: Right, not to . . . (*Chase interrupts*)

CHASE: Hey, I just had a funny idea – oops, sorry for interrupting – I was just thinking about a skit, an idea about using Josh, uhm, I mean, writing a role for Josh where he plays a superior life form and the people around him are just these, these mindless droids, and that, he – this character, I mean – he doesn't have to really do anything but just sit there and think. So of course he doesn't talk to us. But we all think it's because he can't when really it's like normal human beings are too primitive for him to communicate with because *his* form of communication is too advanced for us.

(*All break into laughter!*)

JOEL: Hey, great! I like the idea. And maybe it's like he's saving himself for somebody who will understand, but not really bothering with the rest of us who don't understand.

Conclusion

In her lecture and speech of acceptance upon the award of the Nobel Prize for Literature, the American poet and writer Toni Morrison stated: "Narrative has never been merely entertainment for me. It is, I believe, one of the principal ways in which we absorb knowledge" (Morrison 1993). It is with the same regard for narrative that this research is presented as story – describing events in one class over the course of a fifteen-week semester as its members confronted inclusion. The age-old, but previously unaddressed, questions about mainstreaming were confronted daily in the course of instruction, activity, and interactions. When probed by the researcher, the students articulated greater understandings about disability and offered new interpretations on inclusion that incorporated this new knowledge. The case-study describes how the students attributed thinking to Josh, noted his individuality, viewed their interactions with him as reciprocal, and ultimately defined a social place for him as a fellow actor and friend. These same four dimensions have been reported by Bogdan and Taylor (1992) in their analysis of how non-disabled people come to define and value persons with disabilities. They describe the 'social construction of humanness' (p. 275) as it emerged among individuals involved in caring and accepting relationships with persons with disabilities, proposing that:

> The definition of a person is not determined by either the characteristics of the person or the abstract social or cultural meanings attached to the group of which the person is a part, rather the nature of the relationship between the definer and the defined.
>
> Bogdan and Taylor 1992, p. 276

It is important to consider this research in the context of classrooms where the goal is for a student's disability to become secondary to the student's humanness. Moreover, it is suggested here that the very kinds of learning activities and class structure Janis Avers created enabled the students to come to know and understand Josh, and themselves, a little better.

Also, what came to count as knowledge about inclusion, emerged from the larger context Ferguson (1994) described as membership, "specifically participatory, socially valued, image-enhancing membership" (p. 10). Acknowledging the complexity of defining and achieving membership for students with disabilities as an outcome of inclusion, Ferguson insists:

> The purpose of all of our interventions, programs, indeed schooling in general, is to enable all students to actively participate in their communities so that others care enough about what happens to them to look for ways to include them as part of that community.
>
> Ferguson 1994, p. 10

41

This case-study describes how one teacher approached inclusion, not only for Josh, but for all of her students. Hers was not a conventional intervention, but it was successful beyond her own expectations. During an interview, Janis described one of several unanticipated outcomes from the Issues Theater experience. The students performed their skits in one of her regular English classes, and afterwards, led a class discussion on inclusion.

> It was my fifth hour class – a pretty difficult group, pretty insensitive, or just maybe young . . . immature. But I remember that discussion really opened some ears because it was students talking to students. There was some real dialogue going on there. And see, that's the kind of thing I'm interested in – getting students to talk to other students – serving as examples for what they have learned.

Throughout the interview Janis recounted what Skrtic (1995) describes as the goal of critical pragmatism as she evaluated and reappraised the political consequences of her professional knowledge, practices, and discourse. Further, this perspective evolved because her initial response to inclusion was inspired by her own values, which continuously shaped her response and which she modeled for the students in her classes. In this same interview, Janis eloquently summarized her overall efforts with inclusion and Issues Theater,

> Any time you try to include a student with disabilities in the classroom – by the very act of having them in the classroom – you're making a statement on values. It's like when you have something in your home that you set out, you say, "this is of value to me and I want it to be part of my everyday life. I want to have it here because it brings me pleasure or because it's functional, or because it's somehow important to me." And when you put things away, they're also out of mind. And it's either because they're so valuable you can't bring them out, or because they're not particularly important. So when you put kids away you're saying they're not important. When you bring them in, you're saying, "this person is of value to me." Anytime you do that, what you do is begin a process of opening minds that were not opened before . . . what happened in Issues Theater was a broadening of the mind that had to do with empathy and humanitarian issues. Anytime you invite a student with disabilities into your classroom, you're saying, "I value humanity, I value an open attitude, I believe all persons are created equal, and I'm going to live up to that . . . to walk the walk, you know?"

42

3

USA RESPONSE: LIBERATING VOICES?

Linda Ware's chapter is primarily about an 'issues theatre' class in a high school in the Midwest of the USA which includes a severely disabled student, Josh. He does not communicate through speech or sign-language, and we do not know how much he understands of the communication of others. The focus is on disability, although the theoretical section of the chapter and the voices of the students in the drama class suggest that inclusion is to be understood more broadly. Linda Ware tells us that the central theme explored in the study is to do with 'presumed membership in society' and how this is used by teachers 'to promote inclusion' in classrooms. We are also told that the classroom is the smallest unit for 'creating change' (p. 26). However, we think that there are other important themes in the chapter, and that change in a teacher or student or group of friends may represent smaller 'units' than classrooms. The specification of a single theme may be one illustration of a tension between the summarising academic voice in the earlier part of the chapter and the open-ended narrative that follows, in which readers, as much as the author, create the central themes for themselves.

How does the national context explain and constrain practice?

We are provided with some background literature from the USA on inclusion, and some details of the local education system. Specifically, we are told that inclusion in the USA 'should be viewed as a social movement', connected to a history of reforms about racial discrimination and the de-institutionalisation of psychiatric institutions that preceded legislation about 'handicapped children' and disabled people in the 1970s. However, Linda suggests that the development of inclusion in Longview is largely disconnected from national social movements:

> stakeholders were inspired by various historical events, although in the main they were prompted to action for reasons that were more local than historical.

In describing the local context, Linda discusses the notion of community in a way that has much in common with the Norwegian study. There appears to be a real local concern with maintaining a coherent community and this is seen to be threatened by the creation of a second high school in the town.

High schools in the USA tend to be large, by international standards, though M. Piercy High would be reduced in size with the construction of another high school. Linda asks whether such a large school might be 'too big to successfully implement inclusion'. However, the world beyond the school is bigger and such a view would limit notions of inclusion to small institutions and separate inclusion in education from the social processes mentioned earlier in the chapter.

Linda describes a variety of general features of the school-system which perpetuate exclusion, particularly streaming or 'tracking' which unwittingly preserves inequalities. Repetition of grades, which might further separate students by attainment, is a possible option but rarely invoked in Marge Piercy High. These features of the education system are not discussed further in relation to Josh's experience of the school.

While we are presented with indications of policy in the USA and can pick up through the student voices something about the student culture, we have only limited indications of the way the lives of Josh and others at the school are constrained and liberated through national and local policies and cultures.

Voices and perspectives on inclusion and exclusion

More than any of the others, this chapter allows an extended contribution from students, including an attempt to explore the silent voice of Josh. There are the voices of his teacher and assistant and a selection of academics. There is also the voice of Linda in a variety of incarnations: academic, researcher, teacher and writer.

As in most of our chapters, notions of inclusion or exclusion are not clearly defined in this chapter, although Linda is concerned with drawing a distinction between mainstreaming and inclusion. The transition from mainstreaming to inclusion is described as 'evolution' (p. 24). It is asserted that legislation led to 'mainstreaming', characterised by the presence of categorised students in mainstream schools but 'separated from the regular class for special instruction' (p. 21). This was replaced by a notion of inclusion in the 1990s where a child is *presumed* to be in the regular class. As evidence of this evolution we are presented with figures showing that increasing numbers of categorised students are in 'regular education classrooms'. Yet, as presented, the figures tell us nothing about movement towards greater inclusion, for they may merely reflect an increase in categorisation. There is an implication that inclusion, unlike mainstreaming, involves the reform of mainstream education so that pressures for exclusion are removed. Perhaps this is meant to explain why 'mainstreaming ultimately failed to deliver on its promise' (p. 22).

However, our reading of the literature on mainstreaming and inclusive education, some of which is presented in Linda's chapter, provides strong reasons to criticise the accuracy of the claims about the distinctive uses of the notions of mainstreaming and inclusion. For example, much of the early writings about mainstreaming in the US were concerned with questioning the sense of separating students categorised as 'mildly mentally retarded' out of mainstream classes into special classes within mainstream schools (e.g. Dunn 1968). They were concerned with undoing the separate provision here described as mainstreaming. The literature shows no consensus on the meaning of mainstreaming, integration or inclusion. Linda reports the view of Sarason and Doris, that 'mainstreaming is a moral issue' about broad social relationships: 'how . . . we want to live together'. Whether this is seen as framing mainstreaming as a moral or *political* concern, it links it to wide ranging changes within schools. Nor is evidence provided to show that inclusion has been used in practice to imply the kind of regular class participation that Linda Ware claims. We find mystifying the suggestion on page 23 that inclusion can be both 'ill-defined' and 'widely practiced', since if we do not know *what* it is how can we know *how much* of it there is?

Linda discusses Skrtic's concern that discussions of mainstreaming and inclusion equally lack depth and that a new method, 'critical pragmatism', is required to get to the bottom of special education practice. This is said to reveal the assumptions that lie behind professional practice. We argue that the change of voice from context to classroom in this chapter enables us to address some of the assumptions of academics and researchers in this field, about aspects of *their* professional practice and the extent of its exclusivity.

We are provided with a schema of approaches to inclusion as evolutionary, pilot, phased-in or top-down radical reform, and community-wide conversion. In Longview as a whole there seems to be an attempt at the third form, with hopes for community-wide conversion. However, what we find in Marge Piercy is a variety of the second: Josh's experience in the theatre arts course seems to be a pilot project, since there is no guarantee that it will be repeated, or that he will work again with the same students. Apparently, within the school it is disconnected from lasting change. However, it provides a startling lesson for us and it is hoped that it will provide a lesson for others in the school:

> In a few days you all start different classes, and so will Josh. I'm wondering how we could use your experiences to inform his new classmates in second semester?

Linda appears to conceive of inclusion as primarily about disabled students. Josh is the main focus of the second narrative, although we can see from their offered comments that other students participate in different ways and to differing extents. The conduct of the class permits us to see inclusion as concerned with participation for all. However, it is the students, albeit reported by the author, who assert this most clearly: 'they insisted inclusion applied to everybody and not just to people with disabilities'. They also make a clear link between inclusion and exclusion, and see the latter as the means to understand the former. We are concerned with the inclusion of Josh, because exclusion has taken place and we can change little until exclusionary processes are directly confronted: 'almost everyone chose to define inclusion by going to its opposite – exclusion'.

In describing 'special education students' in the school it seems that decisions about their education are made by professionals, rather than being based on their rights to be present and participate. The categories of students and professionals are presented as unproblematic and we are left intrigued by how an 'inclusion specialist' might respond to such labels. The use of an 'Individual Education Plan' may itself limit the participation of students and the development of more inclusive curricula and teaching approaches. Again, we do not know whether they are seen as part of a discarded mainstreaming or an embraced inclusion.

Linda finds that inclusion within the school is often ill-considered. Typically a disabled student is present in a classroom, but as in other studies in this book, participation is limited by the way the class is taught and support offered:

> Each classroom I observed was tolerant of the inclusion students, as they are sometimes referenced with apology, but interaction among the students was not evident. In many, but not all of these classes, students were supported by a special education teacher, or a classroom paraprofessional, with whom the student would, in most instances, exclusively interact. In effect, support separated the students with disabilities from the rest of the class.

Josh is a student on a 'special programme' described as mainstreaming with his participation within some lessons aided by his helper, Richard. Richard is reported as echoing Linda's concerns as he enters the Theater Arts class:

> He wants to believe this class will be different from the others. In the four years he has steered Josh into regular education classrooms in the name of inclusion, he has yet to feel included, yet to witness inclusion for Josh. In his most honest moments he names their roles: Josh the prop. Richard the appendage. . . . Each class has left Richard perplexed about inclusion; less confident about its possibility, and less convinced that Josh can be known and valued in a non-disabled world.

We then learn about the ways in which the theatre issues class is 'different from the others'; how Richard and Josh's classmates are given responsibility for determining the form and extent of Josh's inclusion as well as the notion of inclusion itself.

The students differed in their views about the value of Josh's inclusion. Most felt that they were better able to live with Josh and it was suggested that this had spread to friends not in the class. One hoped 'he knows it was *him* in our class – not Richard'. Another wondered if the group were reading too much into Josh's reactions:

> Because let's face it, he can't recite lines. Luckily, in his photography class he had his aide take the pictures. You know, he really didn't do anything. So from that standpoint, I kind of wonder if we're fooling ourselves.

But the lessons of the theatre issues class have taught us that inclusion can be approached productively through ideas of exclusion, rights, the removal of inequalities and the lessening of the dominance of self-interest or selfishness in relationships. Viewed in this way we do not need to justify Josh's inclusion, only to understand and counter his exclusion.

Changing voice, changing perspective?

We have already drawn attention to the way Linda chose to present the national and school context using a formal style often termed 'academic', and the observations of the drama class and the discussions of the participants in a freer, more literary form. The chapter returns to the more formal style at its end. Linda reserves the word 'narrative' for her dramatic reporting but we see the two styles as presenting different narratives. The setting out of the national context is a narrative or story whose coherence and truth we have questioned.

At one stage of this project Linda wanted to leave out the opening narrative. She wanted to present the theater issues class without its context, and this should be borne in mind when reading the following comments. She wanted to produce a creatively-written text and felt that this might be jeopardised if policy issues were addressed at the start. It was suggested that there was nothing intrinsic to policy issues that limited the form in which they could be expressed, and argued strongly that a central purpose of the study as a whole was that individual studies should give specific local meaning to notions of inclusion and exclusion. We can speculate whether an ease with the absence of context is more a feature of some writings in some countries than others.

As we hope you will recognise, chapters in this book differ from each other in the perspectives they contain on inclusion and exclusion. Further, within some chapters, notably the one from Ireland, you will find an explicit recognition of differences in perspective between authors of a single chapter. It seems to us that Linda's chapter reveals differences in perspective within one author as we shift from the introductory to the classroom narrative. The juxtaposition of styles allows us to play with the idea of perspectives. The differences in form appear to set up differences in view on inclusion and exclusion. The distinction between the 'formal voice' of the introduction, and the 'personal voice' of the story of Marge Piercy High appears to create a division between the understanding of inclusion conveyed in each.

The formal narrative is depersonalised. Linda refers to herself in the third person as an object: the researcher. The consequence of this style of narrative has different effects on each of the dramatis personae. For Linda we see it as part of a social convention related to her status as a professional and expressing a form of power, even though we might also regard it, ultimately, as emotionally and intellectually impoverishing. However, for disabled people it endorses an ideology of exclusion, exaggerating their objectification and dehumanisation, their treatment as 'other', subject to the categorisations and policy whims of professionals.

If 'academic' means using critical intelligence to investigate and create sense of an area, then there is a strong argument for saying that the dramatic narrative is the more academic. Once we enter the classroom the exploration of practice and the analysis of inclusion becomes clearer. It is as if the change of style, which draws on the experience of the author and the participants in the drama as well as linking into our own experience, allows us to move to a higher plane where connections are made and coherence maintained. Thus the switch of styles prompts us to question the way so-called academic conventions limit the depth to which an area is studied and the sense that is made of it. A concern with tying interpretations into 'the literature' can act as a conservative force, creating the discomforting paradox that the more sophisticated views of inclusion come from the least 'professionalised' participants in the study.

In the conclusion there is a partial return to the formal voice. During the editing process we discussed the switches of narrative with Linda in some detail. We sought clarification of their purpose and suggested that the voice of the conclusion might represent a drawing together, a synthesis of voices, following the formal thesis and imaginative antithesis of the body of the chapter. However, we feel that Linda is still submerged in the final equation as 'the researcher'. She concludes: 'The case study describes how the students attributed thinking to Josh, noted his individuality, viewed their interactions with him as reciprocal, and ultimately defined a social place for him as a fellow actor and friend.' Here she is already pulling away from the open-ended sparking of interconnections that the second section permits, closing down our reactions. The form of this finding is said to match the findings of others. It has validity because it relates to 'four dimensions' identified by Bogdan and Taylor (1992) and a notion of 'membership' espoused by Ferguson (1994). Yet the teacher is given the final word, telling us how Josh's presence in her class proclaims that Josh and the way of life which includes him, are of value.

Linda describes her research method as 'empowerment evaluation', involving both collaborative enquiry and participant observation. It involves handing control of the degree and form of involvement of the researcher/participant to some other participants. These include teachers but may not include students, formally at least. According to Linda, the researcher becomes a 'creative mediator' (p. 28) and she has provided us with a rich source of information on which to place our own interpretations.

Ideas of method and style interact; the 'narrative' style creates research that is accessible to many of the participants. In contrast, in the elliptical 'academic' style much of the information required to generate a contestable story is hidden from view in assumptions about categorisation, procedures or concepts. In Toni Morrison's words 'narrative . . . is one of the principal ways in which we absorb knowledge' and this chapter provides a compelling argument for re-examining the presentation of information about education.

4

SCOTLAND: MAINSTREAMING AT THE MARGINS

Julie Allan

Introduction

This chapter focuses on two students within a Scottish mainstream secondary school: Graham, a 16 year old described as having 'moderate learning difficulties' and Fiona, a 15 year old with hearing impairment.[1] Their academic and social experiences and the support they receive are explored in the context of local decision-making processes and the changing Scottish policy scene. The voices of the students are also foregrounded here. Fiona's and Graham's accounts suggest that their identities and experiences are constructed in the 'disturbing distance in between' inclusion and exclusion (Bhabha 1994, p. 45) and their mainstream peers reveal their part in this process. Inclusion, according to the students, is highly precarious and full of ambivalence and uncertainty.

The Scottish policy scene

A variety of Scottish policies were viewed by local education authority officials and teachers as having had an important impact upon SEN provision. At the time of the research some of these had not yet been implemented. Consequently, some of the views reported here, especially in relation to the delegation of resources and local government reform, are speculative.

Placement policies

The general thrust of national and regional policies within Scotland has been towards the inclusion of as many students as possible in mainstream schools. At the same time, however, there has been a recognition among national and local authority government officials that special schools continue to have an

---

1 The term 'hearing impairment' was used during the research mainly by teachers and educational psychologists, whereas Fiona introduced herself as deaf. A distinction also needs to be made in relation to Deaf culture, denoting the particular linguistic and cultural identities of deaf people. The conventions of using upper case when referring to Deaf culture and a lower case for deaf people generally will be followed.

important place in SEN provision (Allan, Brown and Riddell 1995). This has led to a general trend in Scotland of increased placements in mainstream schools and the maintenance of a relatively static special school population. The region in which the case-study was conducted has a written policy on special educational needs that advocated mainstreaming where possible. In practice, this involves moving students from special schools into units of the kind described above, but the pace of this has been very slow.

Parental involvement in placement decisions

In recent years, an increased emphasis on the role of parents as consumers of education, embedded in the Parents' Charter (Scottish Office 1995), grants parents the rights to select a school for their child, receive information on progress and appeal 'if things go wrong' (p. 12). Parents choosing a special placement, in preference to a mainstream one, could undermine education authority officers' attempts to encourage inclusion. Recent work in this area, however, suggests that in reality, parents' choices are restricted by professionals in a variety of ways (Allan *et al.* 1995).

Officers in the case-study local authority argued that parental choice had influenced placement patterns overall. They said, for example, that the development of special units in the mainstream had been slowed down both by some parents preferring that their child attend their local mainstream school and by others opting for special school placement. As far as the case-study school was concerned, officers claimed that parents were given the option whether or not to transfer their child from the special school, and some had rejected the offer. Yet, the region seemed to operate a highly-structured decision-making process which may have limited the operation of parental choice far more than was implied by legislative rhetoric.

The delegation of resources

Scottish schools were undergoing a major change in the management of resources with the transfer of budgets from education authorities to all mainstream schools by 1996 and to all special schools by 1997. Students with significant special educational needs had these recognised formally within a Record of Needs (similar to a Statement in England and Wales). However, the distinction between those who should and should not be 'recorded' is not clear and has been the focus of debate throughout the UK. Under the new arrangements, headteachers have responsibility for school resources, including funding for non-recorded students with SEN. The budgets for students with Records of Needs, however, remain under local authority control. Officers within the case-study authority said they feared that students without Records of Needs would be particularly disadvantaged if headteachers did not recognise their needs and allocate resources appropriately.

Local government reform

At the time of the research, regional officials were gearing up for a radical reorganisation of local government (effective from 1 April 1996), which would involve replacing the existing twelve regional and fifty-three district authorities with thirty-two smaller unitary authorities. This particular region was split into three and there was considerable concern among officials and school staff about maintaining existing levels of SEN provision. They feared the slowing of the development of SEN policies generally while the new councils found their feet as well as the loss of economies of scale (particularly important for SEN services). This was thought likely to have a particular impact on pupils without Records of Needs who nevertheless depend on centrally-funded resources.

The case-study school

The school, with 1,100 students between the ages of 11 and 17, is situated in a rural town in the North East of Scotland, within commuting distance of a major city and has a mixed population of working- and middle-class students. Traditionally, the local community has been involved in farming, manufacturing and the service sector, but it has expanded in recent years to accommodate people choosing to live out of, but work in, the city.

The school was chosen because it had recently increased its population of students with special educational needs. In 1993, twenty-six students who previously attended a special school for students categorised as having 'moderate learning difficulties' had moved to the mainstream school together with their teachers. Their transition from exclusion (in locational terms) to inclusion, however, was partial, in the sense that the students were placed in a special unit within the school. Unit provision of this kind has increasingly found favour among policy makers in Scotland.

There are formal links between the school and the community in the shape of a School Board, made up of parents, teacher representatives and the headteacher, but this body has limited legal duties and powers (it does not, for example, control the school's budget). More informally, parents have regular contact with the school through parents' evenings and student progress reports. Parents of students with special educational needs, particularly those in the special unit, have more extensive contact with staff.

Graham and Fiona represent two aspects of the exclusion–inclusion relationship within the school. Graham had been identified as having 'moderate learning difficulties', and had transferred from the special school to the unit. From there, he moves into mainstream for particular subjects. Fiona, with hearing impairment, spends most of her time in mainstream, but moves in the opposite direction out of mainstream for individual tuition. The students were shadowed over a period of four days and informal discussions were held with them and their peers. Their parents and a range of mainstream and specialist staff were also interviewed.

Admission procedures for students with special education needs

Prior to the transfer from primary to secondary school, specialist teachers visit the fourteen associated primary schools and discuss students who have experienced difficulties. They then send mainstream staff a list of these students and information about their difficulties. Secondary school staff can also refer any students they consider to have difficulties in learning to support staff or alternatively to the special unit admissions panel. In Fiona's case, mainstream teachers were told of her severe hearing loss and of the family history of deafness. They were also advised that although she was of average ability, her comprehension was limited by a lack of vocabulary development. Staff were given advice on how to help her, for instance by facing light sources and standing still while speaking. Graham's mainstream teachers were told that he was a 'pleasant, rather immature boy who has difficulty making relationships' and whose progress had been hindered by poor concentration.

Selection for the unit

The admission procedures for the unit had evolved from the criteria originally used to select students from the special school. At that time students were transferred provided they were of secondary school age, their parents supported the transfer and they were considered likely to 'cope' within a mainstream school. This last judgement was made on social, as well as academic, grounds. Some students with limited skills in social interaction were not invited to transfer. Those with very low academic abilities also remained at the special school, even if they were of secondary age, and a few parents had declined the offer. Graham met all the criteria. However, although his parents said they supported the transfer, they did not feel that they had been fully involved in the decision. It was something, they said, that 'had just happened'.

Subsequently, once the unit was established, the school set up an admissions panel (consisting of a regional official, an educational psychologist, the mainstream headteacher, the learning support coordinator and the head of the learning support unit) to determine which further students were placed in the unit. These decisions concerned pupils at primary transfer stage, those already in the secondary school or pupils in the local special school. According to the unit's admissions policy, agreed and operated by the panel, the following criteria are used in deciding on placement in the unit:

- A referral is made by an educational psychologist.
- The student has a Record of Needs.

- There is a recognised need for integration from a special school.
- There is a recognised need for a reduced secondary timetable.

These last two points are clearly more subjective than the preceding two and raise questions about whose recognition counts. The so-called need for integration from a special school or for a reduced secondary timetable may well be contested by teachers, parents or the children concerned, but the admissions panel appears to have the final say on this matter.

Systems of support

In this school, all the students who attend the special unit, and a further four in mainstream, have Records of Needs. Graham has a Record of Needs but Fiona does not. In practice, the existence of such a record implies an initial formal assessment, monitoring of progress and additional resources such as staffing or equipment, although these can be made available (as in Fiona's case) without a Record of Needs. Within the school, a distinction is made between recorded students within the unit and those with SEN in the mainstream, creating, in effect, separate administrative streams of 'unit' and 'mainstream' pupils. This was further reinforced by the establishment of a separate staffing complement and budget, school policies and admissions procedures.

There are three separate SEN budgets, held centrally by the education authority, for students within the special unit, those in mainstream with a Record of Needs and those without. The unit budget is the largest of the three, covering its running costs, staffing, equipment and transport of students to and from school. The budgets for students in mainstream cover mainly staffing, equipment and other support. The distinction between those with and without a Record of Needs is an important one, with the former group of students generally receiving more resources than the latter. The policy of the unit specifies the provision available therein, the identification and admission of students, involvement of parents, staff responsibilities and other related aspects. The learning support policy for students in mainstream outlines the kinds of assistance which mainstream teachers can expect, such as consultancy, cooperative teaching and individual tuition and offers advice on identification and assessment.

When in the unit, students are supported by unit teachers and non-teaching assistants. A speech therapist visits the unit regularly and works with individuals or groups. Assistance is also provided by senior students, who may take an optional certificated module on disability. Students who go into mainstream from the unit are usually supported by unit teachers and those with special educational needs who do not attend the unit are supported by learning support teachers. These teachers are members of an Area Special Educational Needs Team (ASENT), which coordinates support for students with special educational needs within the secondary school and its associated primaries. Mainstream departments are required to 'bid' for this provision, since availability is limited.

Fiona receives learning support within mainstream classrooms and is withdrawn daily for a tutorial with a peripatetic teacher for the hearing impaired. The tutorials are aimed at assisting Fiona with developing her language skills, and much of the time is spent introducing her to phrases that other students acquire through informal conversation. Often, Fiona is mystified by expressions such as 'head in the clouds' (day-dreaming) or a 'sweet tooth' (a liking for sweet things), so these have to be explained to her. There are no opportunities for Fiona to learn sign-language within the school, although this might have assisted her language development more generally.

When Graham is in the unit, he is taught in groups of between eight and ten pupils of a broadly similar age. In mainstream, he joins a larger class of about twenty-eight to thirty, but is usually supported by a member of the unit staff. Staff say the unit offers an alternative to a full mainstream timetable, while allowing students some access to ordinary classrooms. If a student is placed in the unit, staff can then decide how much time within mainstream is appropriate. In Graham's case, however, there is disagreement over this between unit staff on the one hand and Graham and his parents on the other; this is explored more fully later in the chapter.

Mainstream teachers rely on support from either the unit staff or learning support teachers, although Graham's English teacher preferred not to have this. According to the learning support handbook, prepared by the head of the Area Special Educational Needs Team, subject specialists are expected to have clear ideas about aims, objectives and content, then to plan a joint approach with the learning support teacher. The handbook states that:

> the Subject Specialist looks after the content and the LS Specialist pinpoints areas of concern. The LS Specialist is not the Subject Specialist. In fact, it is often an advantage to be without knowledge of the subject matter, because the LS Teacher can appreciate the difficulties the pupils are having. . . . A pooling of resources from both teachers can provide stimulus for a learning situation.

In practice, however, a rather different picture was described by learning support teachers and observed during the research. This is a much more one-sided process, in which mainstream staff teach the lesson and the unit or learning support teacher focus on a small number of students with SEN. The traditional 'chalk and talk' teaching style of the history teacher seems to be particularly suited to Graham, who likes to listen, take notes and answer questions. It is less convenient, however, for the learning support teacher who accompanies him to history and who is constrained to listen passively. The class teacher, however, insisted that the presence of a learning support teacher is vital for Graham.

Participation in curricula: the edges of academic life?

Graham and Fiona's participation in the academic life of the school appears to distance them from their mainstream peers in a variety of ways. Some of this may be attributed to the decisions made about their participation in the curriculum.

Both students are exposed to the elements of a mainstream curriculum. Fiona is following the 5–14 programme of curriculum and assessment, Scotland's non-statutory equivalent of a National Curriculum, and Graham is undertaking Standard Grades, the next level of qualifications. In both cases, however, the students are thought to require additional and different provision. Space within the timetable has to be made for Graham's 'life skills' and Fiona's contact with the teacher of the hearing impaired. It was not always clear, however, why certain subjects and not others were cut. Fiona loses out on French, while Graham was persuaded to discontinue drama. Fiona follows a full mainstream timetable, apart from her daily tutorials which, as far as she and her teachers are concerned, are a very important aspect of her provision. Yet, the peripatetic teacher has little opportunity for contact with Fiona's mainstream teachers and therefore is restricted from embedding work of this kind within her mainstream activities. The curriculum followed by Graham and other students in the unit is aimed at equipping the students with life skills such as independent travel, personal hygiene and social education. They also participate in a range of practical activities, including art, environmental studies and leisure activities.

Graham's mainstream timetable accounts for fifty per cent of the school week, but it has recently been reduced from around sixty-five per cent because unit staff thought he was becoming stressed. The head of the unit described what they saw and their response to this:

> Inappropriate behaviour is what usually shows when he is under stress, silliness, cheeking back, which is so out of his character. . . . He was starting to do that, the class clown, and that picked up in me. Nervous habits – starts to write something, then 'no, no, no', that sort of thing. We try and nip it in the bud right away and take away the stress. He can cope with roughly half of a curriculum in mainstream.

The drama teacher offered a similar account and so when Graham's timetable was reduced, drama was the discontinued subject. Both he and his parents said they had been very disappointed at this decision. Graham's view is that he should spend all of his time in mainstream and his peers took the same view, arguing that the benefits are reciprocal:

K: I think it helps us too, to have more respect for them, because I used to think people from the special unit didn't actually have to do anything there, so I didn't have much respect.

T: They do seem quite immature when they're just in the unit. Like, I knew Graham when he was just in the unit, but ever since he's come into our class, he really has matured quite quickly. Because he used to just muck around, make quite a fool of himself. Like, he used to hit the girls and tell them to shut up, but he's changed quite a bit now.

The mainstream students seem to see Graham as exhibiting less, rather than more, of the immature behaviour that the staff attribute to stress. As far as the students are concerned, the special unit seems to be the cause of such behaviour by denying Graham as much contact with them as possible, whereas staff see it as necessary for his protection. The remaining subjects he attends in mainstream are English, maths and history.

Graham's participation in the academic life of the school appears to have a 'businesslike' quality, with little opportunity for him to hang around between classes as his mainstream peers can. He needs to be well organised (which his teachers said he is) in order to get between the mainstream classes and the unit. He arrives at mainstream classes from a different direction from that of his peers and this seems to generate a social distance from them.

Social interaction: negotiating barriers?

Graham's and Fiona's social experiences are portrayed by them and their mainstream peers as unpredictable, oscillating from one moment to the next, but usually marginal in some way. Mainstream students seem to operate their own 'rules' of conduct towards their disabled peers, shifting them in and out of mainstream from one moment to the next. Graham and Fiona are not, however, simply passive recipients of this regime. Rather, they resist and contest attempts to place them at the margins.

Graham: it's all in good fun really

The special unit offers a social space for students during intervals and lunch breaks, as an alternative to the 'rough and tumble' of the mainstream. Thus, students can spend an entire day in the unit without meeting mainstream students. Graham, of course, goes out of the unit to attend mainstream classes, but usually returns to spend his breaks there. His only opportunities for social interaction with mainstream students are, therefore, within lessons, but he rarely speaks to his classmates and they reciprocate by ignoring him. The only exception is when they tease him about his obsession with football:

L: They just tease him a bit.
M: Yeah.
K: It's all, like, good fun, really.
JA: What happens?

M: They'll say things, like, 'did you go to see the match?'
K: Yeah, they'll tease him about another team playing against them and if they beat [his team], they'll take the mickey out of him. It's all in good fun, really.
JA: How does he react?
M: He takes it as a joke.

Graham made no reference to such episodes, joking or otherwise. The mainstream students, however, said that he sometimes reacted to teasing by saying that he was going to tell the teacher. To them, that was going 'a bit far', since other people just 'take it', and so his resistance merely signalled further his difference. They had established limits to the teasing that they saw as acceptable and beyond which they would feel uncomfortable: 'If someone was doing something to him, like picking on him or something, we'd feel a bit of resentment towards them'. The pupils inferred a somewhat passive reaction in their imagined resentment to any treatment of Graham that crossed their own boundaries of decency. Yet, such a situation had not arisen, so it was difficult for them to be more than speculative.

Graham, according to a special unit teacher, has a 'very old fashioned, non-deviant approach to everything, and that is not life'. Yet, staff also said his 'easygoing manner' saw him through any potential difficulties with his mainstream peers. They described him as 'immature', illustrated by his speaking aloud in class, although this had improved recently and he was no longer unable to sit still during a lesson. Graham tends to volunteer inappropriate and irrelevant answers in class and his history teacher commented that this often marks him out from other mainstream pupils. He is regarded as well-organised in mainstream and enthusiastic, which, as one teacher pointed out 'is half the battle', yet his enthusiasm also distinguished him from his peers and contributed to his social isolation.

Fiona: just like us really

Fiona, in particular, seems to work hard at functioning with 'rehearsed carelessness' (Garfinkel 1967, p. 172) by hiding her deafness. Yet she seems to be constrained to act in this way because of the silencing of Deaf culture within the school. As Booth (1988) argued, this amounts to a severe form of prejudice. Fiona seems to find herself marginalised from both the hearing and non-hearing worlds:

> I'm tall, with brown hair and I'm deaf . . . Sometimes in school I can't hear what people say behind my back or if they don't turn their face to me or they speak too fast or when people cover their faces with their hands or I have to keep asking what people said. It's embarrassing and sometimes I don't ask, then don't know what to do.

She said she had learnt some sign-language, but has little use for it. She only knows one person of her own age who is deaf and does not sign with the deaf members of her family. Sometimes, however, her classmates ask her to show them how to say something in sign-language, giving it a slightly exotic quality rather than seeing it as an important element of communication between them. It has been argued that deaf people should not be denied access to Deaf culture (Ladd 1991; Kyle 1993; Lane 1995) and sign-language is an intrinsic part of this:

> The sensory world is a very different world without audition and sign language is possibly the only way of fully expressing the meaning that this world has, for it is a gestural-visual-spatial language.
>
> Corker, 1993, p. 150

The sessions with the peripatetic teacher of the hearing impaired are important to her self-confidence and involve acknowledgement of her deaf identity, but not the explicit teaching of signing.

Fiona has many opportunities for social interaction with mainstream students within classrooms and during break times. She appears to have good relationships with her peers, who help her out with any words she has mispronounced, and otherwise include her in conversations, jokes and other activities. Yet, Fiona said she often finds it difficult to follow conversations with her peers and sometimes pretends she understands what is said, rather than interrupting to ask for clarification. Fiona has recently been introduced to horse-riding through a friend of her peripatetic teacher and has become passionate about horses. This has earned her the reputation among her peers as one of several 'horse-mad' students and seems to reinforce her inclusion in mainstream. Fiona's interest in horses appears to bring her closer to her mainstream peers, in contrast with the distancing response to Graham's obsessive enthusiasm for football.

Fiona indicated that she is happy at school but that this has not always been the case. At primary school she was called 'phonic ear' by students mocking her hearing aid. While she was still at primary, she was aware that her older brother (also deaf) was being bullied at secondary school and so was afraid to make the transfer. However, her parents visited senior staff at the school and Fiona did not experience any bullying when she moved there. Her hearing aid was being repaired at the time of the visit, a situation that suited her, since she prefers not to wear it. Yet, her teachers made it clear that this disadvantaged her. Had there been more explicit attempts to acknowledge and value the cultural distinctiveness of deafness, Fiona might not have felt 'undoubtedly motivated by a desire to conceal' (Lynas 1986, p. 180). She might also have avoided 'struggling to understand' and feeling 'angry and upset' when she could not.

Fiona's mainstream peers said they regarded Fiona as closer to them than to other deaf people: 'well, she knows a couple of people who are deaf, but she's just like us really, just that she's deaf'. Their conduct towards Fiona appeared to be a mixture of ignoring and acknowledging her deafness. They tried to 'treat her normally', but also corrected some of her mistakes. This caused them some anxiety about how Fiona might respond:

> Sometimes if she can't pronounce words, we just tell her what it is, like the other day she couldn't say 'brochure' and I just said 'brochure' and then she kept saying it right . . . We try not to make her feel bad if she's not hearing right.

The mainstream students engaged in a kind of conspiracy with Fiona to improve her linguistic competence by helping her with pronunciation. In this sense, they were important agents in Fiona's inclusion.

Inclusion: a moving target?

Inclusion for Graham and Fiona always appeared more or less conditional, both because of the effects of national and regional policies and due to the actions and attitudes of teachers and students. In terms of changing funding arrangements for example, regional officials and school staff speculated that Fiona would be more likely to be affected than Graham, as she required the services of the peripatetic teacher (which could be difficult for a smaller authority to afford) and she did not have a Record of Needs. However, she was likely to have left school before any impact of the changes was felt.

Graham and Fiona appeared to want as many opportunities for inclusion as possible, but they emphasised different things. For Graham, inclusion meant participation in the mainstream academic curriculum and taking the same formal examinations as his peers. He valued the 'cut and thrust' of the mainstream classroom because it was more challenging than the unit and he enjoyed answering questions and acquiring information, especially in history. Social interaction seemed less important to him and, indeed, he seemed unaware of, or undisturbed by, his isolation in the classroom. Fiona, in contrast, valued her relationships with, and acceptance among, her peers. Extraction from French was a necessary and valuable opportunity to learn vocabulary, obtain help and talk to the peripatetic teacher, to whom she had become very attached. Besides, she had taken French in her first year and had hated it.

Inclusion for Fiona implied assimilation and denial of her deaf identity (Corker 1993). It also meant partial exclusion in the form of intensive, daily withdrawal, to help her acquire the language that was lost through deafness. It could be argued that denying her the opportunity to learn sign-language was limiting her potential for general language development. Inclusion that assimilates Deaf culture and creates abnormality out of deafness (Booth 1988) has the potential to be 'the most dangerous move yet against the early development of a deaf person's character, self-confidence and basic sense of identity' (Ladd 1991, p. 88). Social interaction with her peers was impeded by her deafness, and she chose to disguise this by affecting to hear. Inevitably, this would have meant some restriction on her participation by closing off the 'basic quickfire interchange' (Kyle 1993, p. 216) that is so important to adolescents. She seemed to want, however, to resist a situation in which she might become excluded by those impatient with her lack of hearing.

Graham's prospects of obtaining passes in English, maths and history at the lowest level of certification had clearly delighted him and his parents. Yet, they had been disappointed when he had been withdrawn from drama, unconvinced by the argument that he was becoming stressed and would benefit from a more even balance of his time between the unit and mainstream. Where there was a difference of opinion like this the professionals seemed to assume the right to overrule the parents. In this case, however, the unit staff had also assessed Graham's parents as having an over-estimation of his capabilities. A judgement of this kind is an interesting example of the exclusion of parents in the decision making process. His inclusion in mainstream involved part-time attendance in mainstream classes. While he was there he seemed very isolated, with little evidence of interaction with his peers, except when they were teasing him. His enthusiasm for learning did little to enhance his status among them, yet they had watched him mature and were convinced of the mutual benefits of inclusion.

Mainstream students seemed to have an important role in constructing Fiona's and Graham's social experiences, and their conduct towards Graham and Fiona was mediated by their own rules about appropriate behaviour. This often involved a kind of individualising guesswork about how Fiona or Graham was likely to react, e.g. 'we try not to make [Fiona] feel bad if she's not hearing right'. At other times the mainstream students reflected in a more generalised way about how to 'treat people like them'. They also made judgements about the behaviour of Fiona and Graham. Fiona's peers read her interest in horses inclusively, signalling her closeness to other 'horse-mad' students. Graham's peers, in contrast, saw his enthusiasm for football as a further indication of his difference from them. It is striking that the way he expressed a male concern had the effect of pushing him further into the margins. Social inclusion for Graham seemed to amount to an elusive guessing game, in which his mainstream peers constantly shifted the goalposts and kept him at a distance.

From this case-study, inclusion appears to have the following qualities:

- It is not static, but a continuous process, subject to change. Students were not included or excluded once and for all, but moved in and out of mainstream in response to a variety of factors.
- The physical locations of students (e.g. within a special unit or mainstream) are not significant in themselves. What seems to matter is how

students such as Graham are spatialised by events such as his arrival in mainstream from the unit and the mainstream pupils' perceptions of what he does in the unit.

• Social inclusion is perhaps the most tenuous and can alter from one moment to the next, depending on the interaction between students.

This begins to undermine the binarism that polarises inclusion/exclusion, normal/disabled and other features of SEN provision. In this context, inclusion is something that is done to pupils, and excluded pupils are viewed as the 'undesirable half of a binary pair' (Marks 1994, p. 73). From the accounts in this case-study, however, inclusion seems to be a far more uncertain process, occurring somewhere at the margins and likely to change at any moment:

> What is interrogated is not simply the image of the person, but the discursive and disciplinary place from which questions of identity are strategically and institutionally posed.
>
> Bhabha 1994, p. 47

In other words, Fiona and Graham were placed in a continual state of interrogation, particularly from their mainstream peers. Perhaps we should try to generate more positive versions of this process in which identity and difference are scrutinised and valued by all students. This implies a more explicit recognition of deafness within the school community and opportunities for mainstream pupils to discuss inclusion. Graham's mainstream peers identified their contact with him as mutually educative, yet their influence was at times highly negative and isolating for Graham. With some careful encouragement, mainstreaming at the margins could be a less dangerous thing.

5

SCOTLAND RESPONSE: PROFESSIONALS AT THE CENTRE?

In her chapter Julie Allan explores the 'academic and social experiences' of two students categorised as having 'special educational needs' in the context of 'local decision-making processes and the changing Scottish policy scene'. Julie focuses much of her attention on social processes, revealing through her study of the experiences of two students the complex and at times contradictory ways in which their participation in school life is mediated through their relationships with other students.

Social acceptance is at the top of the agenda for one of the students, Fiona, who spends most of her time in the mainstream, although each day she is withdrawn to work with a specialist teacher. She values highly her relationships with and acceptance among her peers. In order to minimise her difference from them she is prepared to pretend that she understands what they are saying, even when she cannot. For Graham, on the other hand, social interaction seems less important. His main concern, we are told, is to participate in the mainstream curriculum, taking the same examinations as his peers. Yet he spends only fifty per cent of his time in regular classes, the rest being in the unit in groups of eight to ten students where he is said to do 'life skills'.

How does the national context explain and constrain practice?

The account provides us with little background about general educational policies in Scotland. They have been influenced by the principles of introducing market values into education, described in the English chapter, although, meeting with a more resistant culture, these have been slower to take root (Brown 1994). Scottish teachers have retained greater autonomy over the curriculum than their English counterparts and 'opting out' of local authority control has met with little enthusiasm. There is a school board consisting of teachers, parents and the headteacher, but unlike England where in theory and in law the governing body is the main management structure of the school, in Scotland it has no control over the school budget or responsibilities for appointing teachers. However, a drastic fragmentation of local authorities through the redrawing of their boundaries has severely disrupted and curtailed their influence. The emphasis on a rhetoric of school choice in Scottish legislation, similar to that in England and New Zealand, is discussed. The chapter illustrates how, in practice, choice is often restricted by the actions of professionals.

Scottish special education policies are said to encourage 'the inclusion of as many students as possible in mainstream schools'. In the specific region of the case-study school there is a written policy advocating 'mainstreaming where possible'. However, it is reported that officials continue to see special schools as having an important place in provision, and it becomes clear that the notion of possibility relates to a particular vision of the limits of mainstream adaptability, largely under the control of professionals.

In practice, inclusion is said to often involve transfer to a special unit attached to a mainstream school. This strategy has to be seen in the context of changing patterns of funding, with budgets increasingly delegated to the school level. Special needs funding, on the other hand, remains centrally-managed. In Scotland, as in several of the other education systems featured in this book, some students are given an official 'special status' which secures additional money for their education as well as invoking particular reactions of professionals, parents and fellow students. In Scottish special education this is marked by a 'Record of Needs'. It is noted, however, that flexibility within the system allows for additional resources to be made without a 'Record of Needs'.

In the case-study school three groups of 'special' children are defined in relation to three separate 'special' budgets. These are for students in the unit; those in the main school with a Record of Needs; and students in the mainstream, categorised as having special educational needs, but without a Record. Such divisions help to sustain a climate whereby the unit provision is seen as separate from the other support mechanisms in the school, retaining separate staffing and administrative structures. This is highlighted by the way unit attendance is contrasted with presence in the mainstream, applying a language of exclusion to such students even though they are educated within the fabric of a mainstream school and are on its roll. This arrangement has significant impact on the possibility of students from the unit becoming full participants in mainstream cultures.

Voices and perspectives on inclusion and exclusion.

The voices of the students and, at the same time, that of the author herself occupy centre stage in the account. We are invited to tune in to a series of conversations between Julie and the students in which she allows them to speak for themselves while leading us to read their comments in terms of her interpretations. Other voices, including those of parents, teachers and officers, are referred to in passing.

Yet, as we have suggested, it is the perspectives of the professionals which have the most power and exert strong pressures on the way students are categorised and inclusion is conceived. These perspectives remain largely unanalysed and uncontested by the author and therefore, at times, appear to be sanctioned by her. Yet conflicts of view are evident between students and teachers, parents and professionals.

We have little other direct evidence of Julie's view of inclusion, although it becomes clearer towards the end of the chapter that she thinks that an examination of the experience of the students might contribute to the development of a more inclusive policy in the school. The use of what might be called exclusionary terminology in the text, such as 'SEN provision', and 'students with special educational needs' warrants comment, particularly the use of the SEN acronym. This distances a group of students from us, while employing specialist jargon and thus covering it in a cloak of respectability and competence.

The dominant perspective on inclusion, revealed in several practices in the school, is that it arises from benign professional decisions rather than from student or parental rights. This professional view deals in student types who are to be modified and fitted as best they can into an unchanging and unchallenged curriculum and approach to teaching and learning. It is an assimilationist model rather than one that accepts or celebrates diversity. It is a conception that permits the borderline between mainstream and excluded students to be disputed, but the need for a distinction between normal, includable students and abnormal, unincludable students, is held to be self-evident. This retention of a borderline further fuels the idea that decisions require professional expertise.

The operation of the assimilationist model is seen clearly in the way Fiona's linguistic aspirations are limited by the school and herself. The teachers respond to Fiona's difficulties with speaking English by avoiding teaching her French. In Norway, many years ago, one of us encountered students in a school for the deaf learning English. Here there was no question of linking deafness to presumed inability to learn another language. The restrictions on Fiona are part of an attitude to foreign languages that varies from place to place. If it is an aim of Fiona's education to encourage an understanding of language then her language learning might be broadened, for example, by the teaching of British Sign-Language and perhaps making her acquainted with other sign-languages. Certainly, as Julie notes, greater recognition of the Deaf culture and language might be a more productive means of aiding Fiona's acceptance than hiding her deafness.

Graham was 'selected' for the unit from the special school. Those felt to be academically 'very low' or those with 'limited skills in social interaction' were not selected. Among the criteria used are that unit students should have 'a need for integration from a special school' and 'a need for a reduced secondary timetable'. This is a familiar way in which professional values about who should be educated together are made to appear as if they involve the identification of basic requirements of students, like a need for food or culturally self-evident health benefits, like a 'reduced intake of fat'. The conception of the unit, with its separate location, provides a focus for the specialisation of teachers and a rationale for the view that those in the unit need a sizeable dose of what it and they offer.

It is suggested that judgements related to the integration of students into the secondary school can lead to dispute but that the admissions panel 'appears to have the final say on the matter'. In the case of Graham, his parents are reported as being in favour of the decision made but did not feel that they had been fully involved.

The study includes little indication of the interactions that occur between students and teachers. Nor are we made aware of how school and classroom processes impact on the participation of other students. So we are left to speculate as to how far, if at all, the practices of teachers impact on student sub-cultures.

Julie argues that the modifications made in the curriculum of both these students has the effect of distancing them from their peers. The professionals overrule the preferences of both Graham and his parents by removing him from drama lessons because of his 'immature behaviour'. Staff attribute his behaviour to the 'stress' of inclusion whereas some of the other students see these difficulties as arising because Graham is denied contact with them.

Graham, despite being well-organised and enthusiastic, is largely ignored by his peers. Here it is noted that since at breaktimes he returns to the unit ('an alternative to the rough and tumble') 'his only opportunities for social interaction with mainstream students are within lessons'. Graham's enthusiasm for football is seen to distance him from the other students. We presume it is the distance of Graham from them that colours their attitude to his interests which in other circumstances could well be a point of contact. Julie suggests that 'physical locations are not significant in themselves' but Graham's contact with other students becomes increasingly difficult with physical distance. A greater concentration on cooperative group learning within lessons might strengthen Graham's status amongst his peers.

In their own ways, both Graham and Fiona are seen to 'resist and contest attempts to place them on the margins', although their degrees of success in this respect are significantly different. It is argued, for example, that Fiona finds herself 'marginalised from both the hearing and non-hearing worlds', not least because Deaf culture and language are hardly recognised in the school. Nevertheless, she seems to be largely accepted by her peers who, it is argued, are 'important agents' in her inclusion.

Overall, it is concluded that for these two students inclusion remains 'more or less conditional, both because of the effects of national and regional polices and due to the actions and attitudes of teachers and students'. In particular, the study illustrates the roles students can have in constructing the social experiences of one another and how this is influenced by the norms that exist within student groups. Inclusion is seen not as static but a continuous process, subject to change from moment to moment.

The study provides detailed evidence for us of the subtle contradictions that arise in attempting inclusion using an assimilationist model which denies the significance of difference and how this is linked to ideas of selection and fitness for the mainstream. The decision of Julie Allan to focus almost exclusively on students with a professionally derived label of SEN is part of this selective process and could be seen to further contribute to their marginalisation.

Within the study Julie is an external observer, interviewer and interpreter. Representing the voices of others in a text under one's own control is not the same as encouraging or inviting people to speak or write their own stories. The contextualising of voices that takes place raises questions for most researchers in this field about the extent to which a professional narrative colours and reduces the voice of students, or other participants in a way that becomes *less than* them talking for themselves. The first three case-studies in the book in particular, provide interesting comparisons in this respect, and taken with the others offer the possibility of developing criteria for when representation of the voices of others empowers rather than diminishes them.

6

NEW ZEALAND: INCLUSIVE SCHOOL, INCLUSIVE PHILOSOPHY?

Keith Ballard and Trevor MacDonald

Introduction

In preparing this case study we spent time over several months in 'Central School', an inclusive primary school for around 160 children aged between 5 and 12. We talked with parents, teachers and students, and observed in classrooms and playgrounds. We asked to work with Central School because we were interested to learn how and why a school practised inclusion while other schools excluded children on the basis of disability. We set out to describe what went on in the school and to know why the teachers, parents and others had created and maintained an inclusive school. We tried to understand what people did to create an inclusive setting, and why they were committed to education as a non-discriminatory activity. We were particularly interested to know if the philosophy of inclusion advanced by the principal, teachers, and the school's Board of Trustees could be seen in the everyday activities of the teachers and students. As consistencies emerged between what was said and what we saw happening, we became aware of the team approach to problem solving in this school, and the close relationships between the school and its community. We also learned that to be an inclusive school was to attract both support and criticism from the wider educational community, which remains equivocal on the issue of inclusion, despite recent legislation giving all children the right to attend a mainstream state school.

We first outline features of the New Zealand education system that represent the context for this study. We then describe our research approach, the school and the beginnings of its development as 'inclusive'. Next we present the views of teaching staff, the Board of Trustees and other parents on inclusion and exclusion. We then report our observations of classrooms and playgrounds and the views of students. We end by interpreting the work of this school in terms of the concept of metatheory; a world view shared by teachers.

The national context

Central School is in Dunedin, a city of around 100,000 people in the south of South Island. While seventy-four per cent of this country's 3.3 million people live in North Island in relatively more densely populated urban areas, Dunedin is home to the first established of the seven universities in New Zealand, and is a noted centre of teacher and medical training.

Like many industrialised countries, New Zealand has developed a dual system of education comprising mainstream provisions for most students, and a segregated 'special' education system for many students with disabilities (Ballard, 1996). There are 2,808 schools, catering for 672,571 students from primary through to secondary (high school) level. Of these students 0.39 per cent attend fifty-six special schools, and a further 0.60 per cent are in 347 special classes (Ministry of Education, 1995a). In Dunedin there are seventy-nine primary schools, eleven secondary schools, and twelve segregated special education facilities consisting of seven classes or units at primary level and five at secondary level.

Since 1989, the administration of education has undergone radical change as part of the New Right, monetarist policies of successive governments. These have replaced a long-held commitment to an egalitarian welfare state, with an ideology that emphasises the interests of the individual and promotes the reduction of state spending on public education, health and welfare (Kelsey 1993). These changes have been accompanied by relatively high unemployment and increasing poverty. In 1989, the central government Department of Education, responsible for such things as policy, administration, curriculum development, inspectors of schools, and ten regional Education Boards, which employed teachers and provided a wide range of services to schools, was completely dismantled. Each school became a 'self-managed' entity operated and controlled by a parent-elected Board of Trustees. Nevertheless, a new Ministry of Education exerts a high level of centralised control through legal contracts and regular reviews and audits that evaluate compliance with the National Curriculum and the procedures and goals set out in institutional charters (Codd 1993). The National Curriculum for 'all children' may itself be seen as supporting inclusive education.

Alongside these administrative reforms, legislative and other changes have been made that are of particular significance for people with disabilities and their inclusion in the mainstream of education. Amendments to the Education Act in 1989 gave every child the right to attend a state school, for which many parents of children with disabilities had struggled since the 1950s (Sonntag 1994). The right to inclusion within a mainstream state school was promoted by disability and advocacy groups, with calls for an end to the dual 'special–regular' system of education (DPA NZ Inc. 1987) and for all children to be in age-appropriate mainstream classrooms (Interagency Group

1991). The result is that students with intellectual, physical, sensory, and other disabilities now have the legal right to attend age-appropriate mainstream classes in regular schools.

Between 1987 and July 1995, the official guidelines for practice were based on the concept of the 'least restrictive environment' (Department of Education 1988), which promotes the exclusion of some children from the mainstream, and the maintenance of segregated classrooms and schools (Ballard 1991; Taylor 1988). Many schools ignored the provisions of the 1989 Education Act and excluded or placed restrictions on children with disabilities whose parents wanted them in the mainstream.

Under the new law the dual system of special and regular education will continue so that parents may choose separate special education if they wish, and some disability groups now support this position (DPA NZ Inc. 1994). The Minister of Education may still direct that a child must receive special education in a segregated setting, but there are appeal procedures for parents to challenge such a decision.

The position taken on inclusion by the teacher unions has a significant influence on practice in many schools. In 1991 the New Zealand Educational Institute (NZEI), the professional association of primary school teachers, convened an advisory group to recommend policy on students with 'special educational needs'. Adopting the recommendations of this group the NZEI (1991) confirmed its commitment to segregated provisions through the 'maintenance of a full range of special education facilities' (Recommendation 24.1). Qualified support was given to the idea of inclusion by a commitment to the 'mainstreaming of special needs students provided appropriate resources are available' (Recommendation 24.2). Nevertheless, the union would actively promote the exclusion of children by seeking 'the alternative placement of students if appropriate resources are not available at any given school' (Recommendation 24.8).

In April 1995 the Ministry of Education wrote to the boards of trustees and principals of all state schools, telling them of their legal obligation under the Act to include all students seeking enrolment; to ensure that students attend for all of each school day; and to understand that under Section 8 of the Education Act people who have disabilities have the 'same rights to receive education at state schools as people who do not' (Ministry of Education 1995b).

In July 1995 the Minister of Education introduced new Special Education Policy Guidelines (Ministry of Education 1995c). Consistent with the Education Act 1989 and the Human Rights Act of 1993, which legislated against discrimination on the basis of disability, the Guidelines state that 'learners with special education needs have access to the same range of age appropriate education settings as other learners' (Section 1.1) and that schools must 'accept and value all learners' (Section 1.4). While the Guidelines state that 'resources are to be retained in special schools and units while supported by enrolments' (Section 3.3), they would seem to clearly support the right of students to inclusion. What will happen in practice has yet to be seen.

Although the reminders from the Ministry would seem to reinforce their legal rights, the fact that each school is a self-managed entity poses a significant difficulty for parents. When parents are confronted with rejection they must argue their case with each principal and Board of Trustees. As parent advocate Colleen Brown (1995) says, the problem of achieving inclusion is not policy, it is not resources, it is 'teachers who will not teach our children'.

Describing the approach

We spent time in the school observing day-to-day activities. At different times we met with the principal, each of the teachers, and with two parents and five children, to talk with them about their experiences and views. One of us attended a meeting of the four parent members of the Board of Trustees to seek their ideas about their school. Prior to any involvement with us, each participant was given a written statement describing the purpose of the study as 'a case-study of the philosophy and practice of one school, with a particular focus on the inclusion of students who have disabilities in classroom and other school activities'. With this were details of the ethical procedures relating to confidentiality, right to withdrawal and control of their contribution to the study. Also, we gave the participants a brief list of 'some questions to talk to teachers [parents; Board of Trustees] about', so that they had an idea about the purpose of meeting with us. Our talks with the principal, the teachers and with most other participants were recorded on audiotape. Individual contributors reviewed a transcript of their statements. The principal, teachers, and Board of Trustee members read and commented on drafts of this chapter, with particular reference to their own statements used in this account and our interpretations of the information and observations we collected. To protect confidentiality we use pseudonyms for all the people referred to in this report.

This is a participatory approach to research (Heshusius 1994) in which we spent time with people for an agreed purpose, in this case to describe how and why they work as they do. By giving our initial account and interpretations to the participants for their comment, we created a basis for some further reflective interactions with them. We brought our own professional backgrounds to our participation in this school. One of us has been a teacher and a psychologist in the education service. The other has experience as a teacher and as deputy principal of a segregated special school for students with severe disabilities. Writing this account in discussion with participants allowed them to clarify meanings and explanations. Typically, we needed to understand more about the context of a particular comment or observation for a clearer or

71

more accurate account to be rendered. By agreement, some material was deleted where it was sensitive in terms of personal content or relations with other professionals or agencies. Nevertheless, while we made adjustments in these relatively few instances, the general issues involved remain in the report. The participants and researchers believe that we have presented as complete and accurate an account as possible.

Central school

The school describes itself as a 'school for all children'. It is in a community that is poor economically, with high levels of unemployment, single-parent families, and welfare beneficiaries. Nevertheless, over the last ten years, the community and school together have evolved a policy that all children in their school are full-time participants in age-appropriate mainstream class-rooms, including those who may have intellectual, physical, sensory or other disabilities. They have maintained this policy and practice across changes in teaching staff, school administration procedures and, more recently, in Board of Trustee members.

Facilities

The school is of an older design, and most of the single-storey, wooden buildings have been on this site for more than a hundred years. The class-rooms are arranged in a 'U' shape, with the administration block sitting at the centre of the two wings. A separate building houses several other rooms, including the classroom for senior students and rooms used by Rarotongan and Samoan parents for pre-school activities in their own languages. Another room in this block is the focus for Maori and other cultural resources and activities. An assembly hall and small indoor swimming pool sit on either side of the main building. One side of the 'U' houses the junior block and library, while the other has a senior class, staffroom and the resource centre, which is housed in a number of rooms that were previously a segregated facility for students with physical disabilities. Resource centre staff now provide support for students with disabilities in schools within and beyond the city area, and Central School must apply to the Ministry of Education for support from the resource centre in the same way as other schools.

The school buildings have recently undergone some refurbishment. The exterior has been painted and re-roofed, and the junior classrooms have been remodelled. Even so, the foundations of the old wooden buildings have not been attended to, and the floors of the junior classrooms have a distinctive slope to one side.

The school grounds are small by New Zealand standards, covering approx-imately 1 hectare ($2\frac{1}{2}$ acres) in total, including buildings and car park. For outdoor play there is one sealed area and several small grass plots with substantial plantings of shrubs in gardens and borders. There are two 'adventure' play areas in the playground with climbing frames, a swing 'bridge', play-house and sandpits.

Staffing

There is a principal, Janet, six classroom teachers, and one further teacher, Jenny, employed part time for the Reading Recovery programme and part-time in a support role for the junior school. Reading Recovery is an individual instruction programme involving daily withdrawal periods, available in most New Zealand primary schools, to support the reading development of six year olds (Clay 1991).

Janet, the principal, has thirty-two years' teaching experience, twelve of these at Central; Jenny has eleven years' teaching, five years with Central. Of the other teachers, Sue, a recent graduate, is in her first teaching position with four months' experience at Central School; Anne has twenty-four years' teaching experience, eight years at Central; Margaret, three years' teaching, four months at Central; Judith twenty-five years, with four years at Central; Rachel, thirty years with seven years at Central; and Dorothy sixteen years' teaching including her five years at Central.

Students

There are six classes in the school. The New Entrants' room is the arrival point for children who – as is common practice – start school on the first school-day after their fifth birthday. There is a combined class for Years 2 and 3, a class for Year 4 students, a combined Fifth and Sixth Year, a class for Year 7, and a class for Year 8 students who will subsequently go on to high school. Such combinations are also typical, and school and classroom planning ensures that the curriculum is appropriate for each of the age groups in combined classes. Progression through classes (referred to as 'Standards', reflecting their historical basis in standards testing at each level) is by age. Children are not held back for academic or other reasons.

Six of the students had Section 9 Agreements. An Agreement is the mechanism by which the Ministry of Education provides special education support services through enrolment of the student with a resource centre. A further four children received support known as 'discretionary hours'. This is available through application to the Ministry of Education and is usually in the form of teacher aide hours. Resources are scarce in both of these categories and only children deemed most in need receive Ministry support. These and other children who require extra learning assistance from time to time are listed for discussion at the school's weekly 'special programme meetings'. Their needs are catered for within the resources of each classroom and through creative problem-solving among the teachers.

The school includes children who are somewhat transient, moving school several times a year in some cases, and others – about five per cent of the total student group – who come to the school from outside the local community. This latter group includes children with disabilities whose parents want them in an inclusive setting.

The development of an inclusive school

Janet explained that the development of the school as 'inclusive' began ten years ago when she decided that the special unit for children with physical disabilities that was part of the school should be disbanded and all children included in ordinary classrooms. Since then, the school has included all children, including children with intellectual disabilities, vision impairment, autism, severe multiple disabilities, and those with other difficulties and labels, as full-time participants in age-appropriate classrooms. Closing down the unit had been a necessary but difficult decision, as Janet explained:

> I saw all the specialist people making pompoms for the children . . . taking them over to assembly [and saying] 'Look what the children made'. The children didn't make them. There was absolutely no educational value in what happened, and it was being presented in error . . . It was a painful experience, but the unit was really locked into itself and there was no way at that time that you could get policy or philosophy to change to release the children, and so I physically released them and put them into classes.

In doing this she acknowledged that there were not 'good programmes' to support the children in the mainstream at that time, but had decided that you 'can't wait ten years to make the huge philosophical change' that is necessary to set up everything that is needed. Instead, you develop 'new ways of working' and solve resource problems by experiencing the process of mainstreaming.

The principal believed that unit staff had a chance to be part of the new, mainstreamed environment, but all of them had resigned.

> They were still of the mind that the children needed [specialist] adults for their education . . . It [the unit] was really clinical . . . you couldn't get an understanding that these children were there to be educated and [needed to be] in with their peers.

Janet described the unit staff as seeing the children as 'sick' and as 'in need of rescuing'. Her belief was that these and all other children needed access to the curriculum as a way of finding out their own 'strengths and needs'. They also need involvement with peers 'for long-term support in life'. It is these views that are reflected in the school's present commitment to inclusion.

All of the teachers in the present study have come into the school since the closure of the unit. It seems that an inclusive environment can be maintained through staffing changes and through the wish of the school's community to continue with a policy of inclusion.

Talking with the teachers

In talking with each teacher, we explored their concept of inclusion, their reasons for supporting inclusion, and the teaching and other strategies they used to cater for the needs of all children. We asked: 'what is it like teaching at Central School?', 'what kind of school is it?', 'what are your views on having children with disabilities in your class?', 'why do you think in that way?', 'would you ever exclude any children?', and 'if all resources were withdrawn, would you still include children with disabilities in your classroom or would they have to go somewhere else?' We also asked them about planning and teamwork.

What is it like teaching at Central School?

Like other teachers at the school, Judith described teaching at Central school as 'really challenging':

> It's hard work meeting the needs of all children . . . stimulating and interesting working with different cultures . . . much different from the sort of white middle-class school that I was used to before I came here.

Rachel said that while it can be 'really tough to find a way of reaching some [of the students]', she thought that teaching here was 'fun':

> It's an adventure, it's a challenge, a place where dreams can come true. I don't want to sound trite but you're actually encouraged at Central to make [your dreams] come true . . . If you fall flat on your face, no one's going to tell you you're useless . . . we cry a lot as well!

For Sue, in her first teaching job, 'it's sort of been hard and a mixture of a lot of things . . . but [the other teachers] have been really supportive'. This support from other teachers was noted by Margaret who found her work 'busy, very rewarding . . . once you start to get to grips with it . . . tough . . . a lot of support from the staff'. Compared with her teaching experience in England:

there isn't a lot of time when teachers can sit down and have a chat.
[Here] we do a lot more lunch duties and that sort of thing . . . but I
always make time to seek people out to talk.

Dorothy said of her experience of teaching at the school that it was 'challenging, stimulating, exciting and exhausting':

That to me sums it up. . . . Every day is a new challenge . . . it changes
all the time and I think that's the thing that makes it so exciting. . . .
We are not locked into any of 'this is the way we've done it and it
works and we'll do it for the next ten years' sort of thing.

Jenny and Anne also noted the 'challenge' of teaching at the school, and
the supportive network that the staff had created for themselves in what
Anne described as 'a very lively place'. The 'frustration' mentioned by two of
the teachers as part of their experience seems to relate to Judith's comment
that with 'some special needs kids':

You sort of think you're not getting anywhere. . . . All of a sudden,
later on a teacher will say 'Oh so and so's done something' . . . [but]
you don't actually see the results immediately.

What kind of school is it?

The teachers described the school as 'multi-cultural', a 'school for all people'
in a 'lower socio-economic area', and 'a community school where community
members are welcome at any time'. Jenny commented from her experience as
a long-term relieving (supply) teacher in other schools that Central was a
'very caring school' with 'hard-working' teachers. It is also 'an old school
(established in 1865) in an area where a lot of children have elderly neighbours' because of cheap housing and a flat topography in a city with
otherwise hilly terrain.

Rachel thought that many parents wanted 'more' for their children than
they themselves had achieved, and while they demanded 'that real formal stuff
[such as spelling and maths tests], that isn't terribly valid in teaching', they also
supported creative work such as the end-of-the-year show, because 'they recognise the value of that, the creativity that goes into it, the kids' power over it,
because the kids have all the power over it'. She echoed Janet's view that it was
a school that first and foremost was for everyone in the community:

Our policy [is that] this is a school for all people . . . another ten
pages [of policy] wouldn't make any difference. . . . That is the way
we work and that is what we believe in. . . . If you didn't believe in
that you couldn't work here.

While most people noted the multi-cultural nature of the student popula-tion, Anne explained the policy and philosophy that underpinned the approach of the school:

> It is a multi-cultural school but the basis of that is the Treaty of Waitangi. . . . The Treaty creates the framework for the involvement of other cultures . . . [and] the Treaty policy creates an umbrella for Maori language, Samoan language, Cambodian and Chinese lan-guage, and the English framework as well. . . . What has happened possibly is that the Maori community have welcomed the involve-ment of other cultures. Rather than saying the school is bi-cultural, they have said that within the bi-cultural framework the other cul-tural groups are welcomed.

The Treaty of Waitangi, the agreement of 1840 between Maori and the English Crown, is seen as a 'charter for power sharing in the decision making processes of this country' (Bishop 1994, p. 175) under which Maori were to retain unqualified control of their land, culture and language. The Treaty remains a major focus of debate in present-day New Zealand as Maori seek redress for land that was subsequently taken from them, and the right under the Treaty to exercise self-determination in education and other areas. The idea of bi-culturalism is opposed by many Pakeha (New Zealanders of European descent), but the policy of Central School is in line with a Maori view that a bi-cultural partnership is the basis for relations with other cultures that have subsequently settled in New Zealand.

While the school is seen as a community school, the community is not wealthy and so 'fund raising [an essential activity for most schools] has to go outside of the local environment', and support from parents is in 'other ways than financial support'. Parents are welcomed into the school and classrooms at any time. In terms of active help, this seems to centre around a small core of people, and one teacher noted that 'we aim to have parents involved [in the school] but often they don't come because they don't have the skills them-selves'.

What is it like having children with disabilities in your class?

Four people asked what was meant by the term 'disability' and, as Rachel said, the school does not 'identify and label' people, so they were cautious about such terms. She noted that in her class of thirty-four children was 'a young man whose behaviour is very disabling for him', and 'if you've got someone who's a high flyer . . . academically or physically . . . and you can't cater for them in your classroom programme, then that person is disabled too'. Similarly, Margaret, who has twenty-eight children, one of whom uses a wheelchair, asked what was meant by disability:

All children have specific needs obviously. Whether you term them disabilities I don't know. A behavioural need can be more disabling than a visible disability.

Judith, who at present has a class of thirty-four children, five of whom have identified disabilities, saw having children with disabilities in the classroom as:

Part of living in a normal society with kids with disabilities, both physical and intellectual disabilities and behavioural as well. . . . I just see that as part of being in teaching. . . . It makes the other kids aware that there are going to be all sorts of people that they're going to have to live with later on . . . not everyone is going to be the same.

Anne was clear that 'all children are welcome in the classroom and the other children welcome them as part of the group'. We asked if that was true even of her 5 year olds, to which she replied:

Yes. It takes some children longer to recognise they have a supporting role . . . [some] almost like to make the situation worse and see what will happen, whereas others will model for that child the right thing to do.

Dorothy commented on the changes in her teaching now that she taught students with disabilities:

At first, because I'd never had any real experience with people with disabilities, it was a real apprehension, of how am I going to cope with their needs plus keeping all the other kids working . . . I don't think you can plan for any of that. I think it's something that evolves from your day-to-day working.

In her interview Rachel expressed a view similar to Janet's about the problems that arise when people see disability as a 'special' or 'clinical' issue. She thought that in special education there were 'a whole group of people who feel sorry for their kids and you can't do that. As soon as you start to feel sorry and pity them, all you do is give another disability.' Some children that had come into her class from segregated special education 'had learned to be pathetic, to be absolutely helpless and useless', and she had needed to teach them to work and to 'learn about the needs of other people'.

Would you ever exclude any children?

According to Sue, one of the newer staff: 'I don't think that anyone should be excluded in any way. They should just be there in the mainstream with all the children.' Other teachers had one criterion for exclusion, and that was if, in Dorothy's words, the child 'became a danger to themselves and others'. This was seen as applying to all children and not as necessarily associated with disability. Also, the wish was that such a child could eventually be reintegrated back into the class. In explaining her position, Rachel said that, while she would never have thought of exclusion when she was teaching younger children, she felt that it could be a possibility now that she taught 'pre-adolescents':

> My job is to give them an achieving environment, so if there is somebody within that room that consistently interrupts the learning of others, consistently takes the power away from the groups, and I'm talking about very severe levels [of disruption], then a consequence is removal from the group . . . until they are ready [to return].

Anne, who teaches the youngest children, said, 'I can't imagine excluding them – I think it is a case of management and organisation within the classroom to ensure there is safety . . . for [all] students.' She thought that there had to be care, though, as young children did not necessarily recognise the problems that their behaviour might create for themselves or others. Overall, temporary exclusion from class occurred infrequently. When it did, the student concerned and their parents were involved in resolving the precipitating problems.

How would you deal with a shortage of resources?

We asked the teachers whether, if all resources for children with special needs were withdrawn, they would still have children with disabilities in their classrooms or would the children have to go somewhere else.

Anne thought she would just have to 'structure the situation differently' so that she could direct her attention to particular needs while other children worked more independently. Judith said she would 'extend the buddy system' that already operated in her classroom, and ensure that the children with disabilities in her room were getting support from others in group work. Rachel was also emphatic: 'No. Not at all. Because the most valuable teachers are all in the classroom – the other kids.' She talked of the 'huge range' of abilities in her classroom anyway, so that 'there isn't anywhere that a child with a Section 9 Agreement doesn't fit in'. Along with other teachers, she stressed the flexibility of student groupings across subject areas, activities and personalities.

She contrasted her answer to this question with the position taken by the professional body, the New Zealand Educational Institute, to which most primary teachers belong. The NZEI policy is that 'you will only have certain children', and that if you accept a child with a disability then certain levels of support must be provided. She commented that it was 'one of the few areas NZEI [acts as] a union for teachers'. She suggested that there was little support for this position within Central School, and the responses from the other teachers clearly placed the child's needs ahead of the teachers' needs for support. Dorothy, however, did express a degree of uncertainty:

> I think it would depend. Probably I would say that's fine and I'll work around that problem, and then go home and worry myself sick about how to do it. But I think that it is so important for them to be part of real life, and I think at whatever cost it's paramount that they see themselves as normal, ordinary little kids . . . so if support is withdrawn it just means you've got to work a different system.

Dorothy's comment, as well as others recorded above, suggests that the teachers experience stress in their work. In part, the stress relates to the level of support available. Thus in contemplating the withdrawal of support, Margaret had reservations:

> I would be prepared to [still have children with disabilities in the class] but I'm sure I wouldn't be as satisfied with what I was able to do . . . even now I feel guilty if I haven't provided [child's name] with the right activity for her.

For Janet, a child with a disability was 'just one of the group that we have responsibility for'. Such a child was thought of first as 'a child that's coming into this educational setting', and in the first instance teachers and peers needed to get to know them.

> So we're not looking at putting massive resourcing in because we have heard that a child with a disability is coming. . . . If the educational setting is correctly pitched, then there will be things we need to do, but it won't be a massive restructuring.

Nevertheless, Anne noted that teachers can use 'all the help they can get', and Judith spoke enthusiastically about how 'just a little bit of help' had allowed her to focus some planning on one child who had now made 'incredible' progress. This was a boy who had recently come into the school, having spent his first three years of education in a 'special unit'.

Meeting the needs of all children: planning and teamwork

Each of the teachers emphasised that the teacher, support teacher or aide, and the children in the class had to work together to create an effective learning environment for all. Rachel explained the basis of the school policy of 'minimal support'. While a teacher aide might be nominally there to support a particular child:

> they might never come near [the child] . . . learning in the classroom and support in the classroom I would expect to come through me and through my groupings.

Also, as Anne pointed out, 'support might not necessarily go direct to the child with a specific disability. The support going into the classroom provides the climate of support for all students'. Support is planned in a way that will not take away the responsibility that the teacher and children have for supporting their own learning.

Each teacher emphasised the importance of grouping children, sometimes in terms of skill levels, for example in maths, but always with a concern for the effective learning of each group member. For example, according to Rachel:

> You have to have some kind of grouping system that is ever changing and never static that will support everybody with their learning, and that includes me . . . so I am very careful how I group but I also teach my children to recognise who it is they can work with and who it is they can't, and they get very skilled.

Dorothy explained that planning was provisional, depending on specific circumstances:

> I don't think I would work successfully with people with disabilities in my class this year and use the same formula next year. Over the five years [at Central School] I've had to evolve a new plan every year, and it takes weeks and weeks of trial and error.

For children with Section 9 Agreements, formal twice-yearly IEP (individual educational programme) meetings take place, with parents, children, the class teacher, principal and relevant other professionals. Ongoing planning and evaluation of progress for these and other children is undertaken at Special Programme Meetings after school each Thursday. These meetings may be requested by any teacher or parent, and attendance can be similar to that for IEP meetings. For some children their needs may be discussed each week for some time, and then less frequently as programme goals are established and are being met. The emphasis is on access to the curriculum and on social or other needs as identified by those involved with the child.

Where outside health and education authorities have deemed that a child is eligible for particular services then teachers can access support from physiotherapists, occupational therapists, and advisors on children who are deaf and those with visual impairments. In this school, these professionals are required to support learning in the classroom, and are not expected to withdraw children from class for therapy or other activities other than in exceptional circumstances.

From talking with the teachers it seemed that they particularly valued sharing problems and proposals among themselves, either through convened meetings or more often through informal conversation before and after school. For example, at different times, three teachers mentioned a current challenge which was how Mike, a child in a wheelchair and with limited physical strength, could play netball. His teacher said that when Mike chose netball during a session when students were choosing activities, one of his peers said that he could not do it. This person was met by a chorus of retorts from others in the class that of course he could. The three teachers had been thinking about how to achieve this.

Views of the Board of Trustees and other parents

The Board of Trustees comprises four parents elected by the school community. They are the employers of all staff in the school and, in consultation with the principal and a representative from the school staff, determine policy and manage all aspects of the school.

They see their school as a place where everyone is made to feel welcome. In comparison with other schools they experienced as parents, this school is notable for being one where you could 'talk with the principal on a first-name basis', and 'could ring her at home at the weekend' about something with which you needed her help. People seem to spend a lot of time in the school and, as one person said, 'it's like a second home'. Some people sought advice on their personal affairs, and in this regard one person described the school as a 'sort of social welfare department', except that the problems were 'actually dealt with here'. For some people the school is a 'safe haven' where difficult problems could be shared.

In talking about the children at the school, the parents feel that the teachers would 'look for how to help a child', whereas the same child at a different school would either get by with what was available, or 'tough luck', nothing much else would be done.

In terms of involvement of children with disabilities, the general view is that this is important simply because it is 'fair'. One person said that her own child had benefited greatly from involvement with people with disabilities. She said that her daughter 'sees them as children, not the boy in the wheelchair'. Others reported that in the community and at sporting events the Central School children treat children with disabilities in the same way as they treat everyone else. An example was given where one of the Central School children with a disability was at a sporting event. A teacher from another school wanted to make special provision for that child. The Central School children did not appreciate that at all, because to them each participant is to be treated just like everyone else.

When asked 'what would happen if the resources available to help children with disabilities were withdrawn from the school, would the children have to go somewhere else?', the answer was that there was 'no way' that children with disabilities would not be maintained within the school. As one person said, 'there would always be a way'. This prompted one Board of Trustees member to note that some of the foster children for whom she was responsible had 'not been wanted anywhere else', but had been accepted here at Central School, 'and had left here with pride'.

Exploring why the school was like it was proved interesting because people feel that the school is very much a part of the community and that it therefore reflects 'ordinary working-class people' who 'wanted things to be fair for everyone'. It was clear that the school had maintained its policies of openness and inclusion through changes in teaching staff and changes in the Board of Trustees. When asked if the school would change if the principal left, one person responded, with general agreement: 'I don't think that the community would let it.'

The achievements in this school with its community are greatly valued by these parents on the Board of Trustees. We joked about the number of hours that parents and teachers spend at meetings in the evenings, acknowledging that often people leave after 10pm at night. It is clear that there is work to be done, and also that parents and teachers are willing to do it, at significant personal cost in time away from their families and other interests.

We also interviewed two other parents of younger children. Both of these people had consciously chosen Central School for their children. One of the parents lived close to the school but had still considered other schools:

> I did check the schools out before they [her two children] came here . . . and what attracted me was that [Central] school was gaining a reputation for things multi-cultural . . . you're encouraged as a parent to come into the school if we have any queries or problems, and I know that during classroom time it's certainly no problem to come in, you know, quietly, and observe and participate in lessons here, which is very good.

The other parent who lived further away also welcomed the 'open-door' policy. She chose Central School for several reasons:

> The first was that I worked here at Central School a year ago [as a member of the cleaning staff] and I got to know the staff and the school, and what I saw I liked. I liked the attitude of the teachers, the positiveness of the whole school. Second is that [my son] has special needs and Central are very capable of providing him with the extra

care he may need in the school system. . . . He was made to feel very much part of the team . . . anything he did was encouraged, encouraged to work with the other children, to join any activities that they were doing. Anything he did, praise is very good here. . . . It's a very positive school. They – how do I put this? – they don't – race, religion, special needs, they don't appear to be an issue. [My son] was put in the new entrants' class. He was not asked of any special favours. He is expected to do everything the other children do. He's not made to feel any different and yet the help and support is there when he needs it.

The first parent, who does not have a child with a disability at the school welcomed the presence of such children:

I think that it's really important that they are in contact with children who have disabilities . . . that was another thing, that I wanted them to be at a school where mainstreaming was going on . . . involved in just a really wide range of children. For me with my own kids I've never heard any negative comments about children who maybe move differently or anything like that. I really feel that the kids just take it in their stride if there is somebody else in their classroom . . . no negative comments or anything like that.

In general, these parents feel that they are valued as parents, that they are welcome in the school at any time, and that they have as much interaction and information as they want from the school. Most important, they feel that their children – with or without disabilities – are valued and happy in their learning environments.

Observing classrooms and playgrounds

We spent some time in all but one of the classrooms. The layout and instructional activities in each class were similar to that recorded by one of us during a visit to a Year 4 class:

The classroom is brightly decorated, pictures hang on the wall and are suspended from the ceiling. There are a number of tables grouped together around the room. There is a computer at one end of the room. An open space is in the centre with a mobile whiteboard to one side. There is also a ladder-back chair at one end of the room, and a standing frame beside the computer. The class is on the mat. At the edge of the group is Janet who is sitting in a wheelchair. An aide is sitting behind her. The teacher is showing the class some recently completed student work. It is very quiet. The teacher is asking questions of the class about how they could illustrate this work. Janet, along with others, puts up her hand to respond. The teacher gives lots of praise and supportive comment for children's suggestions. The teacher draws this part of the activity to a close by distributing the work books. Students collect work from the teacher as their names are called. Once this is completed, the teacher and the aide discuss the adaptations to the lesson for Janet. The aide takes Janet to a table where there are three other students working. The aide is talking to Janet about the exercise. The other children at the table are looking on.

Apart from some obvious mobility aides or specific adult assistance available to some students, there is little evidence in any of the rooms of arrangements that would single students out. Programmes are essentially the same for all children, with adaptations for individuals identified as having particular learning needs with regard to a given topic, activity, or area of the curriculum. Expectations for participation and contribution to the class seem to be the same for all children, too, and where specialised equipment is present this appears as a natural part of the environment. Nevertheless, it became evident that this environment of 'similar expectations' encompasses some complex understandings as regards particular needs at particular times. For example, an instance of physical violence toward a teacher by a young child required adjustments to class routines for a time to ensure everyone's safety. Also, from some earlier involvement in this school, we had observed how a student with autism had, at times, the right to behave in ways that would not be acceptable for most students. This was understood and seen as unremarkable by students and teachers.

Over the course of our observations we saw some of the children who did not have disabilities using items like wheelchairs or specialised seating to sit in, or to wheel about. Rather than treating these items as toys, or things that were different, the students seemed to accept them as natural supports. For instance, if there was no chair at a table except a special chair that was not being used, students would sit on that. Nevertheless, respect is shown for the personal nature of a wheelchair or other item essential to a disabled student.

Some classes in the school have assistance in the form of a teacher aide or itinerant teacher support for some periods during some days. This assistance is recognised by staff as being of value to the whole class as well as to individual students. From an observation in a combined Year 5 and 6 class, the class teacher had just set the students some activities on the study of planets:

A teacher from the resource centre is in the class for this session. She moves a specially designed chair to a table as the group of students including Peter gets itself organised. The group sits down and the resource teacher asks several questions about organisation and the task at hand. She then leaves the group to assist another group of students with their work. The students sort the planets into their relative sizes. The resource teacher returns and suggests that the names of the planets be written down so that they will be remembered.

The teachers appear to organise instruction to avoid the potentially isolating effect on disabled students of a teacher aide or other support person in the classroom. Later in the observation notes for the Year 5 and 6 classroom session on planets we recorded:

The class teacher claps her hands, gives out points to groups for their application to the task, displays some of the work with comments, and asks the class to please put away their materials and sit on the mat. As students arrive at the mat, the teacher gives out more points. The resource teacher assists Jane and Peter to put things away and help tidy up. Peter stands and turns his chair to face the rest of the class on the mat. The class teacher gives out points to his group but says to him 'Peter, bring your chair around so that you're part of this class please.'

Except in rare and time-limited instances, for example to attend the Reading Recovery programme, students are not removed from class for specific teaching, nor do they typically receive instruction on a one-to-one basis from an aide or other assistant within the classroom. Where specific assistance is required from a teacher, this is usually undertaken within the context of a group. The staff encourage students to assist in the learning of their peers. For example, in the Year 4 class:

The class is working in groups and individually. There are numbers of children assisting others. Some children come up to the whiteboard and pick out words for others who are working at the tables. There are collective boxes of pens and scissors on tables which all children have access to.

The fostering of supportive relationships between students was stated by the principal and teachers to be a fundamental part of the organisation of the school. Senior students take responsibility for the supervision of younger students while they eat lunch in the hall (New Zealand schools do not usually provide a lunch service, and students bring their own sandwiches or other food). From one observation we recorded:

Senior students are standing at various points around the hall. Other students sit near them eating their lunch. The three junior classes are gathered in front of the stage with their teachers. Senior students are asked to come and collect the junior children in their groups. They do so, taking some by the hand back to their groups. As everybody is seated in these vertical groups, they begin their lunch. Apart from the occasional reminder, the senior students have taken responsibility for the entire lunch-time programme.

In the playground the senior students take responsibility for those who use wheelchairs. A student who is not using an electric wheelchair is usually assigned a buddy or two who will wheel them where they need or want to go. During our observations there were often numbers of other students in attendance with these groups, who appeared to be the classmates of those using the wheelchairs.

By and large, students are receptive to the needs of others, and are prepared to offer support. When asked what a buddy has to do, one Year 6 student said that they had to make sure that 'he doesn't get hurt or anything like that. Or when we were over at this park I threw a ball and it flew into his face and things like that.'

We saw students taking their responsibility to others seriously. In the playground, one boy (who has an intellectual disability), angry for some reason, experienced some gentle intervention:

> Joe is throwing handfuls of the small 'pea gravel' that surrounds the climbing equipment. A number of his peers approach him and tell him not to throw the stones. They empty his hands. He rounds quickly on them and squeals out loud. They remove some more stones from him and then get on with their game. Joe turns and talks with a number of children who are climbing down the pole and through the tyres. They encourage him to have a turn. They take him around to the side and show him where he can get into the circle of tyres. Joe doesn't want to try this. Those children who have showed him what to do go about their business. Joe quickly becomes agitated and screams out when left to himself. He goes across to one of the little girls who talked to him about the tyre.

People were also observed to help students with learning difficulties follow routines:

> The bell rings and all of the children move off to form lines at the edge of the playing field. Joe dallies and a young child calls for him to 'come on'. The children line up in class groups. Teachers encourage the children to stand quietly. All of the children respond except for Joe, who is standing out of line. The child behind him tells him to line up straight. Joe does so. The class walks off to assembly. Joe skips along with the rest of the class.

Student perceptions of a supportive environment

We talked with five students from Year 5 and 6 classes about how they saw Central School. We were surprised at the quality and maturity of their comments about the school as a supportive environment. They reflected the teachers' views that students should learn to be responsible for themselves and responsive to the needs of others. As one student said, 'I think they [students with disabilities] will need us here because that will help them to learn much better.' They also recognised that they got something out of the relationship too, as one person said of helping disabled students, 'Oh man, yeah, I enjoy it.'

Also evident is the ease with which these students accept children whose needs are different. This is aptly summed up by one of the students who said that Central School was a good place for 'children with special needs because everybody is the same here':

> If you need help it is here . . . we all help each other . . . it is the same for those who can't speak English, or who can't walk . . . it is a fantastic school.

Another thoughtful, serious student said that Central was a school that would take everyone:

> I was going to say that you [just] have to be born before they come here.
> [Does that mean that anybody can come here?]
> Yeah, they have to breathe.

Students pay little attention to the fact that people are different from each other; they just are and sometimes they need help. They see this help as being available to all those who need it, not just for those of their peers with obvious difficulties. During the interview we talked about the help offered by the resource centre, which they call the special needs centre. They described it as 'where people, um, need, special, extra help than the teacher'. This help includes, 'the teacher aides like Jan and that' who help students to 'write and handwrite and [with] um maths'. The special needs centre provides other assistance, 'like when they need help walking when their legs are stiff like when they're tired, when their wheelchairs get a puncture'. As well as helping with these sorts of problems the centre does things with 'people that kind of, don't know how to swim and that, they help them swim'.

During the interview one child commented that while children with special needs should be at the school, there was not much point in interacting with those students, as 'they can't do very much'. Other students in the group disagreed. They described some of the specific skills and attributes that they believed some of the students with special needs possess:

Peter can do things. Peter can beat us at races.
Amy, she throws balls and she goes in four square [a playground ball game].

In a similar vein, the same student complained about the access that Peter and Amy have to computers, and that these were unavailable to the rest of their class. Another student responded 'Yes, but we only play on the computer. Peter and Amy use it.'

The dissenting voice in this group is important because it confirms that students at Central are diverse in their approach to disability and difference. As in any other naturally heterogeneous community, there are likely to be alternative, even disablist and other entrenched positions. This also confirms our impression that Central School is not without its tensions about inclusion among some students and parents. Sensitivities seem to emerge mostly around resource issues, especially where a disabled student is thought to be getting more equipment or teaching support than other students. Nevertheless, the overall culture of this school, most evident from our observations and conversations with staff, students and parents, is of a remarkable commitment to valuing diversity in both philosophy and action.

The consistency between philosophy, policy and practice at Central School, is best summarised in our field notes, where Trevor had written:

> The point I am left to marvel at from conducting interviews, talking to children and observing them is that the impressions of parents, the ideas that these children have, and their behaviour is absolutely consistent. Parents talk about openness. The school programme is organised around collaboration and fosters a sense of responsibility amongst all students. By their comments, students are, by and large, welcoming of difference, and their behaviour demonstrates a care and concern for others that is extraordinary in my experience [in teaching and teacher education].

Metatheory and action

In this account we have focused on teacher, student and parental views, and experiences that we think impact most directly on student learning. However, the ideology and practice of inclusion permeate other features of school life. For example, there is little emphasis on hierarchical structures within the school, yet clear responsibilities are taken by senior staff. We think that related to this apparently democratic organisation, involving collective decisions and responsibility, is the role in school life of non-teaching staff, the caretaker and others who are very much a part of the whole community that creates this school. Such people, along with parents and Whanau (extended family) of the school's children, contribute to school sport, multi-cultural activities, and fund raising, for the multi-cultural performance group in particular.

The school is not without its difficulties or detractors, and evidently its work makes some educationalists and other professionals outside of the school uncomfortable. Such people seem ready to challenge Central School's policies and practices when opportunities arise through necessary professional interactions. We wondered whether this was because Central School was 'setting free the captives', as Baker and Salon (1986) expressed it, and as the Principal has actually done. Central School had created its own policies and practices of inclusion ten years before the present study, prior to the Education Act (1989), which gave all children the right to participate in ordinary, age-appropriate classrooms and schools, and the Special Education Policy Guidelines (Ministry of Education 1995c) which reinforced the intentions of the Act.

Our interpretation of how and why this has been achieved by Central School is that inclusion has originated, and is being maintained and developed, from a personal commitment on the part of the Principal and of each teacher, to a particular set of values. These values underpin the way teaching is undertaken, classrooms organised, support coordinated, collaboration maintained, and a very heavy workload undertaken in terms of time committed and challenges met. The climate, or 'culture', engendered in the school of a supportive environment for adults and children is clearly recognised and valued by the parents on the Board of Trustees, indicating that a similar value system is shared by these representatives of the community.

Before focusing on the issue of values and a shared metatheory as the central themes to emerge in this case-study, we comment on two less crucial but nevertheless important issues that we initially had some difficulty in understanding as part of the inclusive environment. These were Reading Recovery, a programme that involves withdrawal from the classroom, and the teacher workload, which has implications for sustaining inclusion and for its establishment in other places.

Reading Recovery: including withdrawal?

As a matter of school policy children with disabilities are not withdrawn from class for therapy or other interventions. They receive help as part of the classroom programme or, in the case of some physical or other therapies, outside class times. In the past the school has experienced difficulties with professionals who insisted on working within their medical model of withdrawal for 'treatment', and who found that this was not acceptable within this school. Subsequently, the school has had strong support from other professionals willing to work with classroom teachers to provide physiotherapy and other essential services and expertise as part of everyday classroom and curriculum activities.

However, the school operates the Reading Recovery programme for children who, aged six and after one year at school, show that they are behind their peers in learning to read. They attend reading lessons outside the classroom for thirty minutes per day until they are deemed ready to learn effectively within the classroom programme or until they have been in the programme for about twenty weeks. If they have not made satisfactory progress at the end of that time, they are referred for other specialist assistance. Of course, a child with a disability could also be a child eligible for Reading Recovery, which seems essentially inconsistent with a policy of meeting children's needs alongside their peers within the classroom.

From talking with senior teachers it was evident that they differentiate disability issues entirely from issues of emergent readers in the infant class. Reading Recovery is not seen as problematic in the same way as the removal of children with disabilities, but as a mainstream strategy that operates in most New Zealand schools. It is presented as an 'accelerant' rather than 'remedial' programme and this may explain why children and parents do not seem to attach stigma to being involved in it. All teachers in the primary school system teach reading. When a child attends Reading Recovery, the teacher also works with the classroom teacher on integrating and maintaining the child in the classroom reading programme. Reading Recovery interacts closely with what is happening in the classroom, and is not seen as 'special treatment'.

Thus, the teachers at Central School rationalise that withdrawing some six year olds from class to attend Reading Recovery as part of the mainstream 'culture' of New Zealand schools, and do not associate it with problematic labelling of students or medical-model thinking by professionals. The withdrawal from class of children with disabilities, on the other hand, is constructed as potentially not educational in nature, disruptive of the mainstream educational programme in the classroom, and likely to reflect medical-model thinking that emphasises impairment and difference.

Teacher workload

Some of the teacher statements indicate how hard they work and we were surprised at the long hours spent at school, the evenings at meetings, the weekends at school on preparation, and the work with parents on fund raising and other activities. All of this speaks to a strong professional commitment and perhaps to some personal costs that are not articulated here.

Initially, in our writing we confused teacher workload with the demands of inclusion. Anne, however, pointed out that much of the evening and weekend work to which we referred involved senior staff in school management or community activities. Such demands, she said, were common to New Zealand's 'self-managed' state schools and were not particularly associated with an inclusive school. While it remains our impression that all teachers in this school work hard to ensure that this inclusive environment works for all students and for the community, we note Anne's comment that, from her experience in regular and special education, inclusion is 'no more difficult' than other teaching.

This is an important issue. If inclusion makes excessive demands on teachers, then it could be hard to develop or sustain. With its ten years of inclusive practice, Central School demonstrates the sustainability of inclusion across changes in teachers, children, parents, and central government policies on disability and school management. There are other schools, early childhood, primary and secondary, that are inclusive (Ballard 1991). However, as indicated at the beginning of this chapter, many more schools exclude or place restrictions on students with disabilities. Why then do the principal and teachers hold to certain beliefs that inform their commitment to this school? We believe we have identified a metatheory, an inclusive paradigm or 'world view', that pervades all aspects of the philosophy and practice of the Principal and teachers at this school.

Inclusive metatheory

We thought that what was happening in this school could not be described only in terms of the educational practices we observed but seemed more likely to reflect a particular 'world view' relating to ideas about people and disability. In Tom Skrtic's (1991) terms, a world view is a 'shared pattern of basic beliefs and assumptions about the nature of the world and how it works' (p. 5). It seemed important to explore the basic or 'metatheoretical' (Skrtic 1991, p. 8) assumptions, the paradigm or particular lens through which people view their world and which colours and shapes their ideas and practices (Skrtic 1986).

We believe that aspects of the origins and essence of this world view are evident in the things the Principal and teachers told us when we asked why an issue was important or a practice designed in a particular way. As part of her answer to the withdrawal of resources issue, Margaret said 'I think if you start to exclude children for reasons of disability, you could find a whole lot of other reasons why children shouldn't be there.' Asked why she thought like that, she said 'I suppose it represents an education-for-all philosophy which I think most teachers have, actually.' As expressed by Anne:

> A person with a disability is a human being the same as everyone else, they have the same rights as everybody else, and just as you have a responsibility for providing a learning environment for any child you have to provide a learning environment for a child with a disability.

For Judith, inclusion was 'just part of being in teaching', with a responsibility for all children, a sentiment similar to that expressed by Sue and Jenny. Dorothy said it was a 'personal thing'. Referring to children disadvantaged by economic circumstances as well as those experiencing other difficulties, she said:

> I've got this thing that everybody should be given a fair go . . . everybody having opportunities. . . . After teaching for sixteen years you see kids with so much going for them in one sense and nothing in another sense, and for me I take it very personally. . . . It's such a loss to see untapped potential.

Some teachers told us of experiences of deprivation in their own lives that influenced their philosophy. Nevertheless, whatever the origins of a personal position on inclusion, it seemed to centre around the kind of ideas expressed by Rachel, who said 'It's a trite thing to call it fair play but it's what's right. It's right and it's all kinds of things, but basically it's what is fair.'

As well as children having an absolute right to be included, the principal, Janet, emphasised the importance of all children having 'access to all areas of the curriculum' so that they will come to 'know what their strengths and their needs are and get . . . a balanced view of where their hopes and aspirations may lie'. Janet believed that this could not happen in segregated special education. She thought that without such an opportunity a child would be seriously disadvantaged in terms of their personal and educational development.

By framing the idea of inclusion within notions of fairness, deprivation, and human rights, these people identify disability as a socio-political issue (Barton *et al.* 1992; Biklen 1988), alongside and related to issues of gender, ethnicity and poverty. It is clearly significant that these women have chosen to work in one of the economically poorest areas of their city, that they work closely with leaders of the Maori, Samoan and Cambodian families in their community, and that their strategies for working with students experiencing problems through poverty or abuse are the same as those used for the inclusion of students with disabilities; teachers sharing problem solving, weekly special needs meetings, and so on.

In this school, disability is revalued as an ordinary aspect of diversity, as demonstrated in the way students with disabilities are a valued part of all settings and activities. They are seen as individuals. Their disability is acknowledged as part of who they are, and the personal challenges they may face are not diminished by the philosophy and practice of inclusion. Diversity is valued, not assimilation. Disability as an ordinary aspect of diversity is also evident in the approach to resources at Central School. Here, disability is not seen as necessarily requiring high and ongoing levels of additional support in the classroom. The support needs may vary according to the individual student and the classroom context, so that, potentially, all children can be considered as needing some extra assistance at some time. Resource issues are seen as part of an ordinary continuum of needs applying to all students. This is a more complex model of teacher and student support needs than that created by categorical approaches to disability currently under discussion in New Zealand (Mitchell and Ryba 1994).

At Central School, disability is not a 'fixed state' of an individual that can be categorised, but a result of social relationships that can recreate disability as valued and inclusive, rather than as negatively different, disabling, 'special', and therefore exclusive (Sullivan 1991). By seeing disability as a rights, and therefore political, issue Central School acknowledges the wider social context within which disability is predominantly viewed from a positivist, medical-model paradigm that typically disempowers and marginalises disabled people (Biklen 1988; Sullivan 1991).

Without diminishing the experience of disability, the world view held at Central School recognises that prevailing economic ideologies in New Zealand society 'disable' many other children, including those living in poverty and those from ethnic minorities. From their personal philosophies, and in some cases from their own childhood experiences of discrimination and hardship, these teachers hold strong views on equity and on the right of all children to the best possible learning opportunities. Inclusion for students with disabilities is part of this overriding world view, paradigm, or metatheory, through which these people organise and make sense of the complex ideas and practices that comprise teaching.

Our analysis of the creation of this inclusive school is consistent with the work of Fulcher (1989), who shows how policy is made at the level of the classroom and school and how this may be consistent or inconsistent with government policy and legislation. Where teacher policy and practice is in advance of that evident in other parts of the system, this suggests the significant leadership role that can be played by individual principals (Biklen 1985) and teachers (Dixon 1994). If we analyse disability as a social construction of shared ideas, and as a social creation of institutional and individual practices (Oliver 1988; Sullivan 1991), we emphasise the need to change the assumptions, models, theories and practices that are involved in disabling interactions between people with disabilities and others. From the present study we believe that in their practice of inclusion at Central School, the Principal, teachers, students and parents show that how we relate to each other *matters*.[2]

2 We gratefully acknowledge the participation of the Principal, teachers, students and parents in this study. We thank them for allowing us to spend time in their school and for helping us to write this chapter. We have used terminology related to disability, current in New Zealand. We recognise the preference of some to identify themselves as 'people with disabilities' and of others to describe themselves as 'disabled people'.

7

NEW ZEALAND RESPONSE: ONE PHILOSOPHY OR TWO?

Keith Ballard and Trevor MacDonald describe Central School at the start as inclusive. It is an island of good practice where 'dreams come true', in an education system affected by 'radical right-wing' policies introduced following difficulties identified with the funding of the welfare state (Thomson 1991). These reforms mirror those discussed in the English case-study. The contributions of teachers, students and trustees as well as the considered interpretation of the authors provide a rich array of ideas for developing inclusion.

The staff, Board of Trustees and students in the school espoused a clearly considered and articulated philosophy of inclusion, and this was found to be applied in practice in classroom and playground. Keith Ballard and Trevor MacDonald conclude that the practice is explained by the commitment to a philosophy or 'metatheory', which we take to mean a coherent set of principles that guides day-to-day and moment-to-moment decisions about practice. We ask whether there are additional complexities to be considered about practice in the school, about the beliefs of those who work in it, and about the views of the authors of this chapter.

How does the national context explain and constrain practice?

In terms of the sophistication of its practice on inclusion, Central School is an atypical school and such practice cannot be said to be directly related to national policies. Further, the strength and significance of central requirements in a system that operates as a set of autonomous schools, following radical reforms to the educational system, requires careful examination. The removal of a tier of local government limits possibilities for both preventing and coordinating support for new developments. Although the reforms that have occurred in New Zealand were imported from the UK through advisers to the Conservative Party, we do not know whether the same competitive conditions apply between schools. In England, an apparent devolution of power to schools and their governing bodies has been accompanied by a dramatic increase in central government powers over education.

The chapter emphasises teachers as policy makers, implying that the development of schools is dependent on their personal approach to education. This is given weight by the apparent increase in the autonomy of schools, although their relative autonomy in most countries leaves considerable room for teachers to transform policy as 'street level bureaucrats' (Weatherley and Lipsky 1977). The corollary of this position is that when policies do not develop in schools then individual teachers are to blame. Thus exclusion happens, according to Colleen Brown (p. 71) because of 'teachers who will not teach our children'. Yet even in the absence of direct links between central policies and local practice, teachers are constrained in their actions, culturally and socially as well as personally.

The development of the school is linked to cultural policies concerned with the parity between Maori and other cultures (Pakeha), although for an outside observer this duality cannot capture the cultural diversity of modern New Zealand. The school is a community school with an apparently defined catchment area. One of the teachers refers directly to the Treaty of Waitangi in justifying her philosophy of inclusion and there is an emphasis in the school on sustaining the distinctiveness of its communities.

In terms of general education policies we are told that the National Curriculum is an inclusive force because it is for everyone, but whether it serves to selectively exclude students depends on its precise character. We do not have a detailed analysis of the inclusive and exclusive effects of the National Curriculum. There is no grade retention in schools and mixed-age classes are said to be common in New Zealand primary schools.

The involvement of 'disabled' students is compatible with the official rhetoric on inclusion in New Zealand legislation and government advice. All children are said to have a right to attend a mainstream school through a law passed in 1989 and emphasised in guidelines issued in 1995. However, though the extent of the recognition of the right of students to attend a neighbourhood school may be greater than elsewhere, it is a long way short of universal. The contradictions in the rhetoric and reality of national inclusion policies are not explicitly addressed in the chapter.

Compulsory segregation is still possible (although the numbers in special school are very low by international standards (Pijl and Meijer 1991) at 0.39 per cent with a further 0.6 per cent in special classes) and is advocated by the teacher unions. Some form of special education support is said to be given for three per cent of the school population in total, and further funds weighted according to 'socio-economic status' and to be used flexibly by the schools are to be made available through a 'special education grant'. (Ministry of Education 1996b). Numbers in special schools and special classes have remained static in the years 1991–1995 (Ministry of Education 1996b). The national policy requires a continuum of provision 'so that parents may choose separate special education if they wish'. However, the investment in expensive segregated facilities always provides a pressure to use that provision and avoid the duplication of services in the mainstream. In practice, a dual system only exists on paper across a country as a whole, for in any particular area investment favours one system or another.

As in other chapters, the linking of resources to students on the basis of categorisation creates a mind-set to think of inclusion as applicable to a particular group of students. In New Zealand support is through 'Section 9 Agreements' and discretionary hours, usually in the form of non-teacher assistant time. We do not know if there is a formula giving increasing resources to schools in relatively poor areas or areas where a large number students have English as an additional language.

Voices and perspectives on inclusion and exclusion

This study presents us with a number of clear voices, of teachers, students, and parents as well as the voices of the authors and policy makers. While there is a relative consistency of view coming from teachers, parents and students, we are told of a couple of current 'dissenting voices'. One student suggested that it is a waste of time being with categorised students. There is also a sense that there are other voices, a chorus of doom, around the school watching and waiting for them to slip up.

Although there are two authors, there is no suggestion in this chapter that Keith and Trevor differ in any respect about their perspectives on inclusive education. Can two minds really speak as one on such a complex topic? There is a powerful convention to represent multi-authored works as the product of a consensus. Yet, as soon as one begins to question such groups of authors about their differences, these usually become readily apparent. And as we suggested in chapter 1, even if they are not evident at first, such differences are likely to appear as we explore the views of the individuals concerned in greater detail and depth. However, we recognise that once one has broken the taboo of differences between joint authors, there is a problem about how to represent differences in print without appearing self-obsessed or committing an inordinate amount of time to the preparation of the material.

The chapter contains a strongly-stated 'rights' perspective. The authors imply that they believe that students with disabilities should attend neighbourhood schools as a right through their support for such a perspective when expressed by others, and the notion that in including students with disabilities and disbanding the special class, the school has 'set the captives free'. Notions of the limits to inclusion are tellingly contested by one of the students who says that 'you [just] have to be born', 'they have to breathe' before a student is seen as a legitimate member of the school community. The idea that some students might be excluded from classrooms or the school is related to issues of behaviour and violence, where rights conflict.

On our definition of inclusion, an inclusive school is an ideal never fully attained and inclusion is about changing processes; enhancing participation and reducing exclusionary pressures. In describing Central as an inclusive school, the authors encourage us to think of inclusion as an attainable state. Many of the practices at the school seem admirable, and the coherence and conscious elaboration of approach of teachers, parents and teachers and other staff, are remarkable. Yet, this setting up of the school as 'inclusive' may mean that there are issues which are overlooked, or which would be examined more closely if a more critical approach were adopted. For it must remain possible to ask of this school as of any other: how can the participation of students and others at the school be enhanced? How can pressures to exclusion be reduced or mitigated by the school?

The endless possibilities for enhancing participation *are* reflected in the way the teachers act as if their work has no limit. Several commented on the intensity of life at the school, though the authors point out that the devotion to education is a common feature of schools. However, there are other issues bearing on inclusion that are worthy of comment. All the teachers at this school, as well as all the parents interviewed, are women. We do not know much about language policies at the school, of the possibilities of bi- or multilingual teaching in line with notions of cultural parity between groups. We hear of a teacher giving out points for work in a way that might bear closer examination in terms of the balance between praise and the development of inner reward and pleasure in personal achievement.

The chapter appears to us to interweave two further perspectives on inclusion. On the one hand, it is concerned with cultural diversity within New Zealand society and within the school, and with models of support that are for all children rather than a special categorised minority. However, the main emphasis of the authors is on the inclusion of students with 'disabilities' rather than participation for all and this is indicated through the information that is chosen to form the 'National Context', the questions they ask of teachers and students, and the observations they make in classrooms. It is a view challenged directly by some teachers and students, and also by the fact that in different places in the chapter the authors shift ground themselves.

People also differed in the study in the position that disability occupies in their perceptions of the identity of disabled students. If we think of our identities as consisting of a fluctuating hierarchy of interacting elements, some people see the disability of others as predominant or perhaps the only feature of their identity, and some disabled people may view the world predominantly in relation to their disability. A considerable difference of view emerged in the past between the headteacher and the teachers of the separate special class, who had viewed disabled students as 'sick', requiring a totally 'specialist' curriculum and having no need to mix with other non-categorised students. The authors too, reject the 'medicalization' of disability and see disability as an aspect of 'difference', 'an ordinary aspect of diversity'. Yet, such a view might lead them to identify the study of inclusive education with a study of responses to all difference.

A medical view of disability is commonly contrasted with a social view in which disability itself is seen to be created through the social oppression of people with an impairment, and hence this is connected to a strong assertion of disabled people's rights (Abberley 1987). The implication here is that when oppression ceases, disability dissolves into an ordinary aspect of difference. It might be thought, therefore, that as long as disabled people are subject to exclusionary pressures then a concern with inclusion in education necessarily involved a consideration of disabled students. However, as the authors themselves argue, disability is not the only aspect of difference subject to exclusionary pressures, since differences of gender, race, sexuality, attainment, class and wealth are used to negatively discriminate against less favoured groups. Hence, the issue of disability cannot have favoured status in considerations of inclusion and exclusion. Why it does for many people, owes more to their professional and personal history than the analysis of the concepts and their application.

The authors indicate that they are concerned with inclusion and exclusion more broadly when they discuss the multi-cultural nature of the school, and the way New Zealand society 'disables' children in poverty and those from ethnic minorities. Yet, the teachers and students go even further in linking the inclusion and exclusion of all students – as revealed in their responses when interviewed. When asked 'do you have children with disabilities in your class?' Rachel replies that the school does not 'identify and label' people. She severs the notion of disability from a connection with impairment by suggesting that anyone who experiences difficulties with the curriculum might be termed 'disabled'. Margaret, too, contests the notion of disability: 'all children have specific needs obviously. Whether you term them disabilities I don't know.'

In their practice, the teachers use the support that comes into the school to enhance the participation of all students, a view echoed by a student: 'if you need help it is here . . . it is the same for those who can't speak English, or who can't walk'. They apply a highly flexible notion of support that has the clear aim of encouraging participation rather than exclusion and dependence. Support makes use of all available resources, including the capacity of students to provide support for each other. However, we are not given detailed observations of this inclusive pedagogy, which may reflect further the differences in direction of gaze between researchers, students and teachers.

The underpinnings of this approach to inclusion are further revealed in the way the teachers describe their philosophy in terms applicable to all: it is about 'fairness' and cultural respect, rather than about a commitment to disabled students. Nevertheless, the head reports that the disbanding of the special unit started the school on the path to becoming 'inclusive', and seems, too, to be identifying inclusive education here with increasing the participation of disabled students.

In response to an editorial request, the authors explored the possibility of a contradiction between the withdrawal of students for reading support and the requirement that specialist support for disabled students should be given in the classroom. They distinguish between withdrawal support that increases the medicalization of students and withdrawal support that is not seen as 'special treatment' but as an 'accelerant', an everyday part of New Zealand primary education. We think that this discussion provides an important basis for examining the purpose and detail of inclusion policies. There is a traditional argument commonly put forward by defenders of separate education for some categorised students that they are separated in order to promote greater participation. Clearly, such an argument could be put forward for the Reading Recovery programme. However, whether or not it is true in either case depends on whether the participation of the students is actually enhanced by the separation. If we accept the argument for Reading Recovery then we cannot argue in principle that withdrawal support is never appropriate for other students, including disabled students. The headteacher's observation of the position of students in the special class was that their difference was exaggerated by the separation and participation was not sought. It was separation in the interests of the professionals rather than the students. Within the Norwegian system, for example, class groups for the compulsory years of schooling are 'mixed ability' by law, based on the belief that they cannot be arranged according to presumptions of ability without creating a hierarchy of value. In developing inclusion in education we might allow for flexibility in groupings and places for learning, while carefully scrutinising the rationality of the use of disability or other forms of categorisation, such as relatively low attainment, as a basis for the creation of groups.

The study, like Linda Ware's, was conducted according to an explicit qualitative research code, whereby the contents of the chapter were negotiated with the *adult* participants in it. It aims to be inclusive in conception. Nevertheless, the interpretations and conclusions are the authors' own. They acknowledged that some sensitive personal material has been omitted from the story but that the general issues raised by it have been included. It is not always easy to allude to important sensitive issues in case-study research, particularly where a school such as this is easily identifiable. In other cases the participants may be motivated to censor the research because of a wish to convey a positive professional image. If in this the case the researchers had uncovered practice which gave ammunition to the opponents of the school, would this have created a dilemma about how this should be reported?

8

NORWAY: ADAPTED EDUCATION FOR ALL?

Kari Nes Mordal and Marit Strømstad

Introduction

In this chapter we concentrate on the educational experiences of teachers and students in 'Berg School', a primary school in the Hedmark district of Norway. We pay particular attention to the inclusion of three students with special educational needs in a fifth grade class. We start by outlining the Norwegian educational system, legislation and policies on inclusion, and the terms and concepts used to discuss it. We then report on our observations and interviews at Berg School in the context of its community or 'commune'. We end by reviewing the progress towards inclusive education at Berg and the effects of Norwegian policies.

Education and inclusion in Norway

The history of compulsory schooling in Norway dates from 1739. A law concerning 'The Education of Abnormal Children' was passed in 1881 which created a parallel special education system. Many pupils with severe learning difficulties were regarded as ineducable: until 1964, children in institutions for the mentally retarded had no access to any education and full-time education became available to all children with disabilities only in 1975. The same basic pattern existed throughout the country: children with special needs who were regarded as 'educable' were transferred to special schools or special classes. They were separated from their classmates and a normal environment in a way that reduced their possibilities for inclusion and normal social relations.

During the 1960s the idea of normalisation and integration came to the fore in Norway, as in many other western societies. This shift of paradigm from a psycho-medical to a social-political one was rooted in the economic and political developments that occurred after the Second World War, as described by Vislie (1995). Politicians saw normalisation and integration as the solution for a group of people who had not received their share of welfare. Consequently, policies were introduced for abandoning institutions and the special school system in order to give every child a place in their local school and normal society, irrespective of their difficulty or disability.

In 1975, the legislation relating to special education was repealed and the Norwegian Education Act for compulsory education was extended to cover all children of school age. It required that every child shall be given equitable and suitably 'adapted education', preferably in the local school. However, the parallel special school system still existed, though many handicapped children began to attend their local schools. Institutions for the mentally retarded were finally abandoned in 1991. A year later, the special school system was transformed into a network of competence centres where teachers from ordinary schools can get help and advice to support their work with children who have special needs. Now, practically all children in Norway attend their local schools, though local authorities may, as an exception, choose to establish small part-time or full-time separate special education units within or outside ordinary schools. Probably no more than one per cent of the school population are in special schools or units in Norway, including schools in psychiatric wards (Vislie 1995). The precise national extent of segregated education is difficult to assess as there is no agreement on how or what to count, and there are regional variations. According to information from The Regional Educational Office of Hedmark, in the last two years an average of about 0.3 per cent of the students have been in special schools in the region ('fylke') where Berg, the case-study school, is situated.

The Norwegian school system

Now that the state no longer maintains a network of special schools, compulsory education is the responsibility of the local authorities within each Norwegian commune. Most of the resources for local services are transferred from the government through the national budget, and local politicians have to distribute the scarce funds in compliance with legal requirements. Provision for pre-school children is not legally required and, consequently, is insufficiently developed in the majority of communes, but most children with special needs are granted a place in a kindergarten. Children normally attend primary school (first–sixth grade) from the age of six. The 435 Norwegian communes are sub-divided into fixed primary school catchment areas. These boundaries are defined by tradition and, though the pattern of population changes, it is very difficult for authorities to alter them. Consequently, we have primary schools varying from less than ten to several hundreds of students. Catchment areas for secondary schools normally include more than one primary school area. Since catchment areas are fixed, parents have no choice of school unless they prefer to send their child to one of the very few private schools in Norway. According to official figures the number of students in the age range 7–16 years attending private schools (mostly Waldorf schools or religious schools) in Norway was about 1.5 per cent in 1993–94.

Classes are mixed sex and pupils are grouped on the basis of age. Generally, children must not be grouped according to ability, but such groupings may be used for short periods or for particular purposes, though not for the whole year. Exceptions can be made with parents' consent for children with special educational needs. Students continuously have their work corrected and commented upon, but no marks or examinations are given in primary schools. Secondary schools do have marks and a final exam, but students do not repeat years in either primary or in secondary schools.

The term 'curriculum' usually has a more restricted meaning than in English-speaking countries, where not only the intended but also the realised and experienced plans for teaching are included. (Stenhouse in Nordahl and Overland 1992a). The Norwegian National 'Curriculum Guidelines' is an officially approved document, laying down principles for educational methods and the content of each academic subject for each school year. Schools and teachers are expected to make local adaptations to the 'National Curriculum' and ensure that local culture is part of the curriculum (Ministry of Education, Research and Church Affairs 1987; 1994). For children with special needs, teachers working in cooperation with parents and, sometimes, the student, develop individual learning plans, choose individual learning material and set individual aims for each child. This is relatively easy to do in the primary school where there is no formal grading. However, the formal evaluation systems of secondary schools that apply to all children make it difficult for students with special needs to have individual plans and alternative forms of evaluation.

In accordance with the Curriculum Guidelines, the school day is normally divided into lessons according to traditional academic subjects, such as Norwegian, mathematics, history, Christianity. The distinction between subjects is less explicit in primary school but very evident in secondary school. In primary schools the class teacher is normally responsible for most of the lessons given to one class and the pupils have to relate to few people. In secondary school, teachers teach their special subject and classes consequently change teachers throughout the day and week. Though the school day is divided according to subject, project work or integrated day approaches are strongly recommended.

The reformed Lutheran Church of Norway is the State Church and about eighty-seven per cent of the population have some attachment to it. Christianity used to be a compulsory subject for all children. However, the subject has recently been changed to be non-denominational and more attention is now given to other religions. At the same time, Christianity has played an important part in the shaping of the Norwegian society, and thus a certain knowledge about Christianity makes it easier to understand and relate to our cultural demands. Consequently, even students with different religious background are expected to take part in lessons on Christianity, although they are not in any way forced to believe in or pray to the Christian God.

In addition to class teachers and subject teachers, most schools have special teachers and/or assistants assigned to teach pupils with special needs. In 1993–4, 6.2 per cent of all pupils aged 7–16 received some form of special education following expert assessment ('sakkyndig vurdering'). This number includes students with a whole variety of special educational needs. Special education is organised in different ways in different schools, ranging from completely individualised remedial tuition in a separate room to two or more teachers cooperating to meet the demands of all children in groups bigger than classes. Additional funds for special education are of two sorts: extra resources earmarked for the individual child as a result of assessments, and a grant to each school to adapt general education.

During recent years, parents have been expected to play a more important role in schools. Meetings between teachers and parents are arranged at least twice a year. Parents now know much more about their children's life in school, but it is a matter of debate whether they have much real influence. For a more detailed review of the Norwegian special education development and of the general school system see Helgeland (1992).

Conceptions of inclusion

The terms 'special educational needs' or just 'special needs' are commonly used to categorise pupils with learning difficulties, physical impairments and behaviour disorders. Such terminology implies 'that there is a division to be drawn between "normal" and "less than normal" learners. It implies exclusion', as pointed out by Booth (1995, p. 99). The term integration is still in use among teachers although officially, at least, it has been replaced. When referring to integration, teachers mean the presence in ordinary schools of those children who used to be transferred to special schools or special classes. Of course integration implies that some are segregated and, therefore, need to be returned, but after our school reform this should not be the situation in Norway. One of our writers on normalisation (Solum 1991) has tried to replace integration with the term 'anti-segregation'. This has a more positive connotation in that it takes for granted that nobody is segregated at the beginning and, therefore, the challenge is to see that everybody remains within the regular school. However, the term is seldom used outside certain circles of researchers and lecturers and, in our opinion, it has no significance for most teachers in Norway.

The term 'inclusion' is being used in forthcoming plans for compulsory schooling, but this may be seen simply as a replacement for the term integration. Like the concept integration, it suggests that somebody does not belong from the beginning but has to be included. We prefer to use the phrase 'one school for all' to mean a school with a place for every child who is born and grows up in the school district; a school where nobody needs either integration or inclusion. 'One school for all' represents the unification of two lines of development in Norway. The first is the idea of a comprehensive school system ('enhetsskole') which was introduced in 1936 when seven years of free education were granted to all children. The second line of development involves the term 'one society for all', which came into use in connection with the normalisation and integration of people with special needs during the 1960s. Put simply, one society for all requires one school for all.

In 'one school for all', every child has the right to be given 'equitable and suitably adapted education' ('Likeverdig og tilpasset opplæring'), usually abbreviated to 'adapted education'. This demand was part of the Norwegian Education Act for compulsory education in 1975, but it is by no means easy to understand its implications, nor to put it into practice (Nilsen 1993). Special education is regarded as a natural part of the efforts made by the school to give suitably adapted education to all.

Adapted education has two equally important features. First, there is the *right to belong* irrespective of differences of mental or physical abilities. The same principle applies to differences of culture, race or sex. Second, there is the *right to learn,* whereby every child has to be given equal opportunities to develop their abilities.

Adapted education requires both these demands to be met equally. Indeed, this double message stands out very clearly in the 'Curriculum Guidelines for Compulsory Education in Norway' (1987), which state:

> the pupils must have equal opportunities to face challenges and acquire skills and knowledge. The pupils shall also be given equal opportunities to draw on their own experiences in the learning environment.
>
> (p. 32)

In order to promote such opportuinities:

> the forms of organisation must promote cooperation between pupils and enable the school to exploit the possibilities of learning that exist within the group of pupils. The teaching must be arranged so that all pupils, including those with special learning needs, benefit from learning together and from being part of an organised group – a community. The ways of working and the forms of contact between pupils must give individual pupils an opportunity to contribute to the community according to their own abilities.
>
> (p. 33)

The White Paper concerning principles and guidelines for the new ten-year compulsory school defines an 'inclusive school' as a school where:

> Pupils with special needs shall participate equally in the social, academic and cultural community. This demands that all pupils – also those with special needs – as a general rule should go to school in their own district and get their education within the ordinary class. It also demands that the teaching within the mixed ability class must be organised flexibly. Pupils can work in a variety of small and big groups or on their own. Such groups can also include pupils from other classes from the same or different grades.
>
> Ministry of Education, Research and Church Affairs
> 1995a, pp. 22–23. Our translation.

Adapted education, therefore, has implications for all aspects of the teachers' planning and performance. The teacher must set different goals for the varied abilities of pupils within one classroom, use a variety of materials, differentiate the content of the teaching, organise work flexibly and adapt assessment procedures.

Whether we use the terms 'integration', 'inclusion', 'adapted education' or 'one school for all', for any particular child we still have to ask: is this child really included as a full member of the school community, or have we only made superficial adaptations which leave the child just as isolated as in a special class or special school?

Berg school and its community

In order to examine the practice of adapted education we looked at one school which we have called Berg. We selected the school because for about two decades it has educated a number of pupils with clearly-defined disabilities. Further, it has been working on its own improvement for some years and, as a result, the teachers have been reflecting on questions with a bearing on inclusion and exclusion.

Berg is a small primary school situated in an agricultural area in the central part of southern Norway, about 100 kilometres north of Oslo. It has about ninety-six pupils, nine teachers, one head teacher and two teacher assistants. Except for one child, who is in a children's psychiatric ward, all the children from the local community go to Berg school. While the total Commune population is 18,000, only six to eight hundred belong to the catchment area of the school. Work in the community is on farms and small-holdings and in factories, shops, schools, and social services.

In this part of Norway, class distinctions used to have a considerable impact on life inside and outside school. This persisted well into the last half of the twentieth century. One of our informants said: 'low marks ran in families in those days'. Even in a small community like Berg, people from different classes hardly mixed, for instance, in sports activities. Society has now changed. New housing estates have ruptured the system. Though people surrounding Berg still know where their parents came from, old class distinctions are of little importance to today's children. These days, they play together after school and take part in the same activities. The school has changed too. New teachers have been trained not to make class distinctions between children, but to treat every child with respect and teach them according to their abilities. This development has influenced the relationship between school and parents too, and generally the local community has a positive sense that Berg is their school. The school has no students belonging to language minorities. This varies tremendously in the country; for example, in 1993 in Oslo 23.7 per cent of the students were foreign, whereas in Berg's region, Hedmark, the number was 2.6 per cent (Ministry of Education, Research and Church Affairs 1995b).

The school development activities were originally prompted by constant vandalism of school property but this problem is completely resolved now. Several changes have been introduced. The school day is divided into periods twice as long as the traditional lesson. The pupils can mostly choose for themselves whether to stay in or out in the breaks and doors are not locked. Each day has one 'free' hour in the middle, when the children can choose activities organised by the pupils' council. These latter activities cut across age groups. Another way in which age barriers are crossed is a support system whereby fifth graders are the helpers ('godparents') of first graders.

There is also regular contact between the school and the local community. For example, once a week there is the 'head's lesson' when all children assemble to listen to the headmaster and his invited guest, often a local person who might talk about bygone days, or of the fish and fishing in the lake. Once a month the vicar has a lesson with the whole school to sing (hymns *and* rock!) or to rehearse, as the children – on a voluntary basis – always take part in church with a choir on special occasions. The students often perform at school too, in some way or other, for instance at every 'head's lesson' and at the old age pensioners' open day. Parents come to school for meetings, at Christmas and other social functions. One of the teachers even invites parents to come to the class at any time, and they do attend! All the children take part in these arrangements, taking their turn to contribute to entertainment and in providing refreshments.

Students with difficulties at the school

Students who experience difficulties are identified in a number of ways: before school, through kindergarten in collaboration with the health service and the community pedagogical/psychological support team; by parents involving the health service or their teachers; at school age through regular screening of reading attainment, followed by diagnostic assessment of those in need; or difficulties may be recognised through systematic interviews with students themselves.

About six per cent of the pupils have legal 'Statements' related to their special needs, which is about the average proportion in Norway. The proportion of boys with special educational needs is higher than the national average of approximately two out of every three identified students (see Moen and Øie, 1994). We have not found strong indications of more covert ways of ranking students systematically at the school, though one may wonder if the sex bias in the SEN group is purely accidental.

The extent, content and organisation of the support for the six pupils with special needs are described in their individual learning programmes. Whether the additional support earmarked for each SEN child is given in the classroom or as a withdrawal programme varies and will be discussed later in the chapter. The formal assessment may give directions about the organisation of support, but decisions about this are made mostly by the teachers involved. Two further ways of giving extra support to children are used in the school. In the first grade the group is divided up during parts of the day in order to increase possibilities of individual help. Second, slow readers from any class can join a 'reading stimulation programme' in the school library for a couple of hours a week.

Methods for collecting information

A variety of methods were used to form an impression of the school. A questionnaire on *attitudes* towards 'suitably adapted education' was distributed to the teachers in 1993. Then, in 1994, the teachers were asked to describe their *practice*. Building on the findings from both these surveys, in May and June 1995 we carried out a programme of observations during lessons and breaks. In addition we interviewed the headteacher, teachers, parents, special education coordinator and a pedagogical/psychological adviser; half of the students answered a questionnaire on their sense of well-being at school. Finally, we studied written documents from the school, such as the school plan and individual learning programmes.

Teachers' views of 'adapted education'

In 1993 we had asked the teachers at Berg to express their degree of agreement about 106 statements concerning adapted education. We followed this up by asking for examples of successful practice. About half of the reports were concerned with class organisation and social climate. Several teachers described as 'adapted education for all' a practice very similar to what is known as 'an integrated day'. The children get a plan for their homework and for certain parts of their school-based work for a week at a time and are given responsibility to complete these tasks. As a consequence, in some lessons, different pupils work on quite different subjects at the same time. Most often they work individually, but they may cooperate if they wish. This system requires team planning among the teachers involved, and their role in class becomes more like that of a consultant.

To some extent the pupils may influence the content and amount of work in the programme. Some teachers have developed this further, so that the pupils set their own goals for the week in addition to the teacher's goals. These may concern both academic and social tasks, for example, 'be there on time after breaks', 'improve writing the letter s', 'learn the eight times multiplication table', 'don't interrupt my companion'. These individual goals are evaluated, along with selected parts of the week's work, in sessions with the whole class.

The teachers argued that adapted education had the following benefits for all children, and particularly those with special needs:

- The possibilities for the teacher to differentiate between tasks are improved by making adjustments to the shared weekly programme.
- The teacher can provide help where it is needed without the others wasting their time waiting.
- Pupils automatically help each other, often in a more efficient way than the teacher does.
- Pupils with substantial special needs may have their individual programme within this framework. The child may be helped by the support teacher inside or outside the classroom and still feel part of the class.
- The children get used to working on different topics, at different levels, and often even in different places (e.g. group rooms), at the same time as classmates. 'Being different is normal' is a necessary attitude for the creation of an inclusive climate. This view is strengthened by being talked about openly at the weekly evaluation meeting.
- The responsibility for one's own work and own behaviour increases. This is another important attitude in 'one school for all'.
- By being open about difference, the pupils are continuously being challenged to feel responsibility for and care for each other. The pupils may support or criticise each other ('You nearly made it this week – try again!' or 'You still interrupt me!').

The report of a couple of teachers underlined the importance of practical and aesthetic subjects. One teacher emphasised common experiences – through literature and drama – as the 'glue' to keep the very heterogeneous group together. She finds that this can contribute to each pupil's experiences of being part of the same group while being different and unique. The very shy or the very slow learner can play important parts in the play, even without using many words. As one pupil said in the 'planet period' when he was running slowly in his fixed circle around the flag pole: 'I'm Mercury, because I don't run so fast, you know . . .' (Mercury is the planet with the shortest orbit).

It should be remembered that adapted education is only one of the teaching approaches used at Berg School. Whole class, teacher-directed instruction, followed by individual work, still takes up most of the time in many classes. There are also out-of-classroom events involving trips and camps, celebrations and competitions, which require careful planning and preparation.

The participation of students

We gathered information about the participation of students in a fifth grade class consisting of fifteen 11–12 year olds, five girls and ten boys. We selected the class because it includes three of the six SEN children in the school; Per has Down syndrome; Lars has substantial learning difficulties believed to be due to a turbulent family life, including frequent moving; Jon has learning and behavioural difficulties, recently diagnosed as ADHD (Attention Deficit Hyperactivity Disorder). According to his teacher Jon used to be very aggressive and noisy, but this is improving.

We used observation, questionnaires and interviews to collect information. We were readily accepted into the class, since the children were used to people going in and out and took little notice of us. We paid particular attention to the academic and social participation of the children with special needs. The class seemed to function well socially, as well as academically. The integrated day principle, described earlier, applies to part of the weekly schedule, and changes in the schedule seemed frequent.

Academic participation

The class has twenty-seven weekly lessons. The SEN pupils take part in from six to seventeen lessons with a support or special teacher, or a teacher assistant. Per has one day a week at a neighbouring school in a small group with other mentally retarded children, following an 'Activity of Daily Living' programme. A flavour of the involvement of the children with special needs in class activities and the effect of special help is given by notes of the observation on a Monday morning:

> All students are there with the class teacher (absence from school is rare). Their tables are placed in a U shape. All the girls sit beside one another and the three specially observed children also sit together by choice. The teacher asks about the weekend. Many speak simultaneously and have a lot to tell. Per is the only one of the three who contributes. After a quarter of an hour Jon goes forward to the teacher and asks for his special teacher. He leaves to find her. At the same time the other support teacher comes to collect Per. The teacher introduces the activities for the week and then starts a mathematics lesson. The students are free to cooperate, and Lars is frequently

helped by one of his classmates. Per returns to class after half an hour, finds his maths book and starts working, following his own programme. His place with the support teacher is now taken by Lars, who is out with her for the second lesson. Jon is out with his teacher for the second lesson too. Before the two return the lesson ends by singing grace, and the children start eating their packed lunches.

At the beginning of the week the support teachers make any adaptations to the week's programme for the class that are considered necessary. The individual programmes for the SEN students are mostly concerned with the three Rs. The aims are general and difficult to evaluate, such as 'improve writing' and 'strengthen self-confidence'. In individual lessons, the students follow their own programmes for reading, writing and mathematics. At the end of the individual lesson, students get instructions about how to go on working on their special programme when they get back to class.

The existence of individual plans may affect classroom activities whether or not the support teacher is present, as illustrated in an English lesson:

> The class teacher is alone with all the students present. She goes through a text, and all the students repeat it together. Lars joins in, Per also tries to, with little success, but Jon doesn't try. When asked to write down a message, they all do so. When requested to find the red English book, Jon asks if he can work on his own programme. The teacher says he may, and Jon finds a maths book. Per, too, finds his maths book and starts working in it. The other students answer questions in English – and so do Jon and Per, even though they are also working on their own programmes in maths. Jon explains to Per about the English.

Although a considerable amount of extra support is available to the class, it is not necessarily accessible when it is needed most. For example, sometimes the additional teacher is present when the student can manage well in class without her. This presented a dilemma to the teacher, for example, about whether Per should practise his academic skills according to his individual programme, or be part of the class activity. Sometimes the class teacher could do with help that is being given elsewhere. In a maths lesson two pupils were working on their individual programmes, each with their own teacher in a separate room. The remaining thirteen children were learning about the division of fractions, a topic that many of them found difficult.

At other times the role of the support teacher may be unclear:

> In the music lesson the support teacher takes part – mostly passively – in class, and all the students are present. They are singing, and the class teacher writes the number of the songs in the songbook on the

board. The students also eagerly suggest songs, Per included. Our three friends are able with some trouble to find the right numbers, and partly join in singing, Per with a rumbling voice and much joy!

The choice of whether the special teacher should stay in or out of the classroom is usually made in cooperation with the pupil and the teacher. However, occasionally there are differences of opinion. On one occasion Jon was out on his special programme when the class was to rehearse for a performance during the 'head's lesson'. The class teacher asked one of the students to go and get him for the rehearsal, but the special teacher said (for reasons we do not know) that this was inconvenient, so Jon could not join in the practice.

Views on the place of support

We gathered the views of teachers, students, parents and the pedagogical/psychological adviser on the use of withdrawal teaching. In our earlier questionnaire study there had been almost complete agreement about the importance of social participation between students, but disagreements arose on questions about academic participation and practical organisation. There was marked disagreement on the following statements: 'children with special needs cannot be properly taught inside the ordinary classroom', 'children with special needs have the best academic results if taught in a withdrawal programme'.

Most of the teachers who took part in this survey are still at Berg, and we think the answers reflect a continuing disagreement between the teachers. Though they agree about the importance of individual learning plans and individual goals, some staff seem to have a very strong disinclination to adapt their lessons by giving up teaching 'the same thing to everyone'. Views about the withdrawal of a student with special needs were related to 'the needs of the other children' or the wish to teach a more homogeneous class. Some felt that the academic results of the class were best served if the children with special needs were taught outside the classroom. The view was also expressed, with some force, that children with special needs learn most when alone with the teacher. Teachers emphasised the need to teach the children with SEN as much of the curriculum as possible, and felt that the concentration required often made it necessary to work in a separate room.

They also give practical explanations for supporting withdrawal arrangements, like timetable problems and teachers working different hours. Some equipment, such as Per's computer, which is sometimes used by other students, is kept in the group room. When Per needs to use it he has to leave the classroom. Other teachers felt that they would like to move in the direction of less withdrawal and planned to make some changes towards more cooperation and partnership teaching and more group work. They were supported in this by the view of the headteacher and the pedagogical/psychological adviser.

Teachers also suggested that the children preferred to work on their individual programmes outside the classrooms, and this was confirmed by the evidence from the student questionnaire that children find it quite normal that some pupils leave the classroom for some lessons. Parents also agreed with the teachers' decisions, arguing that these children were so different from others that they needed segregated lessons, so long as these did not exclude them from the social life of the class.

Social participation

In our observations of teaching situations, breaks, sports day and so on, we were quickly struck by the difference between the three SEN students in their relationships to others. Lars appears to be one of the group, actively included by others, though not one to take many initiatives. Per is well-accepted, and takes the initiative, for instance to be part of the football game, which he always is. On sports day he joins in the shot-put and is in the middle of the bunch playing and pushing. But where is Jon in these unorganised out-of-door situations? On the swing on his own most of the time, sometimes talking to younger students. Or he is offering to help the caretaker or to fetch things for the teacher. In the 'head's lesson' some of his classmates refused to sit by his side, and said he was stupid. Per may be scolded, too, for something specific but he is not rejected. There is, for instance, no sign of irritation about his imperfect singing voice. They are all there to perform with the rest when that is planned, preferably in a group. A recent victory for both Jon and Per was to speak two sentences on their own – like the rest – when the fifth grade was responsible for the local National Day speech.

Students' views

In order to find indications of the students' well-being in general, and whether having classmates with special needs influences their attitudes, a questionnaire (based on Nordahl 1992) containing nine statements was distributed to the third, fourth and fifth grade classes – a total of forty-four students. The answers of the boys with special needs did not differ from the others, and there were very small differences between the fifteen fifth graders and the other twenty-nine respondents. They reported that they always, or almost always, enjoyed school, both the activities during lessons and breaks. They liked their classmates, and very few sometimes felt alone or isolated at school. When asked if it was all right to have many different pupils at school or in the class, the whole population scored close to yes, always. The answers to one question were of special interest: 'do you think that other pupils feel alone or isolated at school?' The average score clearly revealed that not all students were regarded as included. But the score of the fifth graders indicates that they may be unaware of the evident social exclusion of one of their own classmates.

Parents' perceptions

The parents of the three children with special needs were also interviewed on this point. They were asked the same six questions concerning their child's schooling and relationships with classmates. We asked them to express their views on a five-point scale, rating from always to never. The answers were not surprising; in fact, the parents confirmed the findings from the other data, with few exceptions. They report that both Per and Lars enjoy school always, or nearly always, including activities during lessons as well as breaks, while Jon's mother scores his liking as 'sometimes'. While parents regarded Per and Lars as always accepted by classmates, Jon's mother was a little more reluctant, but decided to score 'nearly always'. According to their mothers, Lars and Jon spend much of their spare time with classmates. That question was not relevant for Per's mother because their home is situated far from the school. But she said that Per preferred to play with younger children or talk to adults.

Teachers' views

In our earlier questionnaire-study, teachers had agreed on a series of central issues concerning adapted education – especially the ideological demands that are very clearly expressed in law and curriculum guidelines. They gave full approval to the importance of normal relationships between children with special needs and others. They also recognised that if society is ever to change in the direction of more inclusion, different children must come together and get to know each other. For example, we found a consensus of close to one hundred per cent on the following statements: 'pupils with special needs can learn much from other pupils', 'helping classmates with special needs can lead to a positive academic outcome for the other pupils', 'academic achievement is not the most important goal of adapted education'.

In order to inquire further into the teachers' views on the social participation of special needs students, they were given a further short questionnaire, formerly used for this purpose at other schools, which contained questions like: 'to what extent do other pupils accept SEN pupils?' However, the teachers were reluctant to complete it, preferring to express their views verbally. Their reasons included: 'this can't be answered in a general way'; 'these children are as different as any others'; and 'differences in social participation need by no means be related to their having special needs'. Of the 'special' students in fifth grade for instance, one is fully accepted in spite of his handicap (Per), while another is, to a large extent, isolated (Jon). We were informed that the sixth grade had recently completed a sociogram, in which the SEN student in this class was chosen as a potential partner in one activity or another by almost everybody, but another student with no particular difficulties was not chosen by anyone. Generally, however, the teachers look upon the children at the school as predominantly tolerant and caring. For instance, at a mountain camp one girl stood up for her troublesome classmate (Jon) when he was threatened by someone from another school.

The teachers, then, thought that the students' personalities affected the degree of social inclusion. Some also claim that visible handicaps are easier to accept than hidden ones, and that disturbing behaviour is more difficult to tolerate than learning difficulties. In addition, they mentioned the social status of the student's home. It was clear, too, that some teachers make explicit links between 'successful integration', particularly where Per is concerned, and the way the school is organised to develop positive attitudes. For example, the fifth grade class teacher underlined the significance of good leadership at the school and the way pupils are trusted (open doors) and have responsibility ('free' lessons).

Inclusion at Berg school: conclusions or just more questions?

We have emphasised two important rights of students to have adapted education and inclusive schools; the right to learn and the right to belong. Are these rights satisfied at Berg?

Our description of practices at Berg School shows that much is being done to help the students overcome their learning problems. In many ways, the needs of the three SEN boys in the fifth grade are well catered for. They have individual resources and learning plans, as well as separate lessons and participation in classroom activities. But they are more segregated during lessons than we had expected. This was justified by the teachers in terms of the need for concentration and undisturbed individual tutoring. However, in our opinion, the extended use of segregated lessons may be questioned, especially if they are used to drill skills which might just as well be dealt with in the regular classroom. Further, the skills of the support teacher might be of more use if she was available to other children in the class.

Teachers do not seem to have realised that real integration means that children as a rule should take part in all classroom activities. They often ask the question 'how much time can this child spend in the classroom?' A more fruitful question might be: 'is it absolutely necessary to take this pupil out of the classroom?' This second question would better promote inclusion. It is also worth asking whether the mere existence of the special education system works against inclusion. Specialists naturally want to work within their field, and the Norwegian school system provides a specialist for nearly every kind of problem a child can possibly have, though the specialist is not always obtainable in the classroom or at the local school. The intended role of the specialists is to help the teachers adapt their teaching, but their very existence tends to make ordinary teachers doubt their own competence to cope with learning difficulties. They turn to professionals and specialists instead of seeking to solve their teaching problems together through an 'adhocratic discourse' (Skrtic 1991). At Berg School, as well as in most Norwegian schools, we see the dangers of professional bureaucracy as Skrtic describes it. If a specialist is within reach, it is easy for the class teacher to transfer the problematic child from the classroom to the specialist domain, outside the classroom. To stimulate inclusion as well as the competence of teachers, it would be preferable to transfer specialist knowledge to the classroom, where the pupils should be.

At first, we thought that inclusion might suffer because of all the separate lessons; that the right to learn was regarded as more important than the right to belong. However, our observations did not support these suspicions. It looks as if a certain number of segregated lessons need not be a serious threat to inclusion, though there is probably a limit. If that limit is surpassed the student will be 'someone who comes and goes', not a member of the class (Schnorr 1990); but what is the limit, and is it always the same?

We have reasons to believe that Per and Lars *are* accepted and, indeed, *feel* accepted, both by teachers and classmates. Per, Lars and Jon have the same number of separate lessons and are approximately on the same academic level, but Jon is obviously less accepted by his classmates. Are the school and the teachers to be blamed for this? If so, why are the two other boys included? Is it possible that more personal factors are at work? His behaviour has been very disturbing in class, and the children have rejected him. They still often do, though his behaviour is changing for the better. Observations and interviews suggest that he keeps to himself most of the time, possibly by choice, perhaps because he is used to and expects rejection. It seems that his classmates have more tolerance towards learning difficulties than towards behavioural problems, as the teachers suggested. We wonder if they would have been more or less rejecting if he had stayed in his classroom for more of the time.

Do most children at Berg have a sense of belonging, and do they learn and develop effectively? We have reasons to believe that they do. We observed practices that we approve of as well as practices that we might question, but all things considered, we would say that Berg is on its way towards achieving inclusiveness. But that does not mean that the school is unambiguously marching in one direction. We have found a certain comfort in what Clark *et al.* (1995, p. 90) say about schools as organisations. We, too, have found 'complexity, messiness and incoherence', but, nevertheless, in our opinion, Berg is an 'innovative' school.

The influence of the national context

Norway has had a relatively long history of teaching handicapped students in mainstream schools. Inclusiveness is supported by numerous national factors such as the general ideology; favourable legislation; the abandonment, by and large, of the use of special schools and other segregating institutions; a strong tradition of public education, with little parental choice of school and very few private schools available; no marks from first to sixth grade. Notions of competition and school choice are put forward, from time to time, by a right-wing minority, but have little political support. If parents could choose schools wherever they want for their children, this would foster competition, which probably works against inclusion. We argue that if there has to be competition, why not compete in inclusiveness instead of traditional academic results?

But are the students really integrated or included in Norwegian schools? Have schools changed to meet the diversity of all their pupils? Norwegian traditions place considerable importance on justice and individual rights to a modified programme for children with 'needs'. Indeed, you can go to court when your child is not granted what the expert assessment says. Extra resourcing is an important way of supporting the general welfare of those who are in particular need, but we feel that the current approach may contribute to the maintenance of the psycho-medical paradigm, as seen in the emphasis still put on individual learning programmes at Berg School.

Another set of problems arise when major changes are brought in through laws and guidelines with little practical help being given to teachers to implement them. Perhaps that is the reason why there is a surprisingly large gap between the intended and realised curriculum. As we have seen in Berg, efforts to improve the general structures of the school point away from an individual model towards an organisational paradigm (Ainscow 1995b).

The existence of small communities or 'communes', such as Berg, is an integral part of the social and political context in Norway. There is extensive integration between schools and their communities. Though the commune structure is, in itself, no guarantee of inclusion, it probably increases the chance of a general feeling of inclusion among children, and adults for that matter.

Berg School and its surroundings seem to have developed a capacity for dealing with diversity. Eventually the challenge of much greater cultural diversity will reach Berg but through its experience of openness to human variety, the school will be well prepared for it.

9

NORWAY RESPONSE: ADAPTED EDUCATION FOR SOME?

In their chapter Kari Nes Mordal and Marit Strømstad examine the education of three students described as having 'special needs' in the context of an education system that provides a detailed prescription about how students should participate within a common school and curriculum. Like the authors of the chapter from the Netherlands, they are not writing in their first language and while we have endeavoured to take this into account we have not fully investigated the particular hazards encountered by these authors in translating the concepts from Norwegian to English.

This chapter shares the theme of teachers as creators of policy with the previous one. One aspect of the New Zealand story involves a group of committed teachers in one school bringing a distinctive coherence to an ill-defined set of national policies. In this chapter Kari and Marit discuss the reverse process, whereby an apparently coherent set of national policies are diluted in practice. They question the role of specialist teachers and their over-reliance on withdrawal teaching and individual learning programmes, and how these can undermine or hijack 'adapted education'. However, the source of the contradictions between mainstream and specialist approaches to inclusion is unclear. Do the teachers in the school engender them or do national guidelines undermine themselves by the incompatibility of the training and deployment of specialist teachers with national requirements to implement inclusive education? The consistency and coherence of the official voice may be partly illusory if it pushes practice in two incompatible directions. As in the Scottish study, we might also question whether the strong focus of the authors on students identified and depicted by their deficits itself is compatible with a commitment to the rights of students 'to belong and learn'.

How does the national context explain and constrain practice?

Kari and Marit provide considerable background information on the Norwegian education system and policies, albeit from a perspective within special education. It appears that national policies provide a more favourable

118

context for increasing inclusion and reducing exclusion than in any other of our case-studies. There is an expectation that all pupils 'as a general rule' go to a school in their own district, receiving their education in the mainstream class.

There are explicit links to the development of comprehensive education where, in contrast to the system in England when comprehensive schools were being introduced, legislation actually prescribed the form and curriculum content of the comprehensive school in Norway. Comprehensive schools themselves are set in the context of the creation of 'one society for all' from a formerly class-based society. Schooling is mixed in gender and there is very little private education. An explicit pedagogy for inclusion has been developed around the notion of 'equitable and suitably adapted education' that builds on the presence of 'mixed ability' teaching in the compulsory school years, and the absence of examinations and grading within the primary school. All of this contrasts strikingly with the competitive ambience that pervades the English study. 'Adapted education' encompasses cooperative learning within a flexible pedagogy. The authors relate it to students' rights to belong and learn in one school. This emphasis on rights is a feature of the Norwegian system, as it is in the US, and is emphasised within the New Zealand study but is absent within official policies in England, Scotland and Ireland.

The local administration of education is based on a commune structure in which schools have fixed catchment areas and in which it is clearly possible to identify whether students are excluded from the particular school to which they have a right to belong. Kari and Marit argue: 'Though the commune structure is, in itself, no guarantee of inclusion, it probably increases the chance of a general feeling of inclusion among children, and adults for that matter' (p. 117).

The influence of the Norwegian Evangelical Lutheran Church on schools continues to be strong, though it is lessening (see also Fulcher 1989). The authors include religion as a binding force within Norwegian society, although it would be interesting to explore further how it is perceived by those who are not committed to the Church of Norway. The role of religion in facilitating and constraining inclusion is clearly an important issue. It is explicit in the Irish study and we might have made more of it in the England case-study. It would certainly warrant further comparative study.

Special schools continue to teach a small proportion of students. We are told, too, that around six per cent of the school-age population are subject to formal assessment and there is a requirement that these students should have 'individual learning programmes'. Specialist teachers exist for a wide variety of special categories of students. A parallel subsystem of special education continues to exist alongside the mainstream system despite the reduction of segregated education and the metamorphosis of special schools. This relocation of the parallel systems, within the mainstream school, may undermine moves to greater inclusion in different but no less efficient, and perhaps more subtle, ways than a thriving segregated sector. Official notions of an inclusive school pick out pupils with special needs as candidates for equal participation 'in the social, academic and cultural community'. The account suggests that the special education aspect of national legislation encourages what Fulcher (1989) has called 'an individualised gaze', surveilling and separating categorised students within the school community.

The text gives the impression that the changes that have occurred in policy have been orchestrated in a smooth fashion. For example, special schools have adopted new roles, so that perhaps they have not become a barrier to development in the way that has happened in other countries. However, given what we know about human diversity, it is not surprising that in her review of Norwegian education policy Fulcher (1989) concludes that practices are diverse as a result of 'factors such as remoteness and urban–rural differences' (p. 93). In the story of Berg School it is apparent that the discussion of inclusion at the school is heavily influenced by the official context, but the guidelines are treated as background to the school development rather than with an expectation that they will be policed and enforced.

Voices and perspectives on inclusion and exclusion.

Besides the strong official voice in the early part of the chapter, we also hear a combined consensual voice of the two authors. We do not know whether they both equally support their stated views. They also represent a range of views from other researchers, teachers, students and parents. We hear a discordance of view between some teachers, particularly specialist teachers, but also others, who favour withdrawal teaching of categorised students, and that of the authors, the head and some teachers who would prefer this practice to be reduced, advocating more 'partnership teaching and . . . group work'. The research style used involves a sampling of the views of others sometimes constrained around a questionnaire rather than extended inclusion of other voices.

Kari and Marit state their concern with the development of 'one school for all', 'a school with a place for every child that is born and grows up in the school district; a school where nobody needs either integration or inclusion'. Thus, they attempt to move beyond these latter terms. They consider the notion of 'anti-segregation', which similarly starts from an assumption that everyone is included, but reject it as having insufficient currency. Like the New Zealand authors' idea of 'an inclusive school', the adoption of 'one school for all' may encourage a belief that we can reach an ideal beyond the existence of negative discrimination on the basis of student difference. We realise that we need to be cautious in our interpretation here, for the idea of 'one school for all' may simply be a link with the Norwegian equivalent to the English 'comprehensive' school, introduced in Norway in the 1930s. Nevertheless, it is worth repeating that if we think of inclusion as *a realisable state*, this may lead us to ignore or fail to fully analyse the continuing reality of exclusionary pressures and processes, and the interventions required to overcome them.

The authors indicate a broad concern with issues of inclusion in society and education, in addition to their main concern with students categorised as having 'special needs'. In 'one school for all' students also have a right to belong and to learn irrespective of class, gender, culture and race. Cultural and religious diversity is seen to be limited in Berg, although we are left wondering if it is greater than it is assumed to be. All children join in the church choir 'on a voluntary basis', for example, but is it possible that the sense of belonging is dependent on social compliance? We are told that the number of students whose first language is not Norwegian is expected to increase in Norway. Such students are described as 'foreign', although it seems likely that many will be born in Norway. We are, therefore, left unclear as to how far Berg is well prepared for the coming of 'cultural diversity'.

One might have supposed that within 'one school for all' the language of special needs would no longer be used, since as Kari and Marit concur, 'it implies exclusion'. However they persist in talking of 'SEN pupils' and the overwhelming focus of the chapter is on Per, Lars and Jon, three of the six students said to have special needs at Berg School, rather than on the variations in and barriers to participation and learning for all children. They are introduced to us in terms of deficits, 'Per has Down syndrome . . . ; Lars has substantial learning difficulties believed to be due to a turbulent family life . . . ; Jon has learning and behavioural difficulties, recently diagnosed as ADHD.' The overall orientation of the authors is undoubtedly pro-inclusion, yet certain pupils are chosen for attention on the basis of their perceived characteristics, the validity of which is never questioned. Thus the authors appear to use a 'psycho-medical paradigm' that they criticise elsewhere.

'Adapted education' is seen as the means to achieve inclusion, though we argue that the authors describe a mainstream and special version of adapted education which, to some extent, may be incompatible. A detailed plan to make mainstream practice more inclusive was created, initially, in response to vandalism at the school. The account of Berg suggests a school that has close links with the local community and parents in particular. It has a flexible school environment with a curriculum negotiated with students who are allowed considerable freedom as to the ordering of their work and some free choice of activity in a form of 'integrated day'. Children are encouraged to assist one another and there are planned interactions between age groups. The teacher, it is suggested, works as a consultant to the class.

The special version of adapted education can be seen in the planning of the work for Per, Lars and Jon, which echoes traditional special education practice. The authors indicate ways to identify students who experience difficulties and that these lead to the identification of a preponderance of boys. Following categorisation there is 'a formal assessment leading to an individual learning programme' which describes 'the extent, content and organisation of the support' to be provided. These programmes are said to be vaguely expressed but 'mostly concerned with the three Rs'.

Given the general pattern in the school, with children working individually for at least part of the time, these individual programmes might appear to be part of the common approach of the school. However, when they specify more than a small section of the curriculum easily assimilated into mainstream practice the 'individual learning programme' may be a powerful shaping mechanism, encouraging teachers to see the task as one of differentiating or planning for particular individuals. It creates organisational dilemmas for class teachers about their use of time, and for specialist teachers about completing 'their' tasks. In these ways the individual learning programme becomes an end in itself rather than a means to inclusion and learning. An example is given of Jon missing a rehearsal because the support teacher refused to let him return to the class. Such an approach might be contrasted with the accounts from New Zealand and in the US, where emphasis is placed on developing learning contexts within which all students can participate in a range of common opportunities.

Kari and Marit express concern about the roles of specialist staff ostensibly there to 'help teachers adapt their teaching' but who may 'make ordinary teachers doubt their own competence to cope with learning difficulties'. They ask whether the 'mere existence of the special education system' works against inclusion.

The teachers' comments provide a strong indication of how some staff perceive students categorised as having special needs and their relative status in the class. We are told that views about the withdrawal of a student with special needs were related to the 'needs of the other children' or 'the wish to teach a more homogeneous class'. It was suggested also 'that the academic results of the class were best served if the children with special needs were taught outside the classroom' and that such pupils 'learn most when alone with the teacher'. Despite the emphasis on the 'right to belong' in national policy some teachers draw a 'line' that divides children into the majority and the 'others'.

Kari and Marit believe that Berg is 'on its way towards achieving inclusiveness', not least in that most children do have 'a sense of belonging' and 'learn and develop effectively'. However, they express their surprise that categorised students 'are more segregated during lessons than we had expected'. The authors conclude that 'a certain number of segregated lessons need not be a serious threat to inclusion, though there is probably a limit' but argue that 'teachers do not seem to have realised that real integration means that children as a rule should take part in all classroom activities'. They remain concerned that 'superficial adaptations' may leave a child just as isolated as in special provision. This separation within inclusion is a feature of most of the studies in this book.

Their investigations lead them to be aware of 'complexity, messiness and incoherence' in the practice of education, something that we note is absent from certain of the other studies. We are challenged to reflect on how coherent a perspective on inclusion it is reasonable to expect in others or ourselves.

10

THE NETHERLANDS:
A SPRINGBOARD FOR
OTHER INITIATIVES

Gerry J. Reezigt and Sip Jan Pijl

Introduction

In this chapter we explore the development of a part-time special class in De Springplank primary school in Marum, near Groningen, and the way it has emerged from national attempts to change special education policy. We start by examining inclusion and education policy in the Netherlands, then describe the school and our research procedures. Finally, we report on the interviews and observations we made at the school and discuss the implications of our findings.

The national educational context

Compared to many other European countries, the special education system in our country is extensive, and segregated. Almost four per cent of all pupils aged between 4 and 18 attend full-time special schools (Pijl and Pijl 1995). While most children start school at 4, compulsory education starts at 5 and ends at 16. The proportion of special school pupils varies with age; for example, 7.4 per cent of 11 year olds are in special schools. In general, boys are over-represented. The special school pupil population consists of sixty-eight per cent boys and thirty-two per cent girls. Ethnic minority pupils are also slightly over-represented with nine per cent in special schools and seven per cent in regular primary schools. Our Dutch special education system is also very strongly differentiated: currently we have fourteen different types of school, as shown in Table 10.1, which also indicates the number of each type and the number of pupils attending them (Commissie Leerlinggebonden Financiering 1995).

The separation of regular education and special education is created by legislation, separate funding regulations and teacher training. The funding system provides much less money to meet pupils' special needs in regular schools than is available for students in a special school. This acts as a tremendous incentive to refer pupils to special schools.

Table 10.1 Types of special school and numbers of pupils

School type	Number of pupils	Number of schools
pre-school	3,278	119
learning disabled	30,048	279
educable mentally retarded	23,649	237
severely mentally retarded	6,003	129
blind and visually impaired	230	8
deaf	427	5
hearing impaired	1,223	22
speech and language problems	2,563	21
physically disabled	1,378	27
multiple handicaps	3,036	57
severe behaviour problems	2,916	51
hospital schools	422	12
chronic illness	3,036	36
pedagogical institutes	1,157	10
Total	79,525	1,014

Formally, it is parents who make the decision to refer pupils to special schools. However, referrals are usually initiated by classroom teachers in consultation with the school principal, the school support service and the parents. The admission board of a special school (a psychologist, a physician, a social worker and the school principal) conducts extensive assessment in order to decide whether a pupil is eligible for special provision (Meijer 1994). The law permits admission boards to decide on either a special or a mainstream place, but in practice over ninety per cent of the pupils referred are placed in a special school. Since parents rarely object to the decision of the teachers, this procedure effectively makes the regular teacher the one who decides whether or not to place a pupil in a special school. However, parents do have the right to object and if they do so, referral to, or placement in special school is out of the question. The procedures for referral and the role of admission boards are being increasingly criticised. After admittance to a special school, pupils hardly ever return to regular education; less than one per cent of special needs pupils in schools for the learning disabled and educable mentally retarded return to regular primary education annually (Centraal Bureau voor de Statistiek 1993).

Religion has always played a major role in educational planning. We have public, Protestant, and Roman Catholic regular and special schools. Public schools are not allowed to set any selection criteria. All schools are governed by their own school boards. The present system was created out of political struggles at the beginning of this century, and these struggles are invoked whenever a change is proposed. Every suggested change is interpreted by one party or another as a threat to educational freedom. The integration of special schools and regular schools threatens the religious division in education in the special school system. This division by religion results in relatively small schools.

The curriculum offered in Dutch schools, both in regular and special schools, is primarily decided by the principal and the teachers, though sometimes the school board is involved. Our national government sets the time to be devoted to the main subjects, but there is no centrally-prescribed curriculum. However, this situation will change in the near future. Our government has adopted core outcomes for primary education in the main school subjects.

The development of Dutch inclusion policy

The continuous growth in special school attendance has been a source of great concern to policy makers, and numerous attempts have been made to reduce referral. The Dutch inclusion policy has grown out of the policy on primary education. In the early 1980s the Ministry for Education, Culture and Science advocated the amalgamation of nursery schools (for children aged 4–6) and primary schools (initially for children aged 6–12) into the present primary school system for children aged 4–12. In 1985, the Primary Education Act was passed. The major goal of primary schools, documented in this Act, is to offer 'appropriate' instruction to all children and to guarantee all children an uninterrupted school career (Wet op het Basisonderwijs 1985). Teachers should practise 'adaptive instruction', whereby teaching is related to individual needs, and by doing so they should try to prevent learning problems. As a consequence, teachers were supposed to avoid grade retention, and it was anticipated that the practice of adaptive instruction would lead to a more or less spontaneous decrease in the number of special needs pupils.

However, in the years after 1985 it became clear that although most schools supported the new policy in theory, change was slow in practice. Whole class teaching, the predominant model of classroom organisation, did not disappear rapidly and pupils were still being retained in nearly all primary schools (Reezigt 1993; Houtveen 1994; Reezigt and Knuver 1995). In addition, the expansion in special school populations continued. In 1988, the Ministry tried to stop this expansion once again by limiting the numbers of special school teachers. However, this arrangement turned out to conflict with educational law (Pijl and Pijl 1995) and was not implemented.

Since the early 1990s, educational policy has aimed explicitly to include special needs pupils in regular primary education. According to the Dutch Ministry for Education, Culture and Science, the proportion of pupils aged 5–12 in special education should be reduced drastically, and the capabilities of regular primary schools to deal with pupils with special needs should improve. Special needs pupils are supposed to go to regular school again with their 'regular' peers. The inclusion policy is known as the 'together to school again' policy, which in Dutch is: 'Weer Samen Naar School' (abbreviated as WSNS). As a first step, the 'together to school again' policy focuses on pupils with learning difficulties and educable mentally retarded pupils at primary school level. These groups constitute two-thirds of all pupils in special schools and are regarded, in principle, as belonging to regular primary education. A slowly-increasing group of policy-makers, parents and teachers hold the view that special needs pupils are entitled to have their special needs met in regular education. The segregation of these pupils is considered to be socially undesirable, to conflict with widely accepted human rights, and a perhaps convenient, but unnecessary way to provide special services.

The inclusion policy in the Netherlands also has the financial aim of stopping growth in expenditure on special schools (Meijer *et al.* 1993). However, many educational practitioners are sceptical about the commitment to maintain spending at current levels. The average costs for pupils in special schools are twice as high as the costs for students in regular education (Meijer 1994), so a reduction of these costs would be appreciated by the Ministry.

Like the primary policy on adaptive education, the WSNS policy is supported by teachers and principals of regular schools in theory. However, it is hard to find out how much this support really means. Teachers and principals may well have a favourable attitude towards the WSNS policy, as long as they are not really affected by it. Their support may mask a 'not in my backyard' attitude. Teachers in special schools are generally less enthusiastic, probably because they fear that their jobs are at stake, although formally they express concerns about the capability of regular teachers to deal with 'their' pupils (Meijer 1995). They fear that regular teachers do not have sufficient diagnostic skill, for example. In fact, their jobs are not at stake; repeatedly, the government has promised to guarantee employment for all special school teachers. However, the content of their jobs may change. Many special school teachers will work in regular schools, for example as special need consultants, for at least a part of their time.

In general, parents are in favour of the WSNS policy (Meijer 1995). Compared to other countries, parents in the Netherlands were never very prominent in the inclusion/exclusion debates. There is no tradition of parent pressure groups who actively advocate inclusion of pupils with special educational needs. The one exception is the Association of Parents of Children with Down Syndrome. This association has succeeded in influencing regular primary schools to place children with Down syndrome, which was a very unusual practice until recently (Scheepstra and Pijl 1995). The WSNS policy, however, does not apply officially to pupils with Down syndrome.

Regional clusters

Under the WSNS policy, all primary schools and the special schools for learning or developmentally-disabled children have been grouped into regional clusters. Each year, a cluster receives twenty-eight guilders per pupil (approximately equal to ten British pounds) and 5,000 guilders (1,750 British pounds) per special school for extra staff to support pupils with special needs in the regular schools (Meijer *et al.* 1993). Thus, schools are supposed to innovate without a large additional budget. They are encouraged to find new ways of drawing on the expertise of colleagues in other schools. For example, a special school teacher starts to visit regular schools to help pupils with special needs instead of sending these pupils to the special school. In general, clusters were supposed to consist of fifteen regular schools and one special school. In recent years, 290 regional clusters that vary in religious denomination, numbers of schools, organisation and activities were constituted. They were created as platforms for discussion and do not take over any of the powers of school boards; therefore they cannot make decisions about the reorganisation of education in particular schools. Unfortunately, the latest education statistics again show a small growth of special school attendance.

Changes in funding

In June 1995 the Dutch parliament agreed to change the regulations for funding special provision. In the years up to 2000 a gradually increasing amount of money will be placed at the regional clusters' disposal to support learning disabled and mildly mentally retarded students. They are free to decide to spend these funds for pupils with special needs in regular education or to support the special school system. It is thought that the new funding system will stimulate inclusion because it allows services to be brought to the pupils instead of transferring pupils to services. Special schools are uneasy about this new development, which will almost certainly reduce the number of pupils referred to special schools and finally result in the closure of special schools. Considerable numbers of special teachers will experience changes in their work; either they will work as teachers in regular schools, act as consultants to their new colleagues in regular education, or they will be in special schools teaching pupils with more severe and complex special needs.

The school

The activities of the WSNS regional clusters and their schools have not been fully studied as yet, and we cannot provide a full picture of the way that Dutch schools are dealing with the WSNS policy. Van Rijswijk and Kool (1995) have looked at two aspects of WSNS special provisions: arrangements made for a fixed-time period (e.g. special classes for one school year) as against permanent provision, and full-time provisions versus part-time special classes. We decided to study a part-time special class because it gave us the opportunity to reflect on education in both the regular class and the special

127

class. We thought that it would reflect more inclusion in the regular school than full-time special provision.

We chose to study De Springplank ('Springboard') public primary school for 300 children aged 4–12 years, situated in Marum, a village in the north of the Netherlands, near the city of Groningen. The school had established a part-time special class in 1993, initially for four mornings a week, extended to five mornings in 1994–5. By Dutch standards the student population of De Springplank is large, especially since it is located in a rural region. The school building is fairly new and well kept, and the classrooms are well equipped. There is a large playground outside. We did not choose this school as an example of 'good practice', although it can certainly be considered an example of innovatory practice in line with the Dutch inclusion policy.

Marum has 3,000 inhabitants. There is one more primary school nearby, a Protestant school with a population of about 200 children. Some children attend schools outside of the village, for example, a school working according to the Jenaplan ideas of Peter Petersen or a school for a specific Protestant religious group. There are no secondary schools in Marum, so when children have finished primary school they have to go to another city. There are no special schools in Marum either. When children are referred to a special school they are picked up at their homes and transported by bus. About two per cent of the primary school children in Marum attend special schools, a low percentage for the Netherlands.

The student population of De Springplank represents all social classes of the village. 'It is a school for all children in Marum whose parents choose public education', the principal says. There are about twenty children coming from Moluccan families; all of these children were born and raised in the Netherlands and speak Dutch. From time to time De Springplank is visited by some gypsy children.

Most of the teachers have been working in De Springplank for several years. Their average age is 40 years. One of the teachers is qualified for special education.

De Springplank groups its pupils into ten classes. The average class size is twenty-eight, but would be smaller without the Special Group. There is one mixed-age class, a combination of Grades 3 and 4. All other classes contain children of a single age group. Whole-class teaching, offering the same subject matter to all children in a class in the same way and at the same time, is daily practice. However, there are ability groups for reading instruction.

The research procedure

We visited the school twice. We had a preliminary meeting with the principal and the school counsellor in which we explained our aims for the case-study. During our second visit we collected our data.

Research questions

In the course of our study we attempted to find answers to the following questions:

- Why was the group established?
- How is it financed?
- How are children selected for it?
- Who teaches them?
- What are the differences in the educational experience of the Special Group and regular class children?
- What are the effects of the Special Group on children, parents and teaching in De Springplank and other schools?
- What are the views from the special school in the WSNS regional cluster?

Interviews

We interviewed the following people:

- The principal.
- The school counsellor.
- One of the two teachers working in the part-time Special Group.
- A regular teacher who had previously been working as a teacher in the part-time Special Group.
- The alderman of the municipality of Marum, responsible for education.
- A civil servant of the municipality of Marum, involved in educational regulations.
- A parent of a child who has attended the part-time Special Group for almost two years.
- The principal of the special school in the WSNS regional cluster.

Observations

While we were interviewing, two assistants observed four Grade 5 children (aged approximately 9 years) during all their morning and afternoon activities. The children were selected by their teachers, following our request for an appropriate comparison. Two of these children went to the Special Group in the morning. The other children were low achievers, who stayed in their regular class for the whole day. Our observers used mainly low inference procedures, based on instruments by Veenman *et al.* (1986) and Shaffer and Nesselrodt (1992). While they were observing the selected children they recorded for successive five minute intervals the number and type of teacher–child interactions, the on-task behaviour of children, classroom activities and subjects in which the children were involved.

The observers also recorded the behaviour of the teacher using a rating scale of fifty-four items measuring classroom management, quality of instruction, and classroom climate. Each item was ticked as 'yes' or 'no' indicating whether the behaviour described in the item was shown or not shown by the teacher, or inapplicable (Van der Werf, Nitert and Reezigt 1994). In addition to the interviews and the observations, we read several documents on the Special Group written by the teachers and school counsellor at the school (Plattel, 1994).

Our findings

Why was the group established?

In 1993, the school team noted that despite extra support, five pupils were making little progress in reading, writing and maths, and 'were on the verge of a referral to special education'. According to the school counsellor, in line with the spirit of the WSNS policy, 'the school team decided to prevent referral to special education and to develop a special programme within its school instead'. They considered a full-time special class but chose a part-time group to avoid risking the stigmatisation of the children.

How is the group financed?

De Springplank receives money for eight additional teacher hours from the municipality but mainly funds the Special Group from its own resources – hence, the formation of a small special group leads to larger classes for the rest of the school. There are no WSNS funds available for such experiments. The amount of money given to the clusters is insufficient to finance them and other schools in the cluster might object to such a heavy claim from one school on the cluster budget.

According to the alderman and civil servant of Marum, the Special Group leads to municipal savings because it reduces the costs for transportation of children to special schools:

> But even if we wanted to, we cannot use these savings for general educational purposes or give it to De Springplank. Transportation costs are paid from a budget other than the educational budget. Moreover, the municipality is the school board of several schools. Even if De Springplank succeeds in reducing referrals, other schools in our district might show an increase. We have to deal with that too.

He thinks this should change: 'The national government should give more resources to schools for the implementation of its inclusion policy.'

How are the children selected?

The Special Group is meant for children with learning problems from Grades 4, 5 and 6. Children with behavioural problems not clearly related to learning, as perceived by the school team and the school counsellor, cannot be placed in the special class and are still referred to special schools. Children with learning problems are detected by means of the monitoring system: a system of tests taken at regular intervals by all children.

The principal informed us about the procedure followed at De Springplank when children start to lag behind their classmates:

> First, the regular class teacher tries to help. When this does not work, our remedial teacher offers extra instruction outside the classroom [and] one of our teachers acts as a consultant for the other team members.

If the students have not caught up by the end of Grade 3 they are retained for an extra year in that grade; unusually, this may happen in other grades. Grade retention is used for children who lag behind but who may catch up independently or with some additional help, and happens for one or two children in the year. When pupils who are about to enter Grade 4 are consistently under-achieving for their age norms and their progress does not improve after remedial teaching or grade retention the school counsellor gives them intelligence tests. This is the procedure used when a child is referred to special school. The results are discussed with the principal, the regular teacher, the Special Group teacher, the school counsellor, and the child's parents, who together decide about placement in the Special Group.

In its first year, there were five children, and in the second school year, 1994–1995, nine children. The school has set a provisional maximum of ten children. They are all boys, a far greater over-representation than in special education generally. The children are from four different grades: three children from Grade 4, four children from Grade 5, one from Grade 6, and one from Grade 7.

The school counsellor reported that the learning problems dealt with by the teachers in the Special Group comprise dyslexia, memory problems, language problems – sometimes because of a child's immigrant status – IQs below 70, auditory and visual handicaps.

When children have made enough progress they return full-time to the regular class and the expectation is that generally students will have achieved this by Grade 7. As confirmed by the school counsellor 'children of Grades 7 and 8 will stay in their regular class when possible, although they may follow individual programmes outlined by the Special Group teacher'.

Who teaches the Special Group?

In Dutch primary schools in general a classroom teacher teaches all subjects. Children sometimes have more than one teacher, if their teachers are part-time. In the first year, one full-time teacher taught all Special Group children; in the second year, two part-time teachers are working in the Special Group. In the opinion of the school counsellor:

> An appropriate attitude towards children with special needs is more important than certificates or formal qualifications. I think that any teacher willing to change from a subject-orientated approach to a child-orientated approach could teach the Special Group.

However, the only teacher in De Springplank with a special education qualification is now involved in the Special Group, and the other Special Group teacher is an experienced remedial teacher.

The role of the school counsellor

The school counsellor worked very closely with the Special Group teacher in the first year, when he was actively involved in the development of curricular materials. He now adopts a more consultative role. He discusses the progress of all children after testing by the Special Group teachers, and helps to draw up an individual educational plan.

What are the differences in educational experience of the Special Group and regular class children?

Children in the Special Group spend the first half hour in their regular classes each morning. In the Netherlands it is usual to start the day with classroom discussion about varied topics brought up by the children or their teachers. After this period, they attend the Special Group for the rest of the morning. They spend the afternoons in their regular class.

In the Special Group, students have an individual education plan involving the use of their own materials, though there is also whole group teaching. When the Special Group began, the teacher and the school counsellor made individual educational plans for one week in advance, but following criticism from the special school teachers in the WSNS regional cluster, this was extended to four months.

Due to the small size of the group, Special Group teachers can provide frequent individual instruction and guidance. In the regular classes much of the lesson time is taken up with independent individual assignments. According to the Special Group teacher:

Compared to the regular groups, our children are working more often with concrete materials. They are also free to use materials from earlier grades when they want to and when we think that it might be useful. We offer supportive materials such as cassette tapes during reading instruction, and our pupils use the computer more often.

The Special Group teachers use different methods from the regular classroom teacher, for example a maths scheme developed for remedial teaching. The children are assessed frequently using tests related to the curricula used by the teachers. They are also tested three times each year with standardised tests as part of the school monitoring system.

In general, our observations supported the interview data. The Special Group provides a very different education from the regular classroom. There is a higher frequency of teacher–child interactions, more on-task behaviour of children, a larger variety in activities and subjects offered to children, and a somewhat higher quality of instruction by the teacher. Below, we discuss these findings in more detail. While our data does give more insight into Special Group practice, it is based on only one day of observations and therefore must be interpreted with caution.

Teacher–child interactions

We recorded all teacher–child interactions during the morning and the afternoon lessons for two regular, low-achieving Grade 5 and two Special Group Grade 5 pupils, selected by their teachers. Table 10.2 shows the number and type of interactions for the four observed children in the morning when they were in different classes and in the afternoon when they were in the same class.

Special Group children have almost three times more interactions with their teachers than regular pupils, especially task-orientated and procedural interactions. Both teacher-initiated and pupil-initiated interactions are much more frequent in the Special Group. Personal interactions (for example, the teacher asking the child something about his family, or the child wanting to know if the teacher is no longer feeling ill) hardly occur. The same holds for praise of children and criticisms. So in both classes, most teacher–child interactions are directly related to the educational situation.

Time on task

We assumed that the Special Group, with its small size and its potential for individualised instruction, would lead to relatively high proportions of time on task, compared to the regular class situation. Table 10.3 shows that this is indeed so.

Table 10.2 Teacher–pupil interactions

	Regular class		Special Group	
Teacher Initiated				
Task orientated	1 (2)	1 (4)	12	14 (2)
Procedural	2 (1)	1 (1)	6	4
Personal	0	0	0	0
Praise	2	2	2	1
Warnings	3	5 (1)	8 (1)	3
Criticism	0	0	0	0
Total teacher initiated	8 (3)	9 (6)	28 (1)	22 (2)
Pupil initiated				
Task orientated	1 (1)	3 (3)	2 (2)	7
Procedural	1	1 (1)	4 (1)	2
Personal	0	0 (1)	1	2
Total pupil initiated	2 (1)	4 (5)	7 (3)	11
Total morning	10	13	35	33
Total afternoon	4	11	4	2

Note: Afternoon interactions in brackets for comparison

Table 10.3 Percentage of time spent on task during one morning

	Regular class		Special group	
Time	Pupil 1	Pupil 2	Pupil 1	Pupil 2
On task	56	70	70	83
Off task	34	20	8	5
Waiting time	5	5	17	12
Out of class	5	5	5	

Moreover, the time off task is much lower in the Special Group than in the regular group. However, in the Special Group children spent relatively more time waiting for their teacher to help them or to give them new assignments. This may be a consequence of the individualised teaching in the Special Group, since the teacher does not give the same assignments to all pupils, as is common for the regular teacher.

Classroom activities

Our observations on classroom activities show very different patterns for the regular class and the Special Group. In the regular class, the teacher gives a very short instruction, mainly consisting of organisational routines (e.g. 'take your books and start working on page . . .'), and the children do independent individual assignments for nearly the whole morning. The Special Group teacher spends much more time on class discussion and instruction, whole class as well as small group instruction. The whole-class instruction in the special group involves direct teaching of curriculum content. Our observations also show that in the regular group both observed children are expected to complete the same tasks, while the Special Group pupils are treated individually (Table 10.4).

Subjects

There are differences in the subjects offered to regular class pupils and Special Group pupils. In the regular group, both pupils spend equal amounts of time on two subjects: language and maths. In the Special Group, both pupils spend their time quite differently on a much wider variety of subjects (Table 10.5). 'Other subjects' refer to activities such as computer assignments or drawing.

Table 10.4 Time spent on classroom activities in one morning

	Regular class		Special group	
Activity	Pupil 1	Pupil 2	Pupil 1	Pupil 2
Class discussion			10	10
Whole class instruction	5	5	25	25
Small group instruction			10	30
Individual assignments	100	100	35	30
Group assignments			5	
Transitions between activities	10	10	20	10
Other			10	10

Note: Time given in minutes; total time available 115 minutes

Table 10.5 Time given to subjects during one morning

	Regular class		Special group	
Subject	Pupil 1	Pupil 2	Pupil 1	Pupil 2
Spelling			30	45
Writing			10	
Reading			5	
Language	55	55	20	10
Mathematics	55	55	25	40
Science			5	5
Other	5	5	20	15

Note: time given in minutes; total time available 115 minutes

Teacher quality

We attempted to measure differences in the quality of education between the regular class and Special Group by rating the behaviour of the regular teacher and the Special Group teacher on the quality of classroom management, instruction and classroom climate. Table 10.6 shows the scores per teacher.

Table 10.6 Quality of teacher behaviour

	Regular class teacher	Special group teacher
Classroom management	100	88
Instruction	66	93
Classroom climate	86	100

Note: Given as a pecentage of maximum score per subscale

The main differences were on the subscale 'instruction'. Indicators of quality of instruction are, for example, the structure of the lesson, checking the previous knowledge of children, clear presentation, clear instruction on assignments, extra help and instruction when necessary, checking progress by giving turns and frequent monitoring. The Special Group teacher achieves a higher quality of instruction. The differences in ratings cannot be attributed to observer differences: both observers rated the same teacher during the afternoon and achieved an inter-rater agreement of eighty-nine per cent. Also, the fairly high ratings of the observers are not due to rating tendencies. The teacher who was observed during the afternoon (a student teacher) received considerably lower ratings by both observers than the regular teacher and the Special Group teacher during the morning hours.

What are the effects of the Special Group?

We have no systematic data on the pupils before they entered the Special Group and the progress they made thereafter as we did not study an equivalent control group in traditional education or special education. Nevertheless, we gained an impression of the effects of the Special Group from our interviews.

Effects on pupils in the Special Group and their regular classmates

'The Special Group pupils find it easier to ask questions and to talk to us,' the current Special Group teacher told us. 'After some time in the Special Group, they start to feel more confident about themselves and they are very proud of their progress.' The former Special Group teacher also points at the self-confidence of pupils, which was not so great in the beginning: 'when the children started in the Special Group, they said to me: we are not really stupid, are we? Will you be able to teach us something, please?'

The regular pupils seem to accept the Special Group pupils fairly easily; they are not labelled as 'Special Group pupils'. In the afternoons, the Special Group children participate in the programme of the regular class without any special provision. This also enhances the acceptance by the other children. The contacts with regular classmates are considered important not only socially, but it is thought that they may also stimulate the Special Group children to higher achievement than would be possible in a special school. The younger the children are, the more easily they accept the Special Group children. The principal maintained:

> A Special Group child still belongs to his regular class. He is present during classroom talks, special festivities such as birthday celebrations or Christmas parties, presentations by pupils, gymnastic lessons, science, and creativity lessons. He will meet his regular classmates before and after school and during breaks.

And the current Special Group teacher told us:

> Maybe because it is not so unusual to leave the classroom for a while, a lot of children are used to activities outside of their regular classroom, for example ability-grouped reading instruction, remedial teaching, and computer practice. The Special Group children are not considered an exceptional group.

Some children have made remarkable progress in their two years of Special Group attendance. Full-time return to the regular group is a realistic option, although most will stay in the Special Group, or receive assignments from Special Group teachers for independent study in their regular class, during their primary school career.

Effects on the parents of Special Group pupils and other parents

Given a choice between Special Group and special school, all parents have opted for the Special Group. They want their child to stay in the regular school and they do not regret their decision. 'It was not difficult for us to choose between the Special Group or a special school', a parent tells us, 'If our son went to a special school, he would have to leave the village every day. We were afraid that he would become isolated . . .'. For some parents, De Springplank had to stress the fact that placement in the Special Group did not mean that their child did not have severe problems.

The children's parents meet the regular teacher and the Special Group teachers at least twice a year. The current Special Group teacher says 'we have

137

long talks with parents. In general, we meet for half an hour or more.' This is considerably longer than the usual Dutch teacher–parent meeting of ten minutes. When a child is placed in the Special Group, the parents are informed explicitly that this will mean an individual learning programme that might last for several years, maybe until the end of primary school. Parents are also told that the attendance in the Special Group cannot guarantee a school place in regular secondary education.

Now that the Special Group is getting well known as a special feature of De Springplank, parents with children in special schools have started contacting the principal, asking for a place in the Special Group. Some have told the principal that they are considering a move to Marum because of the Special Group. De Springplank is still considering how to respond to these requests. The Special Group started as a provision for the pupils of De Springplank, not as a provision for children who start out in other schools. However, such steps might be taken in the future, if the WSNS regional cluster agree.

Effects on De Springplank as an organisation

The individual approach of the part-time Special Group is in striking contrast to the whole-class teaching in the regular classes, which creates its own failures. Children who cannot cope with the speed of instruction fall increasingly behind. In theory, the Special Group might help regular teachers to use adaptive instruction, although most regular teachers in the Netherlands are resistant to trying alternatives to whole-class teaching. The former Special Group teacher, now working in a regular class, says:

> I think that all of my colleagues should teach the Special Group for some time. Then, in their own school, they can see that they can actually teach children they are now excluding from their classes. In the Special Group, they can learn how to provide adaptive instruction. At least for me it worked like this. In this way practising adaptive instruction in a small group setting might transfer to the regular much larger classrooms.

More individualisation in the regular groups might render the Special Group redundant in the future, but this is seen as a very hypothetical notion. The principal says:

> It takes a lot of time to become an individualised school when you are used to whole-class teaching like we are. As yet, children who fail have to seek extra help outside of their regular classrooms. Still I think that we have taken a step forward. At least we do not have to refer our pupils to special schools.

138

De Springplank offers a continuum of special support, varying from remedial teaching to the Special Group, but this continuum clearly starts outside the walls of the regular classrooms.

It is also possible that the existence of the Special Group might make it easier for teachers to exclude children with learning problems from their classrooms. Referral to the Special Group is not so radical as referral to a special school, and therefore it might become a very attractive procedure for teachers who have to deal with problem pupils. If this happens, the Special Group may expand and have a more diffuse student population. De Springplank thinks that this will not happen because of the strict admission procedures for placement in the Special Group.

Effects on other regular schools

The Special Group has gained some popularity in schools in the municipality of Marum and in the WSNS regional cluster. Some schools have shown an interest in the Special Group as a possibility for their own pupils. The Special Group is supported and advocated by the municipality of Marum and the school counselling service as an organisational model for schools with more than 100 pupils, while smaller schools should be able to provide all children with the instruction that they need in their regular (small) classes. According to the school principal, some colleagues in other schools are somewhat hostile towards the Special Group, maybe because of its exposure in the local media, but he does not think that they fear an exodus of their own pupils to De Springplank because of its Special Group.

Views from the special school in the WSNS regional cluster

Before the Special Group started, the case-study school contacted the special school in the WSNS regional cluster. The principal reported:

> We always had a good working relation with the special school. Before we started the Special Group, I asked the principal of the special school for advice and support. He criticised our plans: we should specify in more detail what we wanted to achieve by the Special Group, how children would make the transition to secondary education. We should spend more time on making individual education plans, he said. I think these were useful comments. We certainly used them to our advantage.

The special school also advised against a full-time special class. Initially all contact was started by the regular school. 'The special school never contacted us,' the school counsellor says, 'but we think that we should cooperate more, especially now that we know what we want.' In the school year 1995–1996 the contacts will be formalised. The school counsellor says:

> A teacher from the special school will work in the Special Group for four hours each week. I think he should participate in all activities: teaching, drawing up individual educational plans, observing pupils.

In our interview with the principal of the special school he insisted that the Special Group children would not have been referred to his school:

> Children in my school are different. They are admitted when they show a cluster of problems: they have learning problems, behavioural problems, and they suffer from concentration problems. The Special Group children only have learning problems. These Special Group pupils do not meet our criteria for admittance to our school.

He therefore disagreed with the regular school principal and the school counsellor, who say that they would have referred the Special Group children. Of course this argument cannot be settled here. It should be noted, though, that referral of a child is almost always followed by admittance to the special school. If De Springplank had referred the nine children in the Special Group, it is very likely that they would have been placed in the special school.

The principal of the special school wondered whether the Special Group can prevent stigmatisation:

> I think that stigmatisation often occurs before pupils are actually admitted to special education, not after. Many children have been isolated in their regular schools for years and are very happy to come to the special school.

Maybe, he suggests, some Special Group children have such deep problems in their school that they cannot be solved by their placement in the Special Group:

> Essentially, young children should be allowed to stay in their own environment, in their own school, in their own village but we have to stay realistic. When children are not accepted in their own environment, in their regular school, they might certainly be better off in a special school.

Although the principal of the special school recognises that he doesn't know everything that goes on at the special class he suggested that:

> Instruction in the Special Group may be too subject-orientated. The

Special Group teachers should try to improve the quality of their instruction, rather than using instruction as a means for class management.

However, the regular school principal argues that the special school may be more critical of the Special Group than their own practice:

Maybe they are so critical because they are being forced to change by the government's inclusion policy. However, I think that they can seize the opportunities of this policy too. They can transfer their knowledge to us, they can help us to deal with pupils with special needs.

Final comments

Due to the Dutch division of regular schools within a community by religion and the relatively short distances to special schools, the negative effects of special school placement are moderate. In the Netherlands, it is quite normal for children within a community to attend different schools.

The initiative to start a Special Group had been taken by the school principal and the school counsellor. We noticed that integration projects were also initiated by school principals or local policymakers in other schools and regions in the Netherlands. In the end, innovation in education seems to depend on enthusiastic, convincing and charismatic leaders at the local level. The part-time Special Group is one of many arrangements now being developed by regular schools in the Netherlands under the heading of the WSNS policy (Van Rijswijk and Kool 1995). Although the formation of the Special Group has been inspired by the goals formulated in the WSNS policy, its practice is a few steps ahead of that policy and of the developments in most other regular schools.

In the main, teachers and principals are keen to support the WSNS policy, but their eagerness may diminish when they consider its impact on their own professional lives. This may explain why several of the initial reactions to the De Springplank initiative from colleagues in neighbouring regular and special schools were rather negative. They questioned the professional skills of the school's teachers, the funding to offer special needs pupils an appropriate education, and suggested that integration in regular education might well prove to be harmful for special needs pupils. Regular schools may fear that such changes may be forced upon them, for example by requests of parents who know about the Special Group in De Springplank. The problems with colleagues, together with the very limited additional funding, make the existence of projects like the Special Group all the more surprising. However, after two years the Special Group and other attempts to integrate special needs pupils are much more accepted and valued. The Special Group model is now being implemented in other schools in the region and special schools are offering full support in starting these Special Groups. The Special Group functions as a *springboard* for other integration initiatives.

We think it likely that the Special Group makes it possible to include pupils in the regular school who would otherwise have been referred to special school. The Special Group involves part-time withdrawal, but its segregating effects are small compared to referring pupils to full-time special schools. The school, the teachers, the children and their parents seem fairly content with the Special Group.

We would have to carry out extensive research over a longer time period to find out more about the procedure that precedes placement in the Special Group, about the quality of the educational arrangements in the Special Group, about short-term and long-term effects of the Special Group on the cognitive and affective development of children and about the effects of the Special Group on the school as an organisation. There may also be influences beyond De Springplank that will affect the development of the group. These might include:

- The admission of children from other schools.
- The role of the Special Group in the continuum of special needs pro-visions, to be set up by the WSNS regional cluster.
- The experiences of other schools with comparable initiatives.
- The effects of changes in the special education funding system.

Irrespective of its future and influence, we regard the part-time Special Group as a way to promote the inclusion of children with learning problems in their regular school, without separating them totally from other children and regular curricula.

11

THE NETHERLANDS RESPONSE: PLUNGING INTO INCLUSION?

In their chapter, Gerry Reezigt and Sip Jan Pijl discuss the efforts of Dutch policy makers to reduce a special school population much larger than in most other countries. Inclusion and exclusion, then, are seen largely in relation to some candidates for special school placement, although there is discussion of the way the development of 'adaptive education' within the mainstream classrooms might reduce the pressure for segregation into special schools or special classes.

They focus on an initiative in one school which has established a part-time special class. They chose this as an example of 'innovatory practice in line with Dutch inclusion policy', and used it as an 'opportunity to reflect on education in both the regular and special class'. Past policy initiatives, with the overt intention of increasing inclusion, failed to reduce special school numbers but the authors suggest that part-time special classes, linked to financial incentives to regional clusters of schools, offer a possible way forward. They discuss the possibility that the introduction of a system of special classes might fuel rather than dampen down exclusionary pressures, and conclude that it will not.

How does the national context explain and constrain practice?

In the Netherlands, the highly-developed system of special schools exists alongside a fragmented mainstream system consisting of exclusive Christian schools and non-denominational public schools. The influence of religion is said to be such that both special school and mainstream school closures are thought to threaten religious freedom.

The negative effects of going to a special school are said to be moderate since 'in the Netherlands, it is quite normal for children within a community to attend different schools'. As there are so many special schools students do not have to travel large distances to attend one. While it may be common for neighbours to attend different schools, we do not know about the relative value that is placed on different schools, mainstream and special, within a community. Williams (1993, p. 306) reported that segregated special schools enjoy a high status and a positive image often missing in other countries (den Boer 1990; Rothbard 1990). In contrast to this view, Gerry and Sip Jan assume there is some stigma associated with attendance at special school. However, Williams follows his suggestion that special schools are valued positively with the apparently contradictory assertion that there is a 'growing unease' about the 'relatively high proportion of pupils' in special schools. Such complexities may be explained by the way different perspectives represent differing interests.

The authors suggest that there has not been strong parental support for integration or inclusion, with the exception of the Down syndrome association, who have achieved a measure of inclusion despite being omitted from official policy moves (de Wit Gosker 1995). We are told that there is no compulsion to send students to special schools and that in theory decisions are taken by parents. Yet, in practice, a 'professional' viewpoint may be perceived as carrying such authority that parents may have considerable difficulty in making their views heard, as is apparent in the Scottish study. That past practice may have dampened down parental support for inclusion is indicated by the readiness with which parents have supported the WSNS policy, in contrast to the opposition from the special schools and the neutral reaction of mainstream teachers, and by the way the grapevine has led to parental interest in the special class at De Springplank.

The discussion of inclusion in this chapter addresses issues about the use of special classes that were explored in the USA in the 1960s around the legitimacy of special classes as opposed to full-time mainstream participation for students with relatively low attainments, and in England in the early 1970s around the use of special classes as an alternative to special schools (Anderson 1973). Special classes, both full and part-time remain a feature of the special education system in both these countries although definitions of innovatory practice have shifted. It is a particular legacy of the high exclusion rates in the Netherlands that the use of part-time special classes should involve new thinking about inclusion.

The Netherlands share a high rate of special school exclusion with some other European countries such as Germany and Belgium (Pijl and Meijer 1991). Once special schools have been established as a significant part of the solution to teaching for diversity within an education system, their growth has been extremely difficult to reverse in many countries. As a solution, it is undermined by the fact that a school's difficulties are rarely resolved by identifying a few students as the cause. But the higher the exclusion rates, the more people have invested in this solution both materially, ideologically and professionally, and objections to it become progressively more difficult to recognise and use to underpin a rethinking of responses to student difference. It is not surprising therefore that the system in the Netherlands, which segregates three times the number of students into special schools as in England, should have displayed such inertia.

As in many other countries, policies to segregate students categorised as having difficulties largely involve the exclusion of boys. This effect is more striking with higher rates of segregation. The fact that the special class at De Springplank contains only boys stands out for us but is not seen by the authors as a reason for extensive exploration. The relationship between gender and school difficulties remains an under-researched area internationally.

Policies to reduce exclusion are said to arise from a mixture of changing views about segregation and a wish to reduce the expenditure on special schools. National policy makers recognised the links between the nature of general education policies and pressures to exclude students by attempting to encourage the practice of 'adaptive instruction' into schools dominated by whole-class teaching. Here, as in Norway, but in contrast to pressures in the reverse direction in England through the 1980s and 1990s, there is official rejection of whole class-teaching. However, we are told that the move away from whole-class teaching has had limited success; embraced in theory but with little effect on practice.

We recognise the need to explore in detail the varieties of practice covered by the terms 'whole-class' and 'child-centred'. Thus, it is possible to have a teacher directing a lesson from the front of a class who draws in many students appropriately into the lesson. In another class, students may work individually on tasks poorly suited to stimulating their learning.

The 'together to school again' or WSNS policy combined the formation of regional clusters with cash inducements for such clusters to reduce exclusion. Financial incentives, initially low, are planned to increase. We are told that the policy itself is exclusive, being for two-thirds of the students in special schools and excluding most of those in special schools in the countries discussed in the other case-studies in this book.

Voices and perspectives on inclusion and exclusion

The voices that we hear most directly in the chapter are those of the school principal, the school counsellor, the special class teacher and the principal of the special school. As we have indicated, however, the voices of the authors and central policy makers, as well as parents, are also represented. There is a solidifying of some of these voices into representations of distinct group interests. There is no hint of any differences of perspective between the authors.

We learn about the views of the authors to a limited extent directly, and slightly more extensively by implication. In discussing observations of special and mainstream class they report that 'the individual approach of the part-time special group is in striking contrast to the whole-class teaching in the regular classes, which creates its own failures'. There is also their final statement that 'we regard the part-time Special Group as a way to promote the inclusion of children with learning problems in their regular school, without separating them totally from other children and regular curricula'. This does not necessarily mean that they themselves favour a reduction of segregation but that they believe the special class can contribute to achieving it.

Inclusion appears to be seen by the authors, in step with official policy and staff at the school, as concerned only with categorised students and expressed using a variety of terms, none of which is called into question. They describe the students who can be candidates for inclusion under law, as 'students with learning difficulties' or 'educable mentally retarded'. We are told that the special class includes students whose 'learning problems' are with 'dyslexia, memory problems . . . IQs below 70, auditory and visual handicaps'. Language problems are also mentioned and partly attributed to 'immigrant status' although we are told that of the twenty children coming from Moluccan families all speak Dutch and were born and brought up in the Netherlands. It would be interesting to find out more about what this means. The liberal use of categories of inability and disability conveys a sense of the separateness and distinctness of these students from other presumably 'normal' students. The language of special education categories, with its selective implications, which is present in most studies in this book, is perhaps most evident in this chapter by Gerry and Sip Jan

Teachers couch their view of educational problems in terms of student difficulties and 'needs'. There is concern that placement in a special class may lead parents to underestimate or fail to acknowledge the defects of their children and that sometimes they have to be told that the special class is for children with 'severe problems'. Nor are they to take their child's presence in a mainstream primary school as evidence that they will be able to transfer to a 'regular secondary school'. Although rights are mentioned as having an influence on national policy, there is evidence of a strong professional perspective in which decisions are to be based on professional judgement rather than student or parental entitlements.

In order to pass into the special class, students have to fail to clear a series of diagnostic hurdles in a similar way to the progression through the stages of the Code of Practice in England and Wales (DfE 1994). In this case, they must have failed to respond to class teaching, remedial teaching and grade retention and their difficulties must not be attributable to difficult behaviour. The apparent precision of the procedures may be less closely followed in practice and the authors recognise a need to study these more closely. It would be surprising, in our experience, if the teachers could resist the temptation to exclude students to the special class whose behaviour they find troublesome. This usually accounts for some of the over-representation of boys in special provision.

In view of the requirement for a succession of failures before admittance to the special class, it is not surprising that a student should ask for reassurance from the special class teacher that he is not 'stupid' and is still capable of learning something. The Principal of the special school reflects the experience of students in a similar position when he reports that they are 'happy to come to the special school' after they have been isolated and stigmatised in the mainstream.

There is an interesting contradiction between the suggestion that the special class is only for students in the Grades 4, 5 and 6 with the later report that once in the special class students rarely leave. This may reveal a distinction between decisions based on professional expertise and those based on professional interest. A need of students for particular professional expertise might lead to a planned intervention for a limited time, the maintenance of professional interests might lead to more permanent separation of students who provoke difficulties.

The authors recognise that if the mainstream class produced less 'failure', there might be less need for the identification and categorisation of failing students. This link between developments in teaching methods and the reduction of failure is also made clear by the headteacher and the former Special Group teacher who argues that the special class could be used to help other teachers develop 'adaptive instruction', relating their teaching more closely to the needs of students. As part of a plan for developing approaches to teaching in the school, such a process might lead teachers to question the sense of attempting to resolve difficulties in learning outside of their classrooms. Yet support is available for students and, by implication, teachers 'only outside the walls of the regular class'.

Unless the process of inclusion moves on to this next stage, it is difficult to assess whether the De Springplank special class represents moves towards greater inclusion or exclusion. The authors recognise that the Special Group might promote greater exclusion as being a 'less radical' way for teachers to get rid of bothersome students than transfer to a special school but report the school as arguing that strict admission criteria prevent this happening. The headteacher of De Springplank argues that the students in the special class would have been referred to a special school, whereas the head of the special school argues that the special group do not have the 'cluster of problems' that would make them special school candidates. The authors tend to support the view of the primary head, 'since referral to special school is almost always followed by admittance'. However, given the fact that some other children are already referred to the special school, the additional three per cent of the school population represented by the nine students in the special class would represent a relatively high proportion for the area. We have experience of special classes being created, ostensibly to increase inclusion in the mainstream and reduce the special school population, which have had the reverse effect, creating additional candidates for exclusion. It remains unclear to us, then, whether De Springplank will provide a springboard to greater inclusion.

The authors are committed to using quantitative methods in a case-study of a single school. This appears to us to lead them to measure and compare things that have limited validity. What do we learn by finding out differences between the amount of time 'on task' in mainstream and special class or differences in the rating of quality of teaching? It is suggested that 'the observations must be interpreted with caution' and indeed we cannot know whether the same findings would have been obtained on a different day. Even if we could say that one teacher consistently used different methods from another or maintained higher levels of curricula engagement than another, we could not attribute these qualities to the place of teaching or even the size of the group. The category of observation reported in the tables tells us little about what was going on in the classroom. For example a high level of teacher initiated interactions in the special class as reported in Table 10.2, depending on their precise quality, might be interpreted as interrupting or supporting the flow of learning or, as the special school Principal suggests, involve 'using instruction as a means for class management'.

In attempting to use the research to help answer whether or not special classes should be used, by comparing outcomes within them to those in the mainstream class, the authors adopt a variant of the professional perspective. The value of inclusion and its form for particular students is to be based on the results of professional researchers. The results of sampling one full-time special class in a special school might produce even higher levels of student engagement and progress. What policy implication would be produced by such an outcome?

12

IRELAND: INTEGRATION AS APPROPRIATE, SEGREGATION WHERE NECESSARY

Jim Bennet, Hugh Gash and Mark O'Reilly

Introduction

This chapter explores inclusion and exclusion within the Republic of Ireland in the context of a national policy that integrates children with special needs where possible, and retains the right to segregate where necessary (Ireland 1993). Overall responsibility for the chapter is shared by the authors, but sometimes our individual voices are presented and differences of view are apparent. We start by giving some of the Irish context, particularly in terms of educational policies bearing on issues of integration. We then present our analysis and description of integration in three schools.

National context

There are twenty-six counties in the Republic of Ireland and six counties in Northern Ireland. The Republic covers 70,000 square kilometres and has a population of three and a half million (Ireland 1994a). Compulsory education is from 6 to 15 years. There is very little legislation about primary education, which lasts up to 13 years. For the most part, the education system has been administered centrally with changes announced by circulars and memoranda. However, recent initiatives are likely to end this legislative lacuna. It is beyond the scope of the chapter to rehearse the benefits or disadvantages of legislation, but the principles which have been advanced for legislation about the education of children with special needs, will be outlined.

A Green Paper, Education for a Changing World (Ireland 1992), refers to the requirement for a continuum of provision for children with special educational needs. This ranges from students having learning difficulties in the ordinary class, who can be assisted by additional support within the school, to those whose disabilities are such as to require specialised attention in a special school. The Irish Government has accepted, as a basic principle, the European Community Council of Ministers of Education Resolution of May

1990 (Ireland 1992, p. 61). This argues that the integration into mainstream schools of children with disabilities should be accelerated in all appropriate cases on the basis of individual assessment, provided that good quality education can be maintained. In 1992, the main issue with regard to special needs education was how to strike the balance between special school and mainstream provision, and how mainstream provision should be developed for a greater number of students. The 1995 White Paper, Charting our Education Future, reiterated the concept of a continuum of provision for pupils with special educational needs. It recommended that the details of each pupil with a special disability be entered into a national data base, and it stated that each of the proposed education boards should have a statutory responsibility for all disabled students in its region (Ireland 1995).

Two publications give numbers of young people in the Irish educational system with mild mental handicap/general learning difficulties: the official government Report of the Special Education Review Committee (hereafter SERC) (Ireland 1993) and McGee (1990). The 1965 Commission of Enquiry into Mental Handicap (Ireland 1965) produced a definition of mild mental handicap that is still in use. Accordingly, children have a mild mental handicap when their handicap, 'though not amounting to severe or moderate handicap, is such that, as children, they appear to be permanently incapable of benefiting adequately from the instruction in the ordinary school curriculum' (Ireland 1977). Children with severe mental handicaps are still not included within the education system in the Republic and the recommendations of SERC are equivocal on this point.

The placement policy for children with special needs is described in SERC as follows: 'we favour as much integration as is appropriate and feasible with as little segregation as is necessary' (Ireland 1993, p. 22). Since 1990, it has been government policy that no further special schools be created for pupils with mild mental handicap/general learning difficulties. In the future, pupils with less severe disabilities will remain in ordinary schools and there will be a need to reduce the pupil–teacher ratio in special schools, which will increasingly cater for pupils with more severe difficulties.

Yet, although SERC recognises the need for a range of educational provisions, there is an emphasis in the report on special schools and special classes within ordinary schools. This lack of support for integration within the ordinary class has been criticised by the Psychological Society of Ireland (PSI 1994). Parents of children with a mental handicap/intellectual disability complained, too, of a lack of both resources and support for mainstreaming in ordinary schools (Finlay et al. 1994). A compromise linking special and ordinary schools, recommended by O'Mahony (1993) before SERC, has both the advantage of being immediately possible to implement, and is in line with recommendations in SERC on the need for a continuum of services, and the desirability of creating and finding resources for links between educational institutions.

There are a number of ways that educational systems facilitate teaching in integrated classes. There have been calls for reduced class sizes in integrated classes (O'Connell 1987), and more adequate material and teaching facilities (INTO 1993). It is recommended that each child with a mild mental handicap/general learning difficulty should count as two children when allocating teachers to a school, and that a 'Special Needs Assistant' should be appointed for each group of four children with mild mental handicap/general learning difficulty in the school (Ireland 1993, p. 186). These regulations would be helpful in ordinary schools with special classes for children with mild mental handicaps, but are unlikely to make a substantial difference to ordinary schools with very small numbers of such children.

The process of integrating children in ordinary classes in Ireland must be seen, then, in the context of class size and organisation. The official pupil–teacher ratio of twenty-seven to one includes teachers in special schools, in special classes, visiting teachers and administrative school principals. Thus, most classes have more than twenty-seven pupils. The exceptions are small rural schools which often have fewer than twenty-seven children in the class, but are organised with more than one grade level per classroom. Urban schools may be crowded with more than forty children in a small percentage of classrooms (1.76 per cent). Teachers with large classes and teachers with multi-grade groups are likely to find mainstreaming difficult (Ireland 1994b).

There are a large number of children who are unofficially integrated in ordinary schools either by choice or because they do not live close to a special school or a school with a suitable special class. The Department of Education has increased the numbers of remedial teachers in the system; however, there are many teachers who remain dissatisfied and ill-prepared to cope with the government policy on integration. In one survey, fifty-four per cent of teachers were not satisfied that the children were receiving an appropriate education, and sixty-nine per cent felt that specialist help was needed in the school (Niland 1993).

SERC made a large number of recommendations to improve special education services, and the effects of some of these are already visible. However, the policy makers of SERC and the Department of Education do not have direct links with the universities and colleges of education, so implementation of recommendations about improvements in training programmes is determined by the readiness or willingness of educational institutions to act. Further, the only research funding mentioned in the recommendations is for test development. This is in stark contrast to the policy in some other European countries, such as Spain, where substantial funds are invested in research on how integration is working. Future policy should develop a similar system for Ireland. The descriptions and analyses of schools reported in this chapter make a small contribution towards the creation of such a research programme.

The nature of the study

Three schools are included in the study. Students in these schools were observed for a school day. School A is a boys' primary school for children aged 4 to 13 years. The background information on this school is presented by its principal. The observer of school A is a psychologist working in a university setting who has an interest in special education. He concentrated on the observation of one student with cerebral palsy and mild mental handicap. There were differences in the perceptions of this observer and the school principal, which became very obvious both in the principal's response to the observation and in the concluding comments that he provided to the chapter. Schools B and C are mixed junior and senior primary schools on the same campus, taking children aged 4 to 9 years and 9 to 13 years respectively. The story of these schools focuses on the educational experiences of two children with Down syndrome who had progressed through school B and were in school C at the time of the observations. They are described on the basis of interviews with their principals by the second observer who is a psychologist working in a college of education. His observations follow the report of the interviews.

School A

The principal's introduction

The school is located in one of the dormitory towns in North County Dublin. It has an enrolment of 544 pupils, ranging in age from 4 to 13 years. All of the pupils in mainstream classes are boys, but there is a co-educational special class for children with mild mental handicap. The pupils of the school are from a wide range of socio-economic backgrounds drawn mainly from the housing estates in the town and its hinterlands.

Primary schools in Ireland are *de jure* non-denominational, but *de facto* most of the schools are managed by the main churches, with many ecclesiastical parish boundaries and school catchment areas being coterminous. This factor can be of vital significance when the question of inclusion or exclusion is being addressed. If schools are full, then one of the main criteria when applications are being processed is whether or not the child is resident within the parish. If, however, there is pressure with regard to obtaining pupils, then the parish rule is forgotten about and schools take pupils from wherever they can get them. However, the 'parish rule' is inevitably brought to bear if an application is received from a potentially difficult pupil, and in this category may be included those children who have special educational needs.

Compulsory education starts from 6 years of age, but because pre-school provision is practically non-existent, primary schools have traditionally enrolled pupils on the September after they have reached their fourth birthday.

The usual criteria for entrance to the schools are for the children to be resident within the school's catchment area and to be at least 4 years of age, but if there is pressure on places, the age requirement may be closer to 5 years than to 4. There is no screening of prospective pupils if they satisfy the age and residential requirements, but it is expected that the principal will be made aware of any special needs that the children may have. Usually, the parents of children with special needs have requested an interview with the principal so that the extent of the pupils' needs may be outlined, and this gives the principal the opportunity to provide details of the school's capacity to meet the child's needs. When the enrolments have been completed, the parents are invited to an induction meeting at which school policy on a wide range of issues is articulated, and parents have an opportunity to question the principal on the basis for these policies.

This school usually enrols approximately seventy pupils each year, and the children are then placed in two classes that are drawn up on the basis of the housing estates in which the children reside. An attempt is made to ensure that the children will be in the same class as their friends. This system of grouping children has been reasonably satisfactory because there is no preponderance of any particular type of housing in either of the two class groupings.

In June 1993, the school had its first application to enrol a pupil with Down syndrome. In view of the implications in this case, the principal consulted the Board of Management of the school. Although the Board asked about the support available for the child and the teacher, it agreed that every effort should be made to accommodate children with special needs in their local school. The proviso was made that each application must be addressed individually so that the school authorities could assess each child's particular level of need.

Apart from the special class all other classes are mixed ability, though pupils may be grouped within classes according to informal assessment of their ability. In the junior classes every effort is made to meet the needs of individual children, and the approach tends to be reasonably informal, given the constraints which class groupings of thirty-five children impose. Unfortunately, as children progress through the school, the approach to the curriculum tends to become more formal due to the demands of assessment tests for entrance to post-primary schools. As a result, children with special needs tend to struggle in senior mainstream classes. In the recent past, this has occurred in the cases of the child with Down syndrome and two pupils with mild mental handicap and cerebral palsy respectively. In all three instances, the children started in the junior section of the school, but then transferred either to the special needs class or special schools.

For the first year of compulsory schooling (junior infants level), one classroom assistant is shared between the two classes. This is part of a job creation initiative, and not a permanent position. In subsequent years support is provided by a remedial teacher, who specialises in the teaching of reading on a withdrawal basis, and an extra resource teacher employed as support to the teachers of the junior classes. The availability of two resource teachers means that remediation is provided from senior infants (the second year of schooling) to the end of the primary school, and it is also possible to give extra tuition in maths to pupils who are struggling. Children are assessed as being in need of remedial tuition on the recommendation of the class teacher or as a result of the standardised reading tests which are held in January of each year.

There is one teacher in the school with specific responsibility for the special class, and four other teachers have had either special class or remedial teaching experience. At a formal level, teachers are responsible for each pupil in their class and the support that is given is simply support and not an opportunity to abdicate responsibility for children with special needs. Great hope was reposed in the peripatetic teacher as support for the pupil with Down syndrome, but experience indicated that this service (one hour per week) was totally inadequate.

The children in the special needs class are integrated for art and craft, music and preparation for the sacraments. They spend a portion of the lunch break in allocated mainstream classes, and then all classes go to the playground for the remainder of the play period. It has been noticed over the years that the children from the special needs class prefer to go to the junior classes because they appear to feel more secure, and it is arguable that they are less conscious of their learning disability. They rarely engage the pupils in the senior classes in conversation, and they do not walk to or from school with them. When the special needs pupils go to the yard, they immediately congregate together and do not interact with the other pupils at all. There have been some instances of pupils asking them to answer tables, to spell words, and some name-calling has occurred. In the recent past the question of the social integration of special needs children has been the focus of a staff meeting and the special class teacher requested that other teachers adopt a proactive stance on this issue. The result of this has been that the pupils from the special class are encouraged to participate in various activities during the lunch break. This approach has met with varying degrees of success.

John is one of the pupils with cerebral palsy who was in a mainstream class for over three years, and then transferred to the special class because his parents were unhappy with his progress and the teacher felt that his needs were not being met adequately. It is significant that he has transferred his allegiance completely to the special class and he rarely interacts with the pupils with whom he was in class for such a considerable period.

The observer's report: physical and professional barriers to John's inclusion

I spent one morning observing and taking notes about John, a 10 year old boy with mild intellectual disabilities and mild cerebral palsy, to gain a picture of his education and inclusion in the school. I had brief interactions with John's teachers and the school principal from time to time during the observations. I also documented these interactions and include the salient points in the following description.

I arrived at the school at 8.45am. It seemed like a typical suburban primary school. The grounds and school building were well-kept. There was the usual scene of children playing in the yard and arriving at school. The principal had asked me to come to the school before the first class period so that he could introduce me to John's teacher and show me his classroom. He escorted me to a prefabricated building, physically separate from the rest of the school. It was the special class for ten children with mild mental handicap. I was introduced to Pat, John's special education teacher, who described John's physical and intellectual disabilities. The principal then suggested that I should observe John's arrival at school. I expected that John would be readily identifiable because of his physical disabilities. In fact, I was not able to pick him out from the crowd. As the students lined up to enter the school, the principal pointed John out to me. John is physically impaired on his left side but not to an extent that it is obvious.

From 9.00am until 10.20am, I observed John from the back of the special education classroom. When the teacher allowed the students to introduce themselves to me at the beginning of class John was the first to offer his name. This was typical of subsequent observations of John's social behaviour; he seemed friendly and outgoing both to students (mainstream and special) and to teachers.

The teacher introduced lessons and assigned tasks. As students completed lessons they approached the teacher for feedback. Those who completed lessons engaged in alternative activities, such as working on the computer, until the next lesson. Both instruction and the curriculum were, in my estimation, well-structured and well-delivered. Similarly, I noted that all students were well-behaved.

At 10.30am, the students went to the yard for break. The whole school was on break at this time so the yard was packed with students. The special class broke up into three sub-groups. John talked with another student from the special class throughout the break. There was some pushing as students bumped one another in the crowd but I observed no formal social interactions between John and other mainstream students. In fact, I did not see any interaction between students from the special class and students in mainstream classes.

The students returned to the special class at 11.00am and continued instruction until 11.30. At 11.30 the special class prepared to go to join a mainstream singing class. The teacher told me that this is the 'integrated class' for this morning. The pupils were escorted by the special education teacher into the main school building and into another classroom. This classroom had the traditional rows of desks. Since there was already a regular class present, together the two classes made approximately fifty students. (I wondered if any of the regular classes went to the special class for integrated activities.) There was the inevitable 'messing' from time to time during the class period but no serious disruptions. Most of the special students sat together, but some were interspersed among the regular students. John sat beside a regular student and talked to him from time to time throughout the class. The regular teacher conducted the class and led it in singing a series of songs. At the end of the class the special class teacher called on his class to line up outside the door. The regular class remained seated as the special students departed. As the students were leaving the mainstream classroom, the regular teacher shook hands with John and told him that he was very good. Obviously, she knew that I was observing John.

Lunch followed the integrated class. Again, the yard was packed with students. The special class students gathered together in the yard near the prefab classroom. One of the students produced a ball and the class played soccer during the lunch period. All the special class students were involved in the soccer game. I observed no social interactions between students from the special class and mainstream students during lunch.

I felt that the students in the special education classroom were physically and socially isolated from the rest of the school. The integration practices that I observed, in my opinion, accentuated rather than mitigated exclusion. The special education teacher possessed excellent teaching and organisation skills. Would it not be more appropriate to place these students in regular classrooms and use the special education teacher as a resource? Maybe one day we will recognise the educational needs of students as having paramount priority above and beyond professional boundaries.

The principal of school A responds

In view of the overt and covert criticisms of the organisation of our school and also the deployment of teachers, I consider it imperative that I respond.

First, there are sixteen rooms in the main building and sixteen mainstream classes, each of which has between thirty and thirty-seven pupils. There is one special class in the school, which at the time of the observation had ten pupils in it. The Department of Education rarely provides permanent extensions to schools, it provides prefabs, and a decision was made to locate the special class in it because it had much smaller numbers than any other class. This is due to factors such as insurance and supervision on days when the classes are not allowed to leave the building at lunch times. On these days, the special class pupils are reallocated to the other classes. (It is easier to reallocate ten than thirty-seven). There were no ulterior motives behind the allocation of a prefab to the special class.

It might be better to ignore the query with regard to whether pupils from mainstream classes are ever integrated with the special class pupils, but to do so carries an implication that it has some validity. Pupils from the special class were also integrated for art and craft lessons and preparation for the various sacraments, and again exigencies of space and organisational issues were factors in having these classes in the main building.

A fundamental question is posed about the existence of a special class in the suggestion about the deployment of the special class teacher as a resource person and integrating the children on a full-time basis in mainstream classes. Each of the pupils in the special class was previously in a mainstream class for at least three years, and each of them encountered resource teacher support for a limited period each day. In the opinion of a number of eminent educational psychologists, it was considered that the children would make more progress if they were placed in a special class where the smaller numbers made it possible to structure a curriculum suited to their individual needs. Our school has no vested interest in maintaining a special class for the sake of it, but we are committed to providing the best possible educational provision for each of the children in our care. There is always a lengthy list of applications for pupils for this class.

The observations on social interactions in the playground simply illustrate the extent to which the observer was unfamiliar with schools. Pupils from different classes, whether mainstream or special, rarely interact with each other unless they are from the same housing estates. Football matches and other recreational activities during this half hour period are usually organised by the pupils themselves on an *ad hoc* basis, and it is more convenient for them to make optimal use of the time available by getting games set up quickly. It must also be stated that choice is involved with regard to social interactions, and it can hardly be expected that teachers should tell the pupils with whom they should socialise.

The unfortunate dichotomy that is presented at the end of the observer's report again illustrates both a lack of knowledge of the organisation of schools and a lack of insight. There is no conflict in our school between the educational needs of pupils in the special class and professional boundaries. The integration of handicapped pupils into mainstream schools and classes is a matter that must take cognisance of context, but it is not the overriding educational aim.

With specific reference to John, his parents are delighted with the progress that he is now making as a result of transferring to the special class. They report that their son is happy, working very well and that he appreciates the extra attention which he is getting in this class. An educational psychologist has assessed his progress and stated that the placement is the correct one.

Introducing schools B and C

Schools B and C, a junior and senior primary school, are located in suburbs on the North side of Dublin. They serve a parish with about 2,400 houses.

157

Most of the houses are privately owned. There is a mix of native Dublin born parents and parents born in the country, but who now live in Dublin. In school B there are 562 children (305 boys and 257 girls) who range in age from 4 to just under 9 years of age. There are twenty teachers on the staff (principal, remedial teacher and eighteen assistant teachers). The children come from a wide variety of socio-economic backgrounds and live in housing estates in the area surrounding the school.

Children from school B transfer to school C when they have completed four years in primary school. In school C there are 591 children (296 boys and 295 girls) whose ages range from 9 to under 13 years. There are twenty-one teachers in the school (principal, remedial teacher, and nineteen assistant teachers).

The principal of school B reports

Bob and Sarah were the first two children with Down syndrome to come to our school in 1989 and they have now moved on to school C. Our initial preparation for them could be described as informal. We discussed their coming at staff meetings and with our Board of Management. We asked that we be given their psychological assessments, access to the Department of Education's psychological service, and that we be allowed to seek help from St Michael's House, an organisation which provides services for people with disabilities in the greater Dublin area, because in our school there was very little support for children like Bob and Sarah in terms of remedial help. St Michael's House maintains a special school not far from our school. Now we have Susan who has Down syndrome, too, is 10 years of age and is in the Primary 3 with children younger than herself.

It would be reasonable for the Department of Education to reduce the class size in the classes in which there is a child with a mental or physical handicap. Grouping occurs within classes for English and maths. Regular weekly or fortnightly tests are carried out by the class teacher.

I have not been in a position in which I have had to refuse to admit a child with a disability, but it has happened that the parents have not asked. There was one case of a parent who had twins, one of whom had Down syndrome. However, when the twin came to the school, the child with Down syndrome was still not toilet-trained and the mother never raised the question about schooling with me.

I think that all of the teachers who have had one of the children with Down syndrome have benefited from the experience. However, I am not sure whether they all feel that they would be happy to repeat the experience if the need arises in the future. Next autumn we are going to have a child with spina bifida. This will be a new experience for us, the first time that a child with a physical handicap will come to our school.

The principal of school C reports

Bob and Sarah transferred to our school and attend Fourth Class (Primary 6). We had tried to get a resource teacher for a long time without success, but the parents were very helpful. They lobbied. I know now that you can get things done by lobbying. It took two years to get the resource teacher. Success depends a lot on your inspector and how helpful he or she is. In the end we were advised to make a list of all the children with a handicap in the area (about 4 or 5 miles radius). We sent in the list to the Department of Education and got a resource teacher. The resource teacher has responsibility for a number of children with Down syndrome in the area. She travels from school to school, so each child is seen at a scheduled time each week.

There is a new parents' association at the school which is mainly concerned with fund raising. This pays for the computer room, for which one parent provided the iron grills for the windows. Besides such practical support from parents in our community, we are also linked with the parish. The parish priest is chairperson of the Board of Management and this guarantees a link of a particular type with the community which is different to links in many state schools in other countries.

We do not have a written policy on integration. Each year we review our policy, but we do not have a written policy. The school policy is at present that we like having the children we have. Indeed, so far we have accepted all comers. We have not had to exclude a child yet! If I had a child who needed special education I would want him or her to be educated as normally as possible. However, the level of disability would be a deciding factor if we were to refuse an application. Also we would insist that the children were toilet-trained, since we have no classroom assistants or nurses.

The only pupils who can be described as integrated are the ones with Down syndrome. We find that the parents of these children are great parents. Generally we know them, because we have had other older family members in the school as children.

We worry about whether we are doing the right thing. I worry about what happens in secondary schools or when the pupils leave. I also worry that I will have a problem in getting teachers to agree to have Sarah and Bob in their classes in the following year. However, a teacher has already agreed to take Bob so I am delighted with the way that the teachers are agreeing to work with integration so willingly.

We like the idea of integration. I feel I have been helped to understand the process by the principal of the Junior School. It is a pity that it depends so much on the child's personality. I find that the children's friendships get more difficult when the children get to be about 10 and they understand more fully how children with Down syndrome will be limited in certain ways – always.

Normally each of the children with Down syndrome in the school will have one hour a day with the resource teacher and one hour a day with the remedial teacher. Also, we allow Sarah and Bob to do Physical Education (PE) with other classes than their own because we find that they are more involved in PE than other lessons.

I am concerned that no extra qualifications were required for the post of resource teacher. There are extra qualifications in special education for teachers who satisfy certain criteria. They can take a course in Special Education at St Patrick's College. There are also potential political problems, namely, that the Department of Education does not want more pressure coming from teachers for courses which will have to be paid for somehow.

I have been able to create class sizes of twenty-six to twenty-seven pupils for the classes in which Bob and Sarah are placed. This is lower than the other classes, but my ability to do this depends on my numbers. I find that the children in these classes are nicer and kinder. I wonder if this is one of the effects of having children with Down syndrome.

Second observer's report: including Sarah in school C

I decided to focus on one child in order to describe the class activities, since similar processes were evident in all three classes I observed. Sarah is 11, has Down syndrome, and is in the Fourth Class with 10 year olds. Her teacher, Anna, made time at the beginning of the school day while the other children were doing set work at their desks, to work with Sarah individually for about fifteen minutes. This was the one concentrated piece of time she gave to Sarah. During the rest of the school day, Anna regularly checked on Sarah, but only for very brief periods of time. This meant that Sarah was excluded from many of the class activities requiring independent study.

There were times when she was included in whole-class activities. For example, in the art class, she sat with the others in the class at one of the tables, and watched carefully to see what they were painting before attempting her own. It was a copy of what looked like a Yucca plant in the desert, with blue sky as background. At the end of the lesson Sarah was asked to return paint that had been borrowed from a nearby classroom. Anna sent another child after Sarah to be sure that she went to the right class with the paint. The other child came back very quickly, and announced that Sarah had gone to the right room. When Sarah came back she had paint on her mouth. The class laughed when the teacher identified the mark, and Anna quickly exclaimed, 'Well you all got it on your hands!' The tone was such that they stopped laughing immediately. Anna did not allow this to be a joke against Sarah, which might exclude her. The teacher sent Sarah and another girl with paint on her hands to go and wash the paint off. They spent about four minutes washing it off in the toilet area.

Sarah also participated fully in a gym class that took place outside. She and the other children with Down syndrome really seemed to enjoy it and could do most of the things which the other children did. Indeed, the children with

Down syndrome often do two sessions of PE in the week, joining another class for their extra PE session. In this instance, PE consisted of a variety of races, some walking and some running, with different groups of children from the class. There was a boys' race, a girls' race, and a race for Sarah to win. Various techniques were used to create opportunities for different children to race each other. For example, children lined up at the fence, and months were called out, such as 'July', whereupon all the children with birthdays in July ran up to the teacher.

There were times when Sarah was involved in her own activities, such as colouring, working on a jigsaw puzzle, and using building materials called 'Construct-o-Straws'. Anna said that she was always on the look out for suitable things to bring to school for Sarah to work on in class.

Anna perceived Sarah to be very popular with the other children. In the lunch break I noticed that it was not always easy for Sarah to relate to the other children sitting at her table. On arrival at the school, I had watched set dancing in the gym. Her 'minder', a girl from her class, was waiting in the gym, by the door. In discussion with the principal I learnt that Sarah had poor coordination, and was noticing that other children were beginning to avoid dancing with her. She was also starting to be excluded socially in some situations, as the children in her class become more self-conscious. As a result, Sarah will sometimes sit cross-legged in dancing class, as the others dance around her. Most of the children dancing are girls but there are some boys who are being taught by girls. Arranging for Sarah to join classes other than her own for physical education and swimming is a response to her relative isolation by providing her with additional opportunities to make friends.

Anna felt that she had been inadequately prepared for teaching Sarah and that she did not know if she was doing the right thing. I thought that she had a lot of extra work making sure that Sarah was fully involved in the classroom. This was inevitable because for the most part Sarah was not doing the same activity as the other children. The experience of the other teachers was similar. However, the opportunities for individualised tuition from the remedial teacher and the resource teacher for Sarah and the others, amount to a maximum ten hours a week. In practice this may be as little as seven hours. The individualised work that I saw seemed very appropriate. Part of the time was spent on language activities, which included talking and questions on the days of week, and on naming Sarah's family members and their relationships.

I met the teachers at lunch time to discuss their attitudes to integration. The resource teacher, David, felt that integration puts great pressure on the teachers because it is a great loss of face to say that it is not working. There is a huge push from the Down syndrome Association in Ireland for integration. Their magazines have regular articles describing children who do very well with integrated programmes. This makes it hard for other less able pupils and their parents to know what it is that is really going to suit their own needs. For example, Bob is 12 and in a Fourth Class of 10 year olds. It is my perception that the teachers consider that the integration of Bob has been a failure. He is totally unable to look after himself; when the class goes swimming, he cannot dress, undress, or even dry himself; if he has a cold he cannot blow his nose. He is far too dependent, and he can do nothing on his own. He perseveres at nothing. He has little or no coordination, he cannot zip up his coat, although he can manage his fly. Indeed, he hates things which require coordination.

Apparently, one of the problems is that his mother cannot be persuaded to allow him to do things on his own. A programme was organised so that Bob would be taken to the school gate by a girl from the class, who was very responsible. This worked for a while but now his mother is back at the classroom door. The staff are unsure why this came about. The principal is trying to see if a programme can be worked out so that Bob will go to a nearby special school one day a week for independence training. However, there are administrative difficulties to be overcome about his registration at school, since a child can only be registered at one school. As an outsider, this seems trivial, but to the principal it requires time-consuming negotiations with officials in the Department of Education.

Concluding comments

It is noticeable from the observations that have been made that the two observers brought very different expectations to their tasks. The first observer focused on the social conditions of John, the pupil with cerebral palsy, and felt that practices in the school increased his exclusion. These observations, however, were at variance with the perspective of the principal of that school. The second observer was anxious to ascertain if the integration was of benefit to the children, given its circumstances and conditions. In school C, the observer reports that children with Down syndrome are physically present in mainstream classes for much of the time, but there is a question mark with regard to the extent to which these pupils are productively engaged, as distinct from simply being busy.

It is evident from the comments of the teachers that considerable goodwill exists towards the concept of integration, but that the structures and procedures for successful integration to occur are not yet in place. Teachers in the Republic of Ireland are attempting to integrate children with special needs into mainstream classes without the support provided by reduced class sizes and extra resources. Goodwill and good intentions count for little, and they can easily dissipate when they are not accompanied by genuine, practical support.

APPENDIX

Imlitir 23/77 An roinn oideachais brainse an bhunoideachais

Circular to managerial authorities and principal teachers of National Schools

Criteria for the admission of pupils to special classes in National Schools

1 Rule 27 of the rules for National Schools lays down that special classes for partially deaf, partially sighted or backward children may be established in National Schools, subject to such conditions as the Minister for Education may from time to time prescribe.

2 Before any child is referred to a special class, the Director of Community Care (Medical Officer of Health) should be contacted, so as to ensure that any relevant information which he may have about the child is made available to the school authorities. Such information must, of course, be treated in strict confidence.

3 A child proposed for enrolment in a special class should have a medical, social and psychological assessment in order to ascertain whether there are any physical, environmental or intellectual factors which may be contributing to his educational problems. These assessments are normally provided by arrangement with the appropriate Health board and with the consent of the parents. Parents may arrange to have their children assessed privately, if they so wish. If it is not possible to provide the medical and social assessments before enrolment, they should be provided as soon as possible thereafter. It is essential, however, that the psychological report be available before the child is enrolled and that this report be acted upon in accordance with paragraph 7 hereunder.

4 Children who are considered after assessment to be mildly mentally handicapped as defined in the Report of the Commission of Inquiry on Mental Handicap, 1965, would, generally speaking, be suitably placed in special classes. The Commission defined mildly handicapped persons as follows:- 'Mildly handicapped persons are persons whose mental handicap, though not amounting to severe or moderate handicap, is such that, as children, they appear to be permanently incapable of benefiting adequately from the instruction in the ordinary school curriculum; as adults some may require supervision and support for their own protection, or that of others. Suitable treatment and education will increase the proportion who will achieve social adaptation and personal independence in later life. In so far as an intelligence quotient can be regarded as a measure of mild mental handicap, the persons concerned would generally have intelligence quotients from 50 to 70.'

5   Certain children in the borderline category between mild mental handi-
    cap and dull normal ability would benefit from placement in a special
    class on account of a special learning problem such as:-
    (a) mild emotional disturbance associated with persistent failure in the
        ordinary class (disruptive behaviour on its own, however, would not
        constitute grounds for special class placement);
    (b) immature social behaviour;
    (c) poor level of language development in relation to overall intellectual
        level.

6   Decisions on placement in special classes for reasons such as those out-
    lined in paragraph 5 above should normally be based on the results of
    objective testing by means of psychometric instruments and should take
    into account the extent to which the pupil is making progress in his pre-
    sent learning environment. In general, placement in a special class should
    be looked upon as serious educational intervention and should be regu-
    larly reviewed by the principal and the special class teacher. The child
    should be re-assessed if there is a doubt concerning the suitability of his
    placement.

7   Reports on prospective enrolments in special classes should be forwarded
    to the appropriate District Inspector of Schools who, following discus-
    sion with the principal teacher, class teacher, special class teacher and
    remedial teacher (if one is employed in the school), will advise the prin-
    cipal teacher regarding placement. Before a final decision is made it may
    be necessary to consult the Inspector dealing with special education for
    the area and/or the Department's psychological service. It is essential, of
    course, that the parents' consent be obtained before a child is placed in a
    special class.

8   A pupil who is at present enrolled in a special class but for whom a psy-
    chological and other reports are not available should not be removed
    from that class without consultation with the District Inspector and
    parents.

                                                                D. _ Laoghaire.
Deireadh Fomhair, 1977.   Rúnaí.

13

IRELAND RESPONSE: LIMITED RESOURCES FOR INCLUSION?

Jim Bennet, Hugh Gash and Mark O'Reilly focus on the education in main-stream primary schools of three children said to have 'a mild mental handicap'. The first is primarily in a special class and the other two in regular classes with some withdrawal. The authors of the study interpret notions of inclusion and exclusion as being about students categorised as having mental handicap, or disabilities, and they accept the sense and legitimacy of such categories. However, considerable differences emerge between the authors in their interpretation of the observations of the participation of students in school. On the one hand, inclusion is seen as allocated according to professional judgement and limited by the quantity of resources; on the other, it is seen as limited by professional assumptions and the way in which resources are deployed. The chapter indicates how education is affected by a distinctly Irish context, but because of the differences of view it contains, it provides a stark illustration of the chimera of single national perspectives.

How does the national context explain and constrain practice?

We are given only a brief sketch of Irish policy, though this is sufficient to sense the bearing on issues of inclusion of important aspects of Irish culture and policy. The emphasis is on the way special education policy affects the education placement of students said to have mild mental handicap. There is no discussion of the detail of general education policy.

All education policy is said to be primarily controlled through government advice, with little education law. In fact the first education law since the Irish constitution was established in 1920 was passed in 1993 (O'Buachalla 1988; Kavanagh 1993). Yet, just as in other countries, there has been a considerable debate, particularly at primary level, about the adaptability of the curriculum to student difference. This is of critical importance to understanding the capacity of schools to encourage the participation of students of differing attainments. A review of the primary curriculum advocated the greater use of child-centred education (Ireland 1971). The 1990 Review Body on the Primary Curriculum documented the lack of implementation of these proposals and highlighted the inflexibility of the upper primary years dominated by teacher-directed class activity (Ireland 1990). In a further review of Irish education policies in 1991 by the Organisation for Economic Cooperation and Development (OECD), it was reported:

> the aspirations and language of the reformers outstripped the willingness of the system as a whole to respond. . . . The reasons given vary from inadequacy of planning, implementation, follow-through and resources to teacher conservatism.
>
> OECD 1991, p. 65.

Compulsory education is from 6 to 15 years, and primary education, including pre-school, is thought of as running from 4 to 13 years. Some of the local terminology is confusing for these English ears. Thus primary schools have junior and senior students aged up to 9 and 9 to 13, respectively.

Primary education is non-denominational but is heavily influenced by the priests' representation on the schools' Boards of Management. Catholic liturgy is part of the curriculum and a student is referred to as 'integrated for learning about the sacraments'. We are reminded of the significance of religion in Northern Ireland where 'integrated' education means Catholics and Protestants in the same schools. This chapte, like those about the Netherlands and Norway, indicates a clear significance of religion for education policies and cultures. Catchment areas are linked to parish boundaries and this can serve to exclude unwanted students. In one of the urban schools the idea of communal allegiance based in housing estates is stressed.

In taking categories of 'inability' or disability for granted, it is assumed that the reader will make sense of the Irish terms. Students said to have mild mental handicap, defined according to government advice in 1965, are said in that advice to be 'permanently incapable of benefiting in the ordinary school curriculum'. Thus their label carries a presumption that they will be in segregated provision. Students categorised as having severe mental handicap are excluded from the education system in Ireland and no law to include them has been proposed even within the 1993 review of special education (Ireland 1993). Similar laws were passed for England in 1970, Scotland in 1974, the US in 1975 and Northern Ireland in 1986. No similar exclusion is still in existence for any other of the countries represented in this book.

Voices and perspectives on inclusion and exclusion

In this chapter we hear the voices of the authors, who are the two observers and the principal of school A. We also hear directly the views of the other two school principals, and indirectly the views of some teachers. The chapter also strongly represents a perspective emanating from official documents.

Clear differences of view are revealed between the authors as the chapter unfolds. The introduction appears as a detached text in which there is an apparent consensus of voice. The first observer then seems to break ground as he tries to make sense of his observations, and then the headteacher of the school responds by defending the policies of his school and asserting the naivity of the observer. The conclusion reasserts a theme of the introduction that 'goodwill counts for . . . little' without 'genuine practical support'.

The report of the Special Education Review Committee is criticised by the authors as having a bias in its concerns with special classes and special schools rather than provision in mainstream classes. However, its central orientations receive little critical examination, including its equivocal stance on the exclusion of some students with severe disabilities from the education system.

The review of special education (Ireland 1993) had argued for the maintenance of a continuum of *placement* for students categorised as having 'special needs', from mainstream to residential segregated schools, which it falsely identified with a continuum of *provision*. It associated more costly provision, particularly in terms of teacher–student ratios, with more segregated placement. Thus, it becomes possible to suggest that a student who requires considerable support to participate in education *needs* segregation. It is this adherence to a fixed notion of where provision is located that results in the formula 'integration as appropriate and segregation as necessary'. The association of continua of placement and provision is also a feature of policies in many other countries in this study and beyond. Continua of placement and provision are 'principles' of the code of practice in England and Wales (Booth 1994; DfE 1994). As has been noted, particularly in discussing the Scotland case-study, such a view asserts professional control over decisions about when 'segregation' is 'necessary', rather than recognising student and parent rights.

The principal of school A appears to support the idea that professional expertise should determine placement decisions, suggesting that students attend the special class as a result of the decisions of 'eminent psychologists'. This may be connected to his strong sense of the benevolence of the status quo; that all is as it is for good reasons. For example, primary schools naturally are less able to respond to individual differences as students get older and hence this explains why the three students with 'handicaps' are transferred to the special class. We are told that 'it is significant that [John] has transferred his allegiance completely to the special class and he rarely interacts with the pupils with whom he was in class for such a considerable period'. It seems that the school principal believes that John is naturally drawn to his own kind, although we might see the shift as partly a process of making John's difference from other students seem natural. The use by the special class of a prefabricated classroom outside the main school building is seen as an ordinary consequence of special class provision and is not thought by the principal to affect the status of these students within the school. Any challenge to the status quo is seen as a challenge to the good sense of influential professionals.

The first observer contests the view of the naturalness of John's placement and educational experience. He finds that John is less disabled than he had expected, that he is friendly towards others in his own class and in the 'mainstream' group, but that by and large his social encounters are restricted to the special class group. He concludes that 'the integration practices I observed, in my opinion, accentuated rather than mitigated exclusion'. He asks whether shared participation between categorised and non-categorised students might be increased. He thus supports the view of the special class teacher, mentioned by the principal, that interactions could be actively fostered. There is no notion of a school inclusion policy in any of the three schools, which might change the way these schools can respond to diversity. The first observer sees the degree of separation of the students as concerned with the prioritising of professional boundaries over educational needs, thus raising the notion of professional interest and challenging the official view. The principal attributes these views of the observer to a lack of 'knowledge and insight'.

There is considerable reference in this chapter to the resources required to support inclusion. The reduction of class sizes is seen as an important way to enable categorised students to participate in lessons. While we would not wish to deflect attention from the difficulty of working in under-resourced classrooms, the inflexibility of budgets has been a long-standing concern of Irish teachers trying to support students in the mainstream, as it is a feature of the early stuttering attempts to develop inclusion policies in the Netherlands. Whereas the first observer argues that greater inclusion would occur with a different use of available resources, the principal of school A argues that more resources are required before inclusion should proceed:

> Teachers in the Republic of Ireland are attempting to integrate children with special needs into mainstream classes without the support provided by reduced class sizes and extra resources.

The call for greater resources to support integration, or for the relocation of resources from special schools into the mainstream, can be interpreted as a challenge to one professional view of when 'segregation is necessary'. There appears to be a contradiction in the argument from the principal of school A that decisions about integration are a matter of the complex professional judgement of psychologists and that they depend most critically on the availability of resources, an argument commonly associated with the teaching unions in a number of countries.

The principal of school B has an equivocal view towards the inclusion of the students with Down syndrome, glad not to have been asked to include a child who was not toilet-trained, and reporting the teachers as unsure whether they would wish to repeat the experience of including Sarah and Bob, despite the fact that they had 'all . . . benefited from the experience'. The principal of school C comes closer to formulating a principle of inclusion when recognising that 'if I had a child who needed special education I would want him or her to be educated as normally as possible'. He is 'delighted with the way that the teachers are agreeing to work with integration so willingly', and says that the staff 'like the idea of integration'. He finds that 'the children in these classes [which include students with Down's syndrome] are nicer and kinder'. He does not link the success of inclusion to resources or the attainment of students but sees it as depending 'on the child's personality'.

But again, there is no school policy on the inclusion of these students, let alone one that links their inclusion to the participation of all students. Thus, the principal asserts that 'the only pupils who can be described as integrated are the ones with Down syndrome'. He also sees the inclusion of Bob and Sarah as depending on the goodwill of individual teachers: 'I also worry that I will have a problem in getting teachers to agree to have Sarah and Bob in their classes in the following year'.

The second observer sees the school experience of Bob and Sarah in a less positive light than the school principle. He observes the variation in Sarah's participation in different lessons and points out the difficulties that her teacher has in giving the time necessary to include her productively. In contrast to the first observer, he does not look for the way participation might be enhanced. He tells us that Bob is an integration failure and then provides a list of deficiencies: 'he is far too dependent, and he can do nothing on his own. He perseveres at nothing. He has little or no coordination'(p. 162). Since these statements could not be true of any living, breathing human being, they are evaluations of Bob, expressions of value and distance, rather than observations. They are rhetorical devices intended to support the contention that Bob's limited attainments preclude him from participation in the mainstream. They do not *report* on what Bob likes to do, and for how long, or evaluate the learning opportunities with which he is provided. The observer appears to attribute the presence of Bob and Sarah in the mainstream to pressure from the Down Syndrome Association. He seems to argue for a reduction of the participation of these students in the mainstream.

In the conclusion, school A's principal supports the view of the second observer, distancing them both from the first observer. The chapter concludes that the students with Down syndrome are 'physically present but not productively engaged' which seems to these readers an oversimplification of the limited data, since we feel that constructive and instructive efforts to support and include Sarah are described, and that these could be built on further. Our reaction to the data, of course, is no less revealing of the assumptions we bring to it than that of the authors of this study.

However, the attention to the differences in perspective of the authors should not obscure the similarities in their positions. They all see inclusion as about categorised students rather than all students. There is only an occasional understanding of the shift in perspective required by an appreciation of the many ways that inclusion and exclusion might be the result of interactions between students and the variety of resources available to support learning. In general, the assumption is made that categorised students require individualised curricula and individual attention if they are to be included. Thus 'Anna regularly checked on Sarah, but only for very brief periods of time. This meant that Sarah was excluded from many of the class activities requiring independent study' (p. 160). There is little exploration of what a pedagogy for inclusion might look like.

There is also a glaring unexamined gender issue in school A. It is a boys' school, yet the special unit is mixed in gender. This must affect the image that the female students in this unit have of themselves. Similarly, for schools B and C the principals and observer make no comment about the fact that Bob and Sarah are not placed with their age group. This disregard of the significance for students categorised as disabled or as having 'special needs' of gender issues or age groupings is common in our experience. It reinforces the notion that such students are 'them', occupying a space beyond normality.

The approach to preparing this case-study raises, in stark form, the issue of diplomacy in research into schools raised about the New Zealand case-study. In that report, as in the USA case-study, the authors argue for the involvement of teachers in research about their schools. Yet teachers may see themselves as the guardians of the good name of their schools and be concerned about the reporting of anything that may be seen to reflect negatively on their work. The authors here present a way forward from such dilemmas by allowing the conflicting voices to be heard.

14

AUSTRALIA: INCLUSION THROUGH CATEGORISATION?

Jeff Bailey

Introduction

This chapter is about the inclusion of Billy Gates, a student with Attention Deficit Hyperactivity Disorder (ADHD), in a small Catholic School, St Pat's. The school is in a regional centre, Toowoomba, in Queensland, the north-eastern state of Australia, a state known for its climate, beaches and barrier reef. Fictitious names are used for the family and the school. After explaining my approach to inclusion I provide details of the Australian and local educational contexts and then look at the inclusion of Billy from the perspective of his school and family. I conclude by looking at the implications of the study for the development of inclusive practice with students with ADHD.

Background to the study

I undertook a case-study of one young boy with Attention Deficit Hyperactivity Disorder (ADHD) to highlight a group of students who present unique educational challenges, but who are often ignored in the debate about inclusion. ADHD is one of the most consistently researched childhood conditions in the medical and psychological literature, but has achieved much less recognition in educational research. It is a syndrome of behaviours characterised by excessive and persistent inattentive, impulsive and/or hyperactive behaviour.

There is a long history of interest in conditions similar to ADHD commencing with the seminal work reported by Alfred Strauss and Laura Lehtinen (1947) on the psychopathology of brain-injured children. In the 1950s and 1960s there was continuing interest in students who appeared to have no organic impairments but who had very substantial learning and behavioural problems. Subsequently, learning disabilities, specific learning disabilities, attention deficit disorder and hyperactivity were attributed to 'minimal brain damage' and then 'minimal cerebral dysfunction'.

However, because of a lack of precise diagnostic criteria, a heavy reliance on parental reports and the absence of well-established psychological or neurological bases, many medical, educational and psychological professionals believe that there is insufficient empirical evidence to confirm the existence of this syndrome. Attempts to clarify diagnoses have been made through the description of three 'types' of ADHD and by expanding the list of criteria. However, inaccurate diagnoses and co-morbidity (in particular the co-existence with ADHD of learning disabilities and emotional disorders) obscure the validity of judgements made about students with ADHD (Sabatino and Vance 1994).

In using the term ADHD (American Psychiatric Association 1994) the cautions of Ballard (1995) about positivist approaches based upon medical and psychological frames of reference are noted. While being part of the professional patois used for convenience, a negative label that does not suggest any useful functional interventions can produce an unhealthy focus on defect, might produce lowered and different expectations and can be detrimental to the welfare and life opportunities of the labelled person. It is commonly assumed that a commitment to inclusiveness implies opposition to labels and their negative outcomes. To be brain-damaged or cerebrally dysfunctional implies an irreversible organic problem which must therefore require medical intervention. Such special considerations promote a perception that the child is 'abnormal'. Worse, the labels tend to avoid any functional emphasis that might be of benefit to the child we wish to include fully in the life of a school.

However, can appropriate services be provided without the use of the ADHD label? The relationship between categorisation and support is very marked in the USA, where the classification of students into approved disability categories entitles the parents and students to receive appropriate services. It was not until ADHD was accepted as a 'handicap' under Section 504 of the Rehabilitation Act that they became 'entitled to a free appropriate public education, due process and related services' (Reid et al. 1994, p. 117). Advocacy groups had to fight to get the services regarded as essential for students presenting with ADHD, and even then only half of the students with ADHD in USA schools qualified under the criteria for this category (ibid.). Funding on the basis of an identified category of disability in Australia is, fortunately, not as rigidly applied as in the USA, and greater weight is given to the views of teachers, but I argue that categorisation is necessary for appropriate services to be provided.

Many educators are wary of the involvement of psychologists and doctors in education and the use of medication in attempts to 'improve' the learning of students with attentional/impulsivity problems. The most commonly used medications are central nervous system stimulants, particularly Ritalin (methylphenidate) and Dexedrine (dexamphetamine). Both are amphetamines; both are designed to stimulate at the neurotransmitter level. There is a huge body of literature on both the adverse and the positive educational effects of such medication for students with ADHD (Garfinkel et al. 1986; Milich et al. 1991; Pelham et al. 1991), on prosocial behaviour (Buhrmester *et al.* 1992), on peer acceptance (Whalen *et al.* 1989), on interactions with mothers (Barkley, 1988) and even on reading (Cotter 1988; Cotter and Werner 1987). The general conclusion is that the use of these stimulants seems to reduce over-activity and impulsivity, and creates the neurological conditions that permit the student to focus on the learning. Parents accept medication very readily. Indeed eighty-two per cent of mothers reported that they had accepted the offer of medication for their ADHD children at the first consultation at which it was offered (Bailey and Curtis 1996). The reality is that students with ADHD are attending school, are often receiving support from medical and psychological professionals and are often taking medication to enhance their prospects for learning and social acceptance.

For the purposes of this chapter, inclusion refers to being in an ordinary school with other students, following the same curriculum at the same time, in the same classrooms, with full acceptance by all and in a way which makes the student feel no different from any other student. Attention to the inclusion of a child with ADHD brings into focus the argument that there has to be a trade-off between a philosophy of inclusion, the social integration it implies, and the provision of specialist services to meet the learning needs of students. Gerber (1994) highlights this issue when he says: 'tension exists about which principle of education for special needs students should have priority – social inclusion or specially designed instruction' (p. 375). My argument is that students with ADHD must be identified in order to receive the support they need to participate fully in the inclusive school and achieve comparable social and instructional outcomes to their non-labelled peers. Failure to do so marginalises them and restricts their educational opportunities.

The national and state contexts

Australia is an island continent of approximately the same land mass as the United States of America but with a population of only eighteen million, consisting of six states and two territories. The system of education is highly centralised and all schools receive government funding. Public schools are funded *in toto*, while for private schools the amount of subsidy depends on the wealth of the school. No local taxes are levied to support schools. Local communities, typically through Parents and Citizens Associations, are responsible for raising additional funds to supplement government funding, mainly in consumables, computers, library books and so on.

There are three loose groupings of schools: the government funded state system of education; the government subsidised Catholic system of education; and the other government subsidised private schools, either schools proposed under the Grammar Schools Act and hence non-denominational, or denominational schools supported by various churches, for example, the Anglican Church of Australia.

The Catholic system of education is very large and dispersed; all cities and large towns, and most small towns in Australia, have local Catholic schools. Catholic schools provide a religious-based education for all Catholic families, regardless of their financial status, in local neighbourhoods. Hence, there are many small Catholic schools. The fees for some Catholic schools are low, in the order of $150 per year, compared to $3,000–$6,000 for some other private schools. Consequently, the amount of money neighbourhood Catholic schools have for the provision of support for included students is relatively small. The relative poverty of the Catholic system, as compared to state schools, makes it unlikely that an area will contain separate special schools or that schools will contain special education units. Catholic students tend to be educated in inclusive settings. The normal support mechanism in the Catholic schools in the Toowoomba region is a full-time or part-time Learning Assistance Teacher. In the Catholic educational region in the city under investigation, there are no 'special' schools.

The role of the national government in determining curricula is of particular current interest. There is an intention to gradually introduce uniformity of curricula and standards across the nation but at this stage the new government has made no statements about national curricula. At the level of the syllabus, for example, in mathematics, science and language arts, state departments of education still produce their own documents and the use of these documents is mandated in government schools. Typically, non-government schools tend to use them in their own planning and instruction.

Policies on inclusion

The Queensland Department of Education has adopted a policy of inclusive schools and curricula within a framework of social justice. Whether the policy is implemented successfully or enthusiastically within schools depends, to a very large extent, on the local school. While many teachers are quite familiar with the concept of mainstreaming, there has not been an extensive campaign about inclusion in Queensland regular schools. In many schools there is a vast distance between endorsement of the principle and provision of inclusive programs and practices.

Indeed, in late 1995, one school in the state system of education sought the judgement of the courts to exclude a young girl with disabilities from the regular school. As well as extensive disabilities, this girl presented with severe behaviour disorders. After many efforts by the school system to accommodate the girl and to develop her skills so that she could remain within a regular school, the state department of education decided to place her in a segregated setting. Despite active lobbying and legal defence by support groups and the parents, the courts determined that the girl would receive her education in a segregated special school. Such an outcome flies in the face of the policy of inclusion. For the parents who obviously believed strongly in placement in the most normal setting, the court's decision must have been a bitter blow. While this case is interesting, it must be stated that such an event is not the norm throughout the state. The legal decision does emphasise, however, the need to be realistic about community attitudes to inclusion.

The organisation of schools

Compulsory education starts from the age of 5. In Queensland, there is normally a pre-school and seven grades. Most classes in Australia are organised on the basis of age. The typical approach to instruction in the state is a self-contained classroom in which a single teacher determines the scope and rate of curriculum. While team-teaching has been very much promoted for many years, it is not a wide-spread practice. Individualised instruction, a goal often revered in educational discussions, is less common than group and whole-class instruction. A range of specialists are typically used, particularly in the larger primary schools. These specialists include music, physical education, art, library and learning support teachers. Smaller schools, particularly in the Catholic system, have fewer specialist resources to draw upon within the school staff. Often, regional resource centres and itinerant consultants are the preferred methods for contributing specialist expertise to the system.

Gathering information

The study was approached with the following questions in mind:

- Does the 'dampening down' effect of the medication leave the student in such a neurologically depressed state that he is incapable of learning?
- Is the main purpose of the medication to relieve the management burdens of the parent and the management and instructional burdens of the teacher?
- As a result of being pharmacologically-controlled will the student fail to learn necessary self-discipline and social skills?
- Will the student develop depressed feelings of self-esteem because of reliance on the medication?
- With regard to social inclusion, will the child be seen as 'different' by the other students and, hence, be teased, bullied and/or socially rejected?

To address these questions, data were collected by interviews with Billy, the school principal, his mother and his teacher, and through the use of a survey questionnaire. The interviews were guided by the development of a teacher and student interview scale, although care was taken to ensure that respondents were able to provide their version of reality, unencumbered by the world view of the interviewer.

Additionally, two scales were developed to gain some idea of the teachers' perceptions of inclusive education. The first scale asked teachers to make a series of professional judgements about six vignettes which described students with different ADHD challenges and to make a judgement about the most suitable placement option from eight choices. The teachers' attitudes to the effects of inclusive education on students with ADHD were measured using a fourteen item, seven-point Likert scale. However, the very small number of teachers in the sample limits the statistical validity and 'generalisability' of conclusions about teacher judgements and perceptions.

The case-study

The Gates family live in Toowoomba, a city of some 86,000 people, on the edge of the Great Dividing Range at an altitude of 800 metres, 130 kilometres from Brisbane, the capital of Queensland. It is an educational centre, with some eighty day and boarding schools, a large College of Technical and Further Education and a regional university with an enrolment of 16,000 students. Known as the Garden City, Toowoomba has an image of being clean and beautiful. There is very little poverty compared to Queensland as a whole, in which it was recently reported that approximately twenty per cent of the state's population live below the poverty line. However, there are areas in Toowoomba which have very low socio-economic status. St Pat's is located in a low socio-economic area and it is likely that most of the families attending the school are low to middle income earners.

Billy's school, one of ten primary and secondary Catholic schools in Toowoomba, has 200 students, eight class teachers, one part-time Learning Assistance Teacher, a librarian and a non-teaching principal. The buildings of St Pat's school are old but very spacious, with quite a few small, vacant rooms available for alternative teaching activities. The grounds are adequate for the size of the school. Students typically come from an area within 2 kilometres of the school. There are virtually no students with significant developmental or learning problems at St Pat's. This situation has arisen from circumstance rather than from a policy of excluding students with disabilities.

Billy, a tall, thin, dark-haired boy in Grade 4, is the eldest of three children. He has a 7 year old sister, Tina, enrolled at the same school and a 4 year old brother, Colin. His father is a labourer in a local timber mill and when he arrives home at 5.00pm, Mrs Gates leaves for her part-time job in a local hotel. Mrs Gates, who bears the major responsibility for the rearing and management of the children, is small, shy and lacking in self-assurance. She is also extremely stressed by the task of managing Billy.

There is no evidence to suggest that this is a dysfunctional family, or one characterised by poor parenting. Indeed, Mrs Gates is well-respected by the school for her relations with the staff and for her efforts in raising her children. A conventional explanation for ADHD, particularly from those who do not believe in the syndrome, is that the behaviour is a result of poor parenting.

Were this the case, Tina and Colin would also present with inattentiveness, hyperactivity and impulsivity. This is not so.

At school, Billy is in his age appropriate grade and, apart from a certain distracted and vague air, is not noticeably different when one first observes the class. He has been in the school for approximately one year, having come from a very small school in a small town in southern Queensland, some 100 kilometres from Toowoomba. His levels of achievement are up to one year behind his current placement. He is receiving reading assistance from the Learning Assistance Teacher for two sessions per week in a withdrawal room close to his classroom. This type of learning support, usually focused on reading and maths, is typical of many Queensland schools. There are no counselling programmes provided within the school.

The views of Billy's mother

If a child is to be fully included in the life of a school, parents should be fully included as well. Parents should be equal partners in the process of schooling, fully involved in all the decisions the school makes about the child. They should feel confident that they can place their child in the school without fear of exclusion because the child is different or difficult. Many parents have had to fight long and frustrating battles to have their children accepted into regular education. These parents have often been regarded as trouble-makers because of their determination to get what is best for their children. In many cases, they have suffered extreme stress and anxiety, with little support from the school system, family and friends. Consequently, they should also be regarded by the school system as needing additional support to help them cope with the problems and additional stresses presented by their children.

At St Pat's, Mrs Gates has been received with a great amount of sympathy and compassion. While she is extremely stressed by having to cope with Billy, she feels that the school has been supportive and interested and has not suggested that Billy should be excluded from the school. This may have something to do with the religious basis of the school. If Christians have compassion and care for people, it should be easier to include difficult students fully into the life of the school.

One problem with ADHD is that few professionals are prepared to make an early diagnosis. Mrs Gates knew intuitively that something was wrong within a few months of Billy's birth, and as he grew older she found him progressively more difficult to control, but the medical professionals did not share her view:

MRS GATES: I kept taking him to the doctors – they just said it was me.
INTERVIEWER: What did they say to you?
MRS GATES: They used to say 'You are just paranoid, it is just you, it's just a typical boy doing boy things.'
INTERVIEWER: Typical boy? Did they tell you you were a bad parent?

MRS GATES: Yes. They told me that it was my fault that I couldn't control him.

She described the scene that took place when he came home from school and she asked him to attend to his schoolwork:

He'd get home. I'd tell him and his sister to get to the table and do their homework. She would get up, no worries, and do hers. Billy would say I haven't got any; we didn't get any today. I'd check his port and it would be in there with a note from his teacher saying what he had to do. I'd say 'How come you told me there was no homework?' and he'd say he couldn't write it down fast enough off the black board so he would only get so far and he couldn't get it down quick enough. I would sit next to him and help him do it for about five or ten minutes. He would do it and then he would lose his concentration. He would start to do like his spelling but there was no way he could do it – he would miss out letters in his spelling. He knew which one it was but he would miss them out.

She was asked how she reacted when he refused to cooperate, and she replied that she would 'just scream at him':

What would end up happening would be I'd probably make him do it and if that didn't work I used to ban him from watching TV. Turn the TV off 'cause he'd watch TV while he was doing his homework. Some days he was OK – he'd do it but it would take hours to do.

Eventually, Billy was diagnosed as ADHD and put on dexamphetamine. Mrs Gates noted the considerable change that this brought in his behaviour. He settles down to do his homework readily without the 'fighting and screaming matches' that regularly occurred previously:

He's a lot calmer – he is not so aggro. He can sit down and do stuff but before he couldn't do it – it's boring, he'd say . . . he'd just crack up – didn't want to do nothing. He can sit down and do his homework – before he used to take an hour or two to get him to even attempt to do it – now I just have to tell him and he goes straight to do it.

At several points during the interview, she burst into tears. Clearly the pressure of dealing with a child who is so difficult to manage is intense. Billy can also be extremely physically and verbally abusive of his siblings, particularly his younger sister. He creates an enormous amount of pain for a young mother who cannot work out why her son is like he is. She feels guilty and worried and that she has very little support in dealing with Billy.

The views of Billy's teacher

Mr James feels that he has a good working relationship with Billy and is supportive and accepting of him. He keeps in touch with the family doctor and has read the reports from the speech therapist and occupational therapist, and has regular contact with the Learning Assistance Teacher. He says that before the medication Billy would not settle down and was disruptive; consequently, he got 'picked on' by some of the teachers. However, 'the day Billy started the medication he was a new boy' and these positive effects lasted all day. There are now no problems with the other teachers. He is happy with the progress Billy is making with his schoolwork and reports that he only occasionally gets into trouble when he 'is just not doing the right thing at the right times'. Billy is now 'a model pupil, he's good, a pleasure to have, and he often wants to stay to finish what he's doing'.

At one time, Billy's mother ran out of dexamphetamine and she used another drug (Norpramin) which had a very different effect. Billy became seriously disruptive, raced around the room upsetting everything and took scissors to his own hair, cutting off very large chunks of it.

Billy has decided that he does not need any more support from the Learning Assistance Teacher, since a new boy in the class started to receive reading assistance. It is possible that he feels some 'difference' by having to go to learning assistance. It is also possible, according to the teacher, that 'Billy does not feel he has to go as he believes he is making progress'.

Billy plays with children of his own age and is not teased, otherwise bullied or socially excluded. He participates in games with other children if he feels like it but if he doesn't he wanders away. His peers are said to be 'very accepting' of Billy and his behaviour even though they know they could not do the same, and they give him 'a lot of support'. Mr James was not sure whether the other students know he is on medication. Despite the erratic behaviour Billy displayed in the past Mr James does not think they see Billy 'as a potential harm to themselves'.

Billy's view

Billy reports that he has quite a few friends, mostly in his current grade, although he has little contact with other students after school, mainly because he lives in an area where there are no other school children. He is never teased, or bullied or left out.

He says that he pays attention all the time during class. He is very happy about taking his medication and feels that he is much better at school when he is on it, although he is not sure that he is much better at home. He said that he would not worry if other students knew he was taking medication. Occasionally he fights with his brother and sister at home, a source of concern reported by his mother, and 'sometimes' it is his fault. He gets into trouble with his teacher, his father and mother occasionally. Sometimes he is unhappy and worries.

To gain some idea of Billy's world view of the support mechanisms around him, he was asked to complete a 'circle of friends and support' form; that is, a model of three concentric circles in which he is placed in the inner, smallest circle and he shows by their placement in one of the three circles how many people provide close (strong) or far (weak) support. Here Billy reported a wide range of support. Specifically, he mentioned his Dad, Mum, and Aunty and Uncle, as well as both maternal and paternal grandparents. He placed his family doctor and paediatrician in the inner circle, along with his class teacher, Learning Assistance Teacher and five friends. He placed his brother and sister in the next circle but it is possible that this was more to do with lack of understanding of the idea of proximal support than a rejection of them. It is also possible that he sees his siblings as competitors, rather than supporters, a view his mother's comments would endorse.

As Billy did not respond readily, a rating scale was used which required fewer verbalisations. The idea was that he would rate himself along a 10 point scale on a number of dimensions, 10 being the very best and 0 being the worst. Billy responded well to this type of task. His results give a clear insight into his self-appraisal of his ability and achievement, his current emotions and his social relations (see Table 14.1).

Table 14.1 Billy's self-ratings

Getting on with people	Rating	Ability/ achievements	Rating
Class teacher	[10]	Cricket	[4]
Father	[10]	Sport in general	[7]
Mother	[10]	Reading	[5]
His sister	[10]	Spelling	[6]
His brother	[10]	Mathematics	[$4^{1}/_{2}$]
Boys in his class	[10]	Intelligence	[$4^{1}/_{2}$]
Girls in his class	[10]	Happiness	[7]

The results of his responses and ratings suggest that he is very happy with his current school circumstances. He sees himself as getting on very well with everyone and indicates that he has a large amount of support. His self-ratings on achievement and intelligence suggest that he is self-aware. He sees himself as being accepted socially and personally by the class. He is not positive about attending reading assistance either because he feels it is not necessary or because he does not like to be singled out for this type of attention.

Teacher attitudes

There are few studies of teacher attitudes toward inclusive education. It is important to ensure when examining such attitudes that the type of special needs is specified in a clear and detailed way. Teachers' attitudes vary according to the type of disability and the extent of instructional adaptations to be made to accommodate the student. It is also essential that consideration be given to all the elements of inclusiveness, that is, being included in the school environment physically, socially and instructionally. It is important, too, to differentiate between a value held about a policy and teachers' feelings about their professional competence and preparation to put that policy into practice.

A study by Wilczenski (1992) found that teachers felt more positive about students who required programmes focusing on social integration than those requiring physical changes to the classroom; they were more accepting of students with physical disabilities rather than those who required academic modifications; and were more positive about accepting into their classrooms students with academic needs than those presenting with behaviour problems.

The instrument used in this study with teachers in the school was developed as a starting point to a more focused investigation of teachers' feelings about inclusiveness, with particular reference to students with ADHD. Six vignettes representing different types of ADHD behaviour were prepared. For example:

> Jane is 9 years of age, in the appropriate grade for her age, shy and withdrawn and under-achieving in most subjects. Her major problem is that she cannot concentrate, she appears to be in a day dream all the time, and she rarely pays any attention to the teacher or to lessons. She is not emotionally disturbed or depressed, she just cannot pay attention. She never causes any problems.

Teachers were asked to recommend in-school and out-of-school interventions, to make judgements about the benefits of inclusive education and to comment on teachers' preparation for teaching students with ADHD. For each vignette they were asked to choose the most appropriate of seven placements:

- Regular class with no intervention.
- Regular class with an Individualised Education Plan.
- Regular class with daily withdrawal.
- A resource room.
- A full-time special class in the regular school.
- A segregated special class.
- A non-educational setting.

A correlational analysis showed that there is a weak but positive correlation between where a student should be placed on an inclusive (high score) – exclusive (low score) dimension and their attitudes toward inclusive education ($r = .235$), and a positive but strong correlation between teacher placement and the level of teacher preparation for teaching students with ADHD ($r = .801$). There is also a positive and strong correlation between teachers' attitudes toward inclusive education and the level of teacher preparation for teaching students with ADHD ($r = .573$). The first correlation suggests that teachers may believe that inclusive education is a good practice but they may wish to place students with ADHD in more exclusive settings. The second correlation implies that if teachers know a lot about ADHD and are well-prepared to teach students with ADHD they will place them in more inclusive settings. Finally, if teachers are knowledgeable and well-prepared it is more likely that they will feel more positive about inclusive education.

Teachers may hold equivocal but not necessarily contradictory views about inclusiveness for students with ADHD. The first ten items of the questionnaire, which is shown in the chapter appendix, were designed to tap teachers' views about inclusive education. It was noticeable that the means varied greatly. While the total mean was 4.9 and most of the means were close to this, there were three outlier scores: items 3 (mean of 6.0), 6 (mean of 4.0) and 7 (mean of 2.6). Item 3 is about the effect of including a child with ADHD in an ordinary classroom rather than a segregated setting on the child's social adjustment. Obviously, the teachers believe in the social value of inclusiveness for the included child, however, when they were asked whether such a placement would have a negative effect on the other children, there was less assurance that inclusion would be so good (item 6). In item 7, when asked whether inclusion would provide more opportunities for the included child to profit from specialised instruction for the ADHD problem, the very low mean of 2.6 indicated their lack of confidence in the provision of relevant instruction for the child in an included setting.

Conclusion: implications for practice

This case-study is exploratory. The measurement of teachers' placement judgements and attitudes toward inclusive education and students with ADHD requires further development. However, several important points have arisen:

- Little is known of the inclusion of students with ADHD. We need to understand better the social and academic implications of having students with ADHD in inclusive settings.
- While Billy seems to be well-accepted socially and academically in his school, other students with ADHD may not receive the same comprehensive and compassionate consideration.

- Information from several perspectives is needed to inform the inclusion debate for students with ADHD (see Rice and Bailey 1996). To maximise the benefits of inclusion for such students, educators may have to learn from professionals whose approaches seem to be in conflict with the philosophy of inclusion. For example, while Billy is medicated he appears to be fully included; when not medicated, he moves towards the 'excluded' end of the continuum. Despite the equivocal results of efficacy studies of psycho-stimulants, clinical and first-hand experience suggests that the use of medication for some of these students increases their chances of effective inclusion.
- While teachers may support the social and developmental benefits of inclusion, in principle, many may feel that a more segregated setting could provide the specialised instruction needed for these students, particularly the very active and physically aggressive.
- A mix of placement/programme options may be perceived to be more practical and helpful than an all-or-nothing approach to inclusion.
- Teachers will be more positive about including students with ADHD if they are well-prepared professionally.
- Different individuals with ADHD may present different inclusion challenges at different times. Thus possibilities for inclusion may be affected by whether a student with attention deficit is also hyperactive, whether the student is male or female, younger or older, and whether there is co-morbidity (i.e. there are additional problems). The gender ratios usually quoted for ADHD are four to six times as many boys as girls. There is a general understanding that while people do not grow out of ADHD, they develop better coping skills in adolescence. There is also a growing appreciation that ADHD often exists concurrently with other problems, particularly learning disabilities and emotional disorders.
- Effective inclusion of students with ADHD will require an integrated approach to their management and education.

Students with ADHD should be brought into the centre of the inclusion debate. This debate must recognise the complexity of the behaviours that characterise these students and their need for planned and comprehensive case management. To do any less is to deny their rights to effective inclusion.

APPENDIX: TEACHERS' PERCEPTIONS OF THE EFFECTS OF THE EDUCATION OF STUDENTS WITH ADHD IN ORDINARY CLASSROOMS

Please respond to each of the 14 items by placing a tick or cross in ONE of the 7 boxes for which the polar labels are Strongly Disagree and Strongly Agree.

The reference is to inclusive education which, for the purpose of this survey, means being in an ordinary school with other students, learning the same curriculum, at the same time, in the same classrooms, with full acceptance by all and in a way which makes the student feel no different from any other student.

The expression ADHD refers to students with attention deficit hyperactivity disorder, a syndrome of behaviours characterised by a large and persistent amount of inattentive, impulsive and/or hyperactive behaviour.

A 'segregated setting' would be a special school or a special full-time resource room with students identified as having disabilities/problems of such a degree that 'regular' teachers could not teach them.

The expression 'regular teachers' refers to those teachers teaching in an 'ordinary' classroom, that is, not one classified as being part of special education.

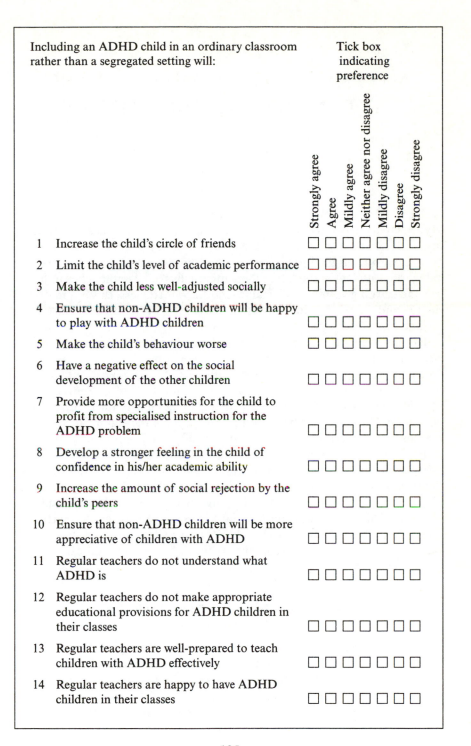

Including an ADHD child in an ordinary classroom rather than a segregated setting will:	Tick box indicating preference						
	Strongly agree	Agree	Mildly agree	Neither agree nor disagree	Mildly disagree	Disagree	Strongly disagree
1 Increase the child's circle of friends	☐	☐	☐	☐	☐	☐	☐
2 Limit the child's level of academic performance	☐	☐	☐	☐	☐	☐	☐
3 Make the child less well-adjusted socially	☐	☐	☐	☐	☐	☐	☐
4 Ensure that non-ADHD children will be happy to play with ADHD children	☐	☐	☐	☐	☐	☐	☐
5 Make the child's behaviour worse	☐	☐	☐	☐	☐	☐	☐
6 Have a negative effect on the social development of the other children	☐	☐	☐	☐	☐	☐	☐
7 Provide more opportunities for the child to profit from specialised instruction for the ADHD problem	☐	☐	☐	☐	☐	☐	☐
8 Develop a stronger feeling in the child of confidence in his/her academic ability	☐	☐	☐	☐	☐	☐	☐
9 Increase the amount of social rejection by the child's peers	☐	☐	☐	☐	☐	☐	☐
10 Ensure that non-ADHD children will be more appreciative of children with ADHD	☐	☐	☐	☐	☐	☐	☐
11 Regular teachers do not understand what ADHD is	☐	☐	☐	☐	☐	☐	☐
12 Regular teachers do not make appropriate educational provisions for ADHD children in their classes	☐	☐	☐	☐	☐	☐	☐
13 Regular teachers are well-prepared to teach children with ADHD effectively	☐	☐	☐	☐	☐	☐	☐
14 Regular teachers are happy to have ADHD children in their classes	☐	☐	☐	☐	☐	☐	☐

15

AUSTRALIA RESPONSE: PAYING ATTENTION TO DISORDER?

In his chapter, Jeff Bailey has brought his concern with Attention Deficit Hyperactivity Disorder to the task of illuminating the issues of inclusion and exclusion through a school case-study. His study of Billy is, perhaps, furthest from our original guidelines in concentrating on the difficulties of a categorised student and relating them minimally to the approaches to teaching and learning within a particular school. Nevertheless, this is a matter of degree and there are similarities in these respects with the study from Ireland.

Jeff argues that Billy cannot get what he needs without a medical diagnosis, pertinently, because much of what he needs comes in the form of tablets, which, he reports, make a dramatic difference to his education. He challenges us to think more widely about the significance of categorisation in identifying the needs of students and in including them in the mainstream of education. His study can be used, too, to reinforce the significance of connecting a consideration of the exclusion of students on the grounds of difficulties in behaviour to concerns about attainment and disability and other exclusionary pressures in education. He reminds us that different students may pose different challenges for inclusion and that we may need to check that we share a common understanding of who should be included in and excluded from education (see Booth 1983). Whatever the particular merits of labelling Billy as having ADHD, this latter interpretation would put this chapter at the centre of discussions of inclusion and exclusion in education.

How does the national context explain and constrain practice?

Jeff describes the Australian education system as 'highly centralised'. This conflicts with the view of Ward (1993) who has noted that as far as special education is concerned, at least, the Australian states present a 'bewildering diversity of philosophies and practices' (p. 135). Jeff describes a mixed economy in all Australian schools with some being more private than others because they receive less public funds. This system, overtly stated here, is a feature of education in all countries, since the resources available to support learning always depend on the material, human and cultural capital in the students' homes, whether or not money actually changes hands from home to school. He mentions the particular features of Catholic education, in which a low level of funding has led to the establishment of less segregated provision than in the rest of the education system.

There is interest in Australia in the idea of a national curriculum but currently the curriculum is mandated at the state level. Jeff suggests that the Queensland department of education has adopted policies of inclusive schools and curricula within a framework of social justice. However, he argues that in practice the implementation of these policies is largely determined by individual schools. This flexibility in the system is echoed in arrangements for providing additional resources for categorised students. Jeff notes that 'funding on the basis of an identified category of disability in Australia is, fortunately, not as rigidly applied as in the USA, and greater weight is given to the views of teachers'. However, he provides little explanation of the details of such funding policies.

Looking elsewhere for insights into the development of policies for inclusion in education in Australia, Swan (1994) suggests that inclusive education, defined as the 'right to equitable education access, participation and outcomes for all students', is now official policy throughout the country (p. 361). However, Roger Slee, who has written extensively about this theme, is much less certain (Slee 1995; 1996). He notes that certainly many legislative conditions, not least the Commonwealth Disability Discrimination Act 1992, are in place so that parents can reasonably expect that their disabled child will have the choice of attending a regular school. However, he remains unconvinced that this happens in practice, pointing to the continuing disputes that occur between parents, teachers and administrators over matters to do with inclusion and exclusion. Speaking specifically about Queensland, he describes how a teacher union and parents of non-disabled students lobbied the state authorities 'for the retention and extension of segregated special school provision for disabled students' (Slee 1996, p. 20). In general, Slee's own conclusion is that the main difficulty arises from the way in which inclusive schooling is conceptualised as but a 're-articulation' of the 'dividing practices' of special education. Inclusion, as it is currently interpreted, he argues, 'doesn't challenge the disabling foundations of school organisation, pedagogy and curriculum' (p. 26). Looking to the future he is also anxious about current proposals in Queensland, possibly influenced by English reforms, to introduce performance standards and achievement benchmarks at various stages of schooling.

Voices and perspectives on inclusion and exclusion

The chapter presents the voice of the author, his focus on a medical view of school difficulties, and examines the views of Billy, Billy's mother and teacher. We are also presented with a quantitative study of the attitudes of the teachers in the school to inclusion in education. There seems to be something of a hole in the story. We are told about a child whose mother is said to be 'the main carer' yet, from 5pm every day, Billy is in the care of his father. It would have been informative to have been given some knowledge of the father's point of view.

Jeff argues that the Christian orientation of the school may provide it with a distinctive perspective on inclusion. He argues that the readiness of Billy's school to include him, a commitment to its community, 'may have something to do with the religious basis of the school'. It seems that this may be a persuasion he shares when he adds, 'if Christians have compassion and care for people, it should be easier to include difficult students fully into the life of the school'. Yet, while religious schools may reach out to include students within a defined community, they may also exclude students overtly by admissions policies and informally within aspects of the culture and curriculum of the school.

From the chapter we learn that Jeff's view of inclusion is to do with the placement, participation and acceptance of categorised students. Thus, we are told that 'there are virtually no students with significant developmental or learning problems at St. Pat's', and this can be taken to justify the sole concentration on Billy. Jeff defines 'inclusive education' as 'being in an ordinary school with other students, following the same curriculum at the same time, in the same classroom, with full acceptance by all and in a way which makes the student feel no different from any other student'. In our study and in relation to the New Zealand and Norwegian studies, we have discussed the disadvantages of setting up inclusive education as an ideal state, rather than a set of never-ending processes. In the version of the definition here, we would argue that an undesirable state is described, populated by a homogenised normality. The idea that all students can follow the same curriculum at the same time ignores a reality of the way students learn and implies a view of curriculum as the plans of a teacher, executed under very tight control. An unintended consequence of the aim that no students should 'feel any different from any other student' can be an intolerance to diversity. In our view inclusion requires support for and celebration of difference. Through the case-study of Billy it is apparent that inclusion is partly seen as about the acceptance of Billy's difference and the legitimacy of him responding differently within lessons. Yet if it is his label, and the negative connotations that are associated with being described as having Attention Deficit Hyperactivity Disorder, which grants him a special licence to be treated differently, then this may suppress an acceptance of the difference of others.

The caricature of inclusive education, that it involves treating all students the same, underpins Jeff's argument that 'there has to be a trade-off between a philosophy of inclusion, the social integration it implies, and the provision of specialist services to meet the learning needs of students'. What is the status of this argument? In an earlier version of it, in England, Peter Mittler (1979, p. 101) argued that decisions about whether a child should go to a special or a mainstream school involved 'reconciling the child's educational and learning needs with the need to maintain contact with ordinary children'. It seemed then that integration was being given an educationally unacceptable definition in order to persuade people to oppose it.

In several of the other chapters students are labelled using a series of terms to depict disabilities and deficits without critical examination or a clear explanation of the meanings of the term within that country or to the particular groups of people who feature in the case-study. It seems, then, that the terms are assumed to have international currency even though it must be clear that different expressions are used in different countries. Jeff makes such an assumption explicit, attempting to give the notion of ADHD international status as a 'disorder' whose meaning can be tied down by the American Psychiatric Association, the imperial standard. We argue that this involves an unrealistic view of the possible degree of international control over language and social practices. For we can still ask, as we did of Jeff after an early edit of the chapter, how the term is used in Australia, and Towoomba. More specifically, what similarities can we assume between Jon categorised as having ADHD in Berg in Norway, and Billy in Australia? We are given the definition of ADHD as 'a syndrome of behaviours characterised by a large and persistent amount of inattentive, impulsive and/or hyperactive behaviour'. We can be sure that the vagueness and breadth of such a concept will result in different professionals and parents giving it widely different interpretations. Roger Slee provides an alternative Australian perspective in which he deplores the rise in categorisation of students as having ADHD (Slee 1996).

As in several chapters, we are meant to accept that it is not only correct to apply a particular label to some students, but that it is in fact correctly applied to the students in the study. Yet, although we are told that there are three types of ADHD, there is no discussion of which type Billy has. There is a recognition of the contested nature of ADHD, acknowledged to be a reincarnation of earlier notions of minimal brain damage. It is not mentioned that another attempt to medicalise difficulties of behaviour through the notion of 'hyperactivity' syndrome, using treatment with the same drugs, was also subjected to strong critique in the 1970s particularly through Schrag and Divoky's (1975) 'the myth of the hyperactive child'. Problems associated with diagnosis need to be answered if the apparent scientific precision of Jeff's approach is to be maintained.

Jeff argues that 'to be brain damaged or cerebrally dysfunctional implies an irreversible organic problem which must therefore require medical intervention'. From a careful reading of the text it seems that he believes that ADHD is similarly 'organic'. There are several difficulties with the argument here, not least a dualism between mind and body that is involved in contrasting organic and non-organic 'problems'. But, further, there is no logical connection between impairment and the need for medical intervention.

He rejects an alternative to his position – that Billy may be like he is because of the way he has grown up:

> A conventional explanation for ADHD, particularly from those who do not believe in the syndrome, is that the behaviour is a result of poor parenting. Were this the case, Tina and Colin would also present with inattentiveness, hyperactivity and impulsivity. This is not so.

Yet, this implies a mechanical view of parenting that denies everything we know about the complexity of family relationships. Not all the differences between children can be attributed to their congenital condition. It seems, too, that the fact that more boys are diagnosed as having ADHD than girls is seen as evidence of congenital origins. Such vast disparities between the identification and categorisation of boys and girls as difficult in behaviour, leads us to conclude that it is social rather than medical intervention that is required.

Jeff's central argument is that categorisation of students with ADHD is essential 'for appropriate services to be provided'. He does not argue this on the pragmatic grounds that the funding system requires it as in the US. Funding systems that depend on categorisation actually encourage the creation and extension of medical labels for educational difficulties and may result in a competition for special funds between different categories of student.

Jeff's argument is quite specific: medical categorisation is essential in order for tablets to be prescribed, and these are the key to educational improvement. This is his trump card in the face of problems over diagnosis or a concern that such labelling is damaging; medical intervention works generally for students categorised as having ADHD and particularly in Billy's case. We are told that there is a 'reality' that 'students with ADHD are attending school and are often taking medication to enhance their prospects for learning and social acceptance'. In support of the sense of giving children medication it is reported that in one study 'eighty-two per cent of mothers reported that they had accepted the offer of medication for their ADHD children at the first consultation at which it was offered (Bailey and Curtis 1996)'. Such high rates of compliance with drug use may say more about the power of the medical profession than the wisdom of forgoing a pause for thought when drugs are offered.

However, we are provided with strong evidence that medication makes a considerable difference to Billy's behaviour and his readiness to learn. His mother thinks he is 'a lot calmer'; his teacher now sees him as a 'model pupil'; 'there are no problems with other teachers'; and Billy 'feels that he is much better at school' when on medication. Yet the fact that medical intervention has a 'positive' effect is not sufficient evidence for the desirability of its use. It leaves unanswered a range of questions which might tip the balance to alternative approaches to Billy's problems. What are the short- and long-term side-effects of taking the drugs both directly in Billy's bodily reactions, and indirectly in a dependency on a medical approach to solving problems that may prevent us looking at solutions that, ultimately, may be more productive for Billy and for other students?

One side-effect of adopting a strictly medical view of difficulties is that it leads Jeff to speak about students in particular ways. Thus a girl *'presented with severe behaviour problems'*; students who appear to have more than one problem have *'co-morbidity'*, and a difficulty traced to family interactions makes that family *'dysfunctional'*. It seems to us that such language is likely to separate some children and families from others in the minds of teachers, establishing them as 'abnormal'.

Such an approach also fosters the idea that certain children cannot be the responsibility of the mainstream teachers, because their disorders can only be alleviated by specialists. In the appendix to his chapter, Jeff defines a 'segregated setting' as 'a special school or a special full-time resource room with students identified as having disabilities/problems of such a degree that 'regular' teachers could not teach them'. This implies a degree of precision that sustains an image of special educators and those who advise them as expert scientists. While a clear case can be made for specialist knowledge in some circumstances, for example in teaching sign-language to deaf students, such knowledge does not have to be located in segregated settings and can be acquired by mainstream teachers. Further, in practice segregated settings contain a wide range of students taught by people with widely differing aptitudes for teaching.

We agree that the educational prospects of some students are enhanced by the diagnosis of physical difficulties which are then ameliorated medically: the treatment of the heart defects associated with Down syndrome provides a useful example. However, the history of the education of students with Down syndrome over the last twenty years has involved an attempt to shift away from educational interventions based on generalisations about people with that label, towards making an appropriate response to the real skills and interests of individuals. Treating a large proportion of students thought to behave badly as if they have a medical condition which requires a single solution would appear to threaten such progress for many students.

Jeff suggests that those who display a 'commitment to inclusiveness' are generally opposed 'to labels and their negative outcomes'. While some people may talk as if we can dispense with all 'labels', it makes no sense to suggest that we should dispense with all characterisations of people. It is the negative effects of some labels that may have an exclusionary effect if they accentuate difference, distort perceptions of identity, and, in amalgamating a variety of students, mislead teachers and others about how these students might learn, what they should be taught and by whom.

Jeff suggests that, as well as being written for this book, the case-study was pursued in order to develop research instruments. He questions the value of the statistics he obtains on the small sample of teachers but then presents and discusses them. We have doubts about the precision of such methods. For example, we find it highly questionable whether teachers can give an unequivocal meaning to the items on Wilczenski's questionnaire (Wilczenski 1992) that Jeff draws upon in his case-study. We argue, too, that Jeff's sampling of attitudes to 'children with ADHD' actively promotes a view of the legitimacy of such a category of student and the extent of their difference from the 'norm'.

The study does not provide us with a sense of the interactions that occur within the classroom, the curriculum and pedagogy that is experienced, nor, indeed, the way other students apart from Billy are behaving. So we have little impression of what Billy's school is really like. Without this information it is difficult for us to judge whether his medication serves to ensure his compliance to a regime that is largely irrelevant or insensitive to him and, possibly, others in his class. The study thus points to potential dangers in traditional special education research which focuses almost exclusively on individuals or categorised groups of children and their characteristics without close attention to the wider context.

16

ENGLAND: INCLUSION AND EXCLUSION IN A COMPETITIVE SYSTEM

Tony Booth, Mel Ainscow and Alan Dyson

Introduction: approaching inclusion

You can imply by all sorts of ways in the hidden curriculum that some students are more estimable than others and I hope that we are very much alive to that. We would always celebrate a student getting a job or a student getting a place on a scheme [an employment training scheme] or a student getting a place in an FE [Further Education] college and announce it and talk about it and celebrate it just as much as a student getting a place at university.

Head of Sixth Form, Richard Lovell High

In this chapter we explore the processes of inclusion and exclusion in education by examining how Lovell Community High School recognises and responds to student diversity and how this is affected by local and national policies. The school is a mixed-sex school for 1,550 students aged 11–19, and a provider of day and evening courses and activities for adults in the surrounding area. We examine the contradictory pressures on schools that seek to include and value students in a competitive educational climate which creates economic and social pressures to devalue and exclude students. Thus we link the processes of inclusion and exclusion operating within and on schools.

We follow this introduction with an account of government pressures towards selection by attainment between and within schools, and then describe the history of the school. We asked ourselves what an international audience might need to know in order to make sense of the processes of inclusion and exclusion at the school. We then present our analysis of how this school responds to diversity in terms of the ways students are categorised, grouped, taught, supported and disciplined. We suggest that such 'organisational responses to diversity' provide a framework against which students are valued, and inclusion and exclusion within the school can be understood. We then report our observations of classroom practice and the variation in participation of students they revealed. We conclude by looking at how national policies are shaping the future of the school.

Some people talk as if we can identify schools which are or are not 'inclusive' (see, for example, Mittler 1995). An inclusive school might be said to be one that includes, and values equally all students from its surrounding communities or neighbourhood or catchment area, and develops approaches to teaching and learning that minimise groupings on the basis of attainment and disability. However, by this definition there are no inclusive schools in England. For such an inclusive school is an elusive ideal, existing when no difference is devalued within society. The ideal of an inclusive school is undermined specifically by government policies, which encourage competition and selection between and within schools as well as by the continued exclusion of students on grounds that include disability and low attainment. The development of an inclusive school might be seen, then, as a goal of education, never fully attained.

We regard inclusion and exclusion as processes rather than events, and define them respectively as the processes of increasing and reducing the participation of students in the curricula, cultures and communities of neighbourhood, mainstream schools. Any real school, at any one time, reflects a complex interplay of including and excluding forces, acting on individuals and groups of students.

Approaching the school

There was some disagreement between us about the choice of school. The school includes a large number of students categorised as having 'severe learning difficulties'[1] and students with visual disabilities. At first, we differed about whether selecting a school that included a group of students who had previously attended special schools was an advantage because it demonstrated a concern of the school with inclusive education, or a disadvantage because it might distract us from examining critically inclusion and exclusion at the school and the processes of inclusion and exclusion affecting all students. Alan and Mel were keener on the choice of school than Tony, as revealed in the memos that we wrote to each other at the time. Alan felt that 'this is a school which sets out to be inclusive . . . in addressing overt forms of exclusion, it will make it easier to see more covert forms'. Mel too welcomed that:

we have agreed to observe the work of a school where there are

---

1 'Severe learning difficulties' is a broad informal category that in former times was given apparent precision by IQ test scores. The category covers students with the lowest attainments and encompasses those with limited or even no apparent understanding of language. However, students with the most severe disabilities were not included at Richard Lovell.

pupils who are generally excluded from English secondary schools . . . it allows me [to ask]:

- How does a school in our highly segregated system come to swim against the tide?
- What impact does this have on thinking and practice for *all* students in the school?

Tony had felt that 'we should deliberately steer away from selecting a school that could be thought to represent "good practice". A large number of students categorised as disabled or as having "severe learning difficulties" . . . [might] divert us from scrutinising the processes of inclusion and exclusion throughout the school'. However, we agreed finally that the presence of a large group of categorised students could enrich the study, provided we subjected all aspects of the school to critical scrutiny.

For most of the students with visual disabilities or categorised as having severe learning difficulties, the school was not their neighbourhood school. It might be seen as a 'mainstream special school', where there is a concentration of resources formerly allocated to an isolated separate special school. This is an increasing practice in England, and is often the preferred option for local policy makers when a special school closes. We discuss below how the idea that children should attend their neighbourhood school has been eroded for all children.

To prepare this study, the three of us visited the school together for three days in each of three terms, as part of our commitment to reflect the changes in the school over a three year period. We sent a letter to the school which set out our interest in 'researching and developing the ways in which ordinary schools can respond to the diverse needs and characteristics of their students and hence provide effective education for all students in their localities'. We asked the school to arrange a link person: in the event, our visits were coordinated by two people, the deputy head in charge of the school curriculum and the head of what the school called its 'special needs department'.

We had expressed a wish to shadow groups of students, and when we arrived we were each presented with timetables which attached us to groups for the whole period of our first visit. The groups had been selected because they contained one or two students who had Statements, documents which are meant to guarantee additional 'special' provision for students identified as having learning difficulties. We were handed 'pupil profiles' about these students which began with the identification of their difficulties in terms of a labelled condition: 'Charlie has Down syndrome, which has resulted in moderate to severe learning difficulties'; 'Mary has had optic nerve damage from birth – educationally blind'; 'Diane has physical difficulties resulting in locomotor and coordination difficulties. She also has learning difficulties.' The assumption that we were concerned primarily with students labelled as having 'special needs' was evidently conveyed to some students. One of us was greeted by a student in the first lesson of the first day, with 'you can be with him [*pointing to his friend*], he's . . .' [*here he placed his finger by his temple and rotated it, indicating someone with scrambled brains*].

However, although our timetables had been highly organised before we arrived, they proved to be extremely flexible. After the first day, we were free to follow our interests and choose where to observe and who to interview. On our first visit we observed and tape-recorded sections of lessons and interviewed both teachers and non-teacher support staff. We attempted to map out the way the school and individual lessons were organised to respond to differences between students. On subsequent visits after this initial study, we interviewed groups of teachers and students, and these are examined in further articles about the school (e.g. Ainscow, Booth and Dyson 1996). At various times during the day, for longer sessions in the evenings and in separate meetings between visits we pooled our perceptions of the school and challenged each other's understandings of it.

There was considerable debate between us as we compared and contrasted our reactions to the school. In an earlier stage in the development of the chapter we retained a sense of difference and debate between the views and interpretations of the three of us by allowing different sections to reflect different views. We concluded that such apparent self-regard and absence of coherence would be unsatisfactory from the point of view of the reader. Nevertheless, we remain unsatisfied with the present form, which largely obscures the differences of perspective that remain between us.

Setting the context: schools for all?

The extent to which secondary schools in England encourage the participation of all students in a neighbourhood is intimately connected to the fluctuating history of selection for secondary education. Lovell calls itself a high school but it might also be called a 'comprehensive community' school. This latter label places it as part of the developments in secondary education that gathered pace in the 1960s. These reversed policies that assigned students at the age of 11 to different secondary schools on the basis of their attainment. In theory Lovell is a non-selective school, but there are continuing political conflicts about the desirability of selection between schools and central pressure to increase selection within schools. It has been affected, too, by successive policies connected by the slogan of 'school choice' which have undermined the relationship of schools to particular catchment areas.

The 1944 Education Act paved the way for the creation of a tripartite system of state secondary education, consisting of grammar, technical or trade schools, and secondary modern schools for which students were selected at the age of 11. About thirty per cent of students were rewarded for their achievement by a place at a grammar school and sixty per cent attended secondary modern schools. The development of technical schools, intermediate in status, never became widespread and catered for about five per cent of students. The remaining students attended comprehensive schools in the very few areas that had them and a few attended special schools. The system was based on a notion that there were three types of child who should therefore be catered for in three types of school. One might add that these were seen as three types of 'normal' child, since special schools and their students were not considered in these plans for the development of secondary education and are missing from histories of it (see, for example, Simon 1991).

A significant percentage of students have always been educated privately in a sector of education with its own highly developed hierarchy, topped by the so-called 'public schools'. About six per cent of students of compulsory school age (aged 5–16) were in private schools in 1996 (DfEE 1996a). Most students in private schools would view themselves as more privileged than those in the state sector. Special schools in this hierarchical system might be seen as providing a devalued education for devalued students.

The advocacy of inclusive education has a particular political significance in England if its relationship to comprehensive education is made explicit. The tripartite system had been set up by the wartime coalition government dominated by Conservative MPs and was put into effect during the post-war Labour government. However, subsequent advocates of the selective state system and of private education were drawn primarily, though not exclusively, from supporters of the Conservative Party. Moves to abolish the selective secondary system, though not its special school element, came from supporters of the Labour Party and were partially implemented following the return of a Labour government in 1964, through a mixture of advice and budgetary control, though not through legislation. A degree of autonomy allowed to local government permitted the continuation of grammar schools in a few areas, but by the mid-1980s, ninety per cent of students were in comprehensive schools (Benn and Chitty 1996). However, in many schools their previous history and culture as a grammar or secondary modern continued to affect the participation of students and the way they were valued.

Many comprehensive schools did develop an approach to curricula and teaching which recognised the diversity of their intake, but the parallel set of changes in primary schools freed from the straitjacket of preparation for a selective secondary system was deeper. The development of mixed attainment teaching, flexible collaborative group work, team-teaching, project work, integrated curricula and use of community resources parallel the full range of ideas later drawn upon in formulating a pedagogy of inclusion. The English progressive primary school provided a model for those considering the integration of students from special schools (Levine 1979; Booth and Jones 1987). By the 1980s several large local education authorities were exercising their powers to coordinate the development of comprehensive education that met the needs of all students, and were putting in place policies to remove discrimination against black students and girls in schools.

In 1979 a Conservative government came to power with a determination to change any institutions within their control that were seen to embody socialist principles. Education was subjected to radical reforms. The powers of local authorities were reduced, a curriculum was introduced under central government control and schools were to be run as businesses competing for customers in the education market place. Parents were exhorted to select schools on the basis of league tables specifying examination successes and truancy rates. However, in reality, the system of so-called parental choice of school permitted oversubscribed schools to choose students and parents. Schools competed to attract middle-class students with 'cultural capital' or 'surplus value' that could be converted into success in league tables.

At first, overt attempts to re-introduce secondary selection were confined to so-called policies of school choice and to encouraging grouping by attainment within schools. With successive terms of office these policies were reinforced by introducing centrally-funded 'grant maintained schools', almost entirely free of local authority influence, which was further reduced by requiring governing bodies to consider annually whether to put the possibility of 'opting out' to a parental vote. By 1994–5 about seventeen per cent of secondary schools, two per cent of primary schools and two out of 1,200 special schools became grant maintained (DfEE 1996a). In addition, a small number of City Technical Colleges were created through partnership with industry.

In 1988, a national curriculum was introduced for students aged 5–16 in state schools, but not the private sector, to be phased in over several years (DfE 1988). It appeared to take the academic, subject-based curriculum of the grammar schools as the model for the whole of education. When it was first introduced in Parliament it did not refer to students who might experience difficulties, and the existence of students categorised as having 'special needs' was inserted by amendment. The resulting Act included the notion that some students could have the National Curriculum disapplied, but subsequent government guidance and professional practice have undermined the exclusion of students from it (NCC 1989). This gave an unanticipated inclusive twist to the law which was seen by some as an entitlement curriculum and may have had its biggest effect on the content of teaching in the special schools.

The new curriculum heavily overloaded the schools and introduced a time-consuming and bureaucratic assessment system. The pressures that it created for teachers were so overwhelming that in 1994 a new slimmed-down version with a simplified assessment structure was produced and applied to students aged 5–14, (DfE 1994). The government, however, pressed ahead with introducing national tests at 7, 11 and 14, despite strong objection from the teaching unions.

It is difficult to convey the turmoil created in education by the hasty implementation and revision of ill-considered reforms, and the effect these had on teachers and learners and on the possibilities for considering issues of equity and participation. There was a persistent criticism from central government and their advisers of so-called 'child-centred' or 'progressive methods'. Group work and cross-curricular project work were discouraged and the submission of coursework in public examinations was curtailed. Whole-class teaching was encouraged in primary as well as secondary schools. Thus, the methods used to support the wider participation of students in schools, a pedagogy of inclusion, came under attack.

Before the advent of the National Curriculum, the then Prime Minister Margaret Thatcher had ridiculed local authority attempts to introduce multicultural and anti-racist education. Nevertheless, a working party was subsequently established to examine issues of multi-cultural education and a series of strong recommendations on the multi-cultural adaptation of the National Curriculum were made. However, the report of this group was never published (Tomlinson 1993).

Throughout this period, and intensifying in the 1990s, there was an emphasis on failure in schools and teachers. Schools were to be improved by identifying, remedying and, where necessary, rooting out failure. A four-yearly system of national inspections in state schools by the Office for Standards in Education (Ofsted) was introduced, with plans added later to include the grading of teachers on the basis of the observation of two lessons (Ofsted 1996a). The consequences of a bad inspection on school popularity and teacher redundancies created an atmosphere of fear and stress in many staffrooms up and down the country. Teachers were publicly humiliated by having details of failed inspections emblazoned across the front pages of local papers. This emphasis on failure, paradoxical in that it persisted in a government that had been in power for seventeen years, was given a further twist by being supported by the education spokespeople of the Labour Party (TES April 12th 1996).

With the prospect of a Labour government at the election held in May 1997, political capital was made of the fact that the leader of the Labour Party and his wife chose to send a son to a prestigious school outside his immediate area, and Harriet Harman, the Shadow Secretary of State for Health, and her husband opted for a grammar school place out of their local area for their son. Ironically, at the same time, commentators supportive of the Labour Party were calling for a return to some form of selection to stem or even reverse the growth of the private sector (Gray 1995; Hutton 1995). In an attempt to create 'clear blue water' between the policies of the Conservative and Labour parties, the government published a White Paper – a discussion document that precedes the attempt to pass legislation on the issue discussed – in 1996 promising the partial re-introduction of grammar schools if re-elected (Simon 1997). In the event, a Labour government was elected with a landslide majority built on its shift towards the 'centre ground' of politics. Apart from a partial reabsorption of grant-maintained schools as 'Foundation Schools' under local government control, and a scaling down of the National Curriculum in primary schools to make way for more teaching of literacy and numeracy, the new Secretary of State for Education promised more of the same.

Conceptions of special education and integration

The articulation of principles of comprehensive community education and the developments of a pedagogy and curricula to teach diverse groups together provide a starting point for understanding inclusive education in England (Booth 1983; Ainscow 1995a). The changes that have taken place in the education system since the late 1970s, however, have profoundly limited its development. Yet, it has not been common to understand the development of inclusion policy in relation to changes which affect the education of all students.

At the levels of both central and local government, special education policies have usually been developed in parallel to policies for education in general, in a way that further undermines inclusion. Policy has continued to be framed according to a selective philosophy in which school students are divided into 'normal' and 'abnormal' learners, those with and without 'special educational needs' or 'learning difficulties'. The Warnock Report of 1978 had criticised the categorisation of students according to 'handicap', but had suggested that one in six students at any one time should be regarded as having 'special educational needs' (DES 1978), thus advocating a huge increase in categorisation overall. The legacy of the report has severely impeded the introduction of an inclusive philosophy into special education. The notion that educational difficulties in schools can be resolved by identifying and responding to a large group of students defined as having special educational needs dominates all levels of policy making, and thinking and practice in schools.

In general, discussions about integration, inclusion, selection and segregation do not concern students subject to disciplinary exclusion, either formally or informally, and other groups such as pregnant schoolgirls and traveller children who are especially vulnerable to mainstream exclusion. 'Exclusion' is usually interpreted in England to mean disciplinary exclusion and is mainly unrelated to other forms of exclusion (Booth 1996). There has been a dramatic rise in disciplinary exclusions in the 1990s (Blyth and Milner 1996), much of which has been attributed to competitive pressures in schools. In response to rising disciplinary exclusions, the 1993 Education Act required local authorities to establish Pupil Referral Units, a type of school not subject to the National Curriculum, where excluded students could be taught. This was a form of provision previously heavily criticised, not least by the government's own advisers (Ofsted 1995). One of the major teaching unions, the National Association of Schoolmasters/Union of Women Teachers, has suggested that there are a further 150,000 students who should be excluded from the mainstream on disciplinary grounds.

Integration according to the law?

Comprehensive education, education for all in a common school, was debated and introduced as we have suggested, without a discussion of special school exclusion, and at a time when a group of students said to be 'severely sub-normal' were excluded from education altogether. An educability law, giving all students an entitlement to education, was introduced in 1970 (DES 1970). The 1981 Education Act introduced a qualified presumption of a mainstream place for students with 'a Statement of special educational needs', provided it was compatible with their appropriate education, the appropriate education of others in the school and the efficient use of resources. The 1993 Education Act, which incorporated most elements of the 1981 Act, introduced a slight increase in the effect of parental preference, but compulsory segregation of some students categorised as having special needs, against the wishes of parents and students, is still possible in English schools at a time when the concept of school choice has been elevated to a moral imperative for others (DES 1981; DfE 1993; DfEE 1996b).

Generally, recommendations by Local Education Authority (LEA) employed professionals for mainstream education tend to correspond to traditional practice and available provision in an LEA. Parents who disagree with the school recommended by an LEA or the contents of a Statement of special educational needs, can appeal to a legally constituted tribunal. However, most of those who sit on tribunals have the presumption that students with statements should be educated in special schools (Crabtree and Whittaker 1995).

The percentage of students in special schools in England is about 1.2 per cent or about 95,300 students (DfEE 1996a). This varies considerably from LEA to LEA, from three per cent to less than half per cent (Norwich 1994). The overall percentage has stayed relatively stable in the 1990s, falling slightly from a peak in the mid-1980s following the introduction of a so-called integration law. While accurate statistics are difficult to gather, it seems that students with physical disabilities and sensory disabilities are more likely to be educated in the mainstream, while students categorised as having emotional and behavioural difficulties or as having moderate learning difficulties are beginning to show increasing rates of segregation.

In 1995 a Disability Discrimination Act was introduced which may affect inclusion in education in two ways. It applies to all employers of twenty or more staff and thus affects all LEA schools and most non-LEA maintained schools, and could have the effect of increasing the numbers of disabled teachers. The law also requires that school governors must publish details of how their schools are being made accessible to disabled students. This adds a stronger presumption of inclusion to the details of school policies required by the 1993 Act. It also adds an interesting twist to the legal definition of disability in England. Most people in education had assumed that 'disability' meant physical disability. The Disability Discrimination Act defines disability to include people who have a 'physical impairment' or 'mental impairment' which has a 'substantial effect on their day-to-day lives' (Department of Employment 1995, section 1). Leaving aside the lack of a social model of disability in this definition, the Act applies the presumption of inclusion to both physically disabled students and others whose attainment is such that it substantially disrupts their lives. These students, one might argue, fall within the official category of severe learning difficulty and have commonly been excluded from the mainstream.

Guiding the implementation of policy?

The 1993 Education Act also introduced the Code of Practice to guide the identification and support of students categorised as having special needs (DfE 1994). This document had intermediate legal force between law and advice, since schools had to 'have regard to' it in formulating their practice. It reproduced a five-stage model of severity of 'special need' set out in the Warnock Report (DES 1978), specified at what point schools were expected to call on additional expertise to support students, and borrowed the notion of the individual educational plan from earlier legislation in the USA. As soon as they are identified as having special educational needs, students are to be placed on a special register, a practice which it is argued may be stigmatising and against the wishes of parents (Wearmouth 1996). While claims were made by officials in the Department for Education that the Code could be used to support an approach to overcoming difficulties in learning for all students, seventy-five per cent of its pages were concerned with the formal assessment and statementing process for what it estimated as two per cent of the school population. Despite the odd disclaimer, it encourages a view of difficulties in learning as arising from deficits in students rather than as a result of a relationship between learners, teachers, curricula and other resources to support learning. There has been very limited acknowledgement or acceptance of this 'social model of learning difficulties'.

In fact, the attachment of 'additional resources' to the statementing procedures is fuelling a rate of statementing higher than two per cent in many areas. An increasing proportion of students are provided with statements in mainstream schools, running at 1.4 per cent of the school population in 1994–5, in addition to the 1.2 per cent in special schools, (DfE 1996a). Under tight financial controls, the obligation to provide the resources specified through formal procedures appeared to some schools to represent additional finance for students. However, overall budgets for students tended to remain unchanged, the net effect of increasing statementing is to take resources away from students and put them into assessment procedures. The statementing procedure thus becomes a way in which schools compete for a share of resources rather than a way to benefit the education of students.

Paradoxically, the law requires that students who are the subject of Statements and other children identified as having special needs should be educated where possible *alongside* students who are not identified as having special needs. This would appear to require mixed attainment teaching in schools and it is a measure of the separation of special and mainstream policy that such a contradiction should remain in law.

The Code elaborated on the role of a 'special educational needs coordinator', required in every school. The use of this term, often abbreviated to SENCO and sounding, fittingly, like a newly-privatised company, could be regarded as a move backwards from the more inclusive notions of 'learning support' that had been growing in popularity previously, or the idea of learning development in which notions of curriculum development and learning support for students were combined in some schools (Gilbert and Hart 1990).

In theory, LEAs retain the power, under the 1993 Act, to coordinate support for students officially defined as having 'special needs', but this is restricted by the relative independence even of those schools which nominally remain within control of the Local Education Authority: even special schools can become grant-maintained, and schools can opt in and out of LEA learning and behaviour support services. Part of the budget devolved to schools is earmarked for 'additional needs', and local inspectors are meant to see that this money is used to overcome difficulties in learning, but this is notoriously difficult to ascertain and enforce. Although their powers have been severely curtailed, Local Education Authorities have more power to coordinate special education and inclusion policy in accordance with the selective philosophy of official policy than they have to foster the development of schools in general. This makes it relatively more difficult for them to conceive of education policies that are about enhancing the participation of all students.

The development of Richard Lovell school

An understanding of recent changes and pressures in education helps to make sense of the responses to student diversity at Richard Lovell School. It is located on the eastern edge of Letham, with open fields on one side reflecting its status between the most popular out of city schools and the inner city schools, some of which are threatened with closure. It is linked to fourteen primary schools which send many of their students to Lovell, one of a 'family of schools'. This is a consortium for the development of educational policies to combat 'under-achievement' and support the social regeneration of the area. It has strong links with the Labour-controlled city council and the Labour Member of Parliament.

In the period between 1972 and 1974 Letham Education Authority dismantled its selective secondary schools and at the same time introduced a system of first (taking students from 5–8 years), middle (taking students between 9–13 years) and high schools (taking students between 14–18 years). Such a scheme was never very widespread and was largely confined to England. Only one middle school exists in Wales, and Scotland, which had two, now has none (Mackinnon, Statham and Hales 1995). Lovell shared its campus with one of its feeder middle schools.

There is an immediate welcoming atmosphere in the school from staff and students, and there are striking art displays in the corridors. Behind them is a school fabric in considerable need of refurbishment, formed from the amalgamation of buildings in two adjacent schools. For example, one classroom/corridor, next to a toilet, is also a thoroughfare. It is lit by a large expanse of windows, none of which open. It is cold in winter and like a greenhouse in sunshine.

The current head joined the school in 1983. He felt that the school had a 'tremendous spirit', but 'in terms of its discipline and its aspirations it was dreadful. The first summer of 1983, the first [public 16+] examination results, there was not a single child out of a 360 pupil entry who got a grade A in any subject.' He attributed difficulties at the school to 'union militancy' which reached its height in the mid-1980s when the government, determined to reduce union power, managed to remove teachers' collective bargaining rights. The teachers' actions at that time failed to persuade central government but disrupted the running of schools, curtailing extra-curricular activities and according to the head, included a series of twenty-minute stoppages of lessons.

> We weathered that storm . . . the years from about 1988 . . . were very positive . . . examination results improved year on year . . . and the spirit of the school was really quite superb amongst the staff – we'd lost a lot of the militants, there was a strong ethos within the school with a lot of new developments, like the special needs development.

In 1989, the school became an area resource for students categorised as having severe learning difficulties, starting with seven students. The teacher with special responsibility for these students had worked in the nearest special school, and had just spent a year on a Fulbright exchange trip to Connecticut where she had worked with a group of similar students in the mainstream. She told the head of her special school that she would like to work with a group of students in a Letham mainstream school. To her surprise the scheme was supported and Lovell agreed to collaborate. Together with the head of physical education (PE), she set about devising a model to support the students in the mainstream that would not reproduce the relative isolation of the group with whom she had worked in the States. She established a resource base from which students are supported in mainstream lessons, usually by non-teacher learning support assistants.

Her colleagues at the special school regarded her as 'the black sheep'. Since the integration plans did not include students with the most severe difficulties of communication and movement, she was accused of 'taking away the cream', who were seen as the role models for the remaining students. She replied: 'Well, where were the role models for the students who are leaving?' According to a Local Authority administrator the inclusion of these students was given considerable impetus by a major fire at the special school.

In 1991 the school also became the secondary resource for students with visual disabilities for the whole of Letham, though some students with visual disabilities are included individually in other schools. This occurred during a major reorganisation of special schools in the city whereby the twenty-four special schools were all closed and then fourteen new 'rationalised' schools were opened. The coordinator for provision for visually disabled students is employed directly by the LEA. She also coordinates the activity of two special needs assistants. In addition, there is occasional involvement of peripatetic teachers.

Then, in 1993, a further reorganisation was carried out in Letham mainstream schools, largely in response to a wish to economise on surplus places. By this time the previous system of dividing schools seemed obsolete, since the National Curriculum had introduced the notion of 'key stages' for the years of compulsory schooling following the more traditional form of infant (aged 5–7, Key Stage 1), junior (aged 7–11, Key Stage 2) and senior school (11–14, Key Stage 3 and 14–16, Key Stage 4). It also borrowed the American and Continental system of year grades. The compulsory school years are now described as running from Year 1 at age 5–6 to Year 11 at age 15–16.

Letham decided to switch to the more conventional system and instituted a complete upheaval of the schools at the end of the 1992–3 school year. This process affected the composition of the city schools because of the presence of outer Letham secondary schools, which had always taken students aged 11–18 year. A plan to shift all post-16 schooling into a single tertiary college for the whole of Letham was rejected by central government and hence the relative stability of the outer Letham schools exacerbated the competitive system of school choice. As soon as the plans to change city schools emerged many parents opted to avoid disruption and send their children to these 'havens'. As the head of Lovell described it: 'we had two good feeder middle schools, that basically took the more middle-class element . . . and they virtually disappeared overnight'. This process was variously described to us as 'losing the top end' and 'haemorrhaging the aspirational middle classes'. The choices of parents had meant that a further two secondary schools would not survive the reorganisation process and were planned to close. These were the schools that came bottom and next to bottom in the English league tables. One of these is in the heart of a housing estate, described as an area of high deprivation and unemployment, from which many Lovell students are drawn. Many of the 300 students currently at that school would swell Lovell numbers.

The middle school on the campus, and whose buildings were to be incorporated into the reborn high school, had been active in the campaign to save middle schools and relations between the two schools were fraught. The head described the middle school staff's last stand:

> They had banners up in the windows for two years prior to reorganisation, saying 'STOP REORGANISATION' and 'SAVE THE MIDDLE SCHOOLS' . . . We took over those buildings two days before the end of the school year . . . they had a barbecue while our staff were trying to move materials in and out, and then they left the place, and it was just left as if they'd trashed it. It was absolutely amazing. But it created in the staff a Dunkirk spirit.'

The school re-started with a large majority of new staff including a management team, re-deployed, in the main, from other schools. Most staff were unused to teaching the age range in their new workplace, which in the first year also included Year 6 children. As the head argued: 'I defy anybody to be able to pick up that sort of organisation and immediately create the sort of ethos which you need to run a school.'

The school population

In the first year after reorganisation Lovell's student numbers increased from 900 to 1,700, then fell subsequently to 1,550. Attendance rates at the school are high, currently running at eighty-seven per cent. Most of the students come from a reasonably well-defined area of East Letham. There are only a few non-white students at the school. As the head informed us, Lovell was the only Letham city school that appeared in the top half of the secondary examination league tables. Although there is an all-boys school and an all-girls school nearer to the threatened schools, Lovell is seen, according to the head, as the school of choice between these three: 'we're regarded very much as a "posh" school you see, . . . because our kids have a uniform and we're the other side of the ring-road'. However, some parents and teachers suggest that the competition from one nearby school may be much greater than this indicates.

The catchment area for the students with Statements of special educational needs is much wider than for other students. There are sixty students with Statements at the school, or 3.8 per cent of the school population. This is three to four times the numbers at other secondary schools in Letham. Students with visual disabilities may come from anywhere in the city. There are seven such students in the school, two of whom are regarded as 'educationally blind'. Thirteen of the seventeen students who are overseen by the specialist teacher for severe learning difficulties have Down syndrome, though some of these students are described on their Statements as having moderate rather than severe difficulties. Of these thirteen students, four are in the catchment area of the school, a further five are the catchment area of the nearest special school while four are way out of the catchment area of even the special school. Thus the school serves as a city-wide 'special' mainstream school for students with Down syndrome, as well as for students with visual disabilities. This concentration of categorised students is unusual in England. A few other secondary schools in England include groups of students categorised as having severe learning difficulties, though many more schools include one or more such categorised students. Nationally, about twenty per cent of students with Down syndrome are in mainstream secondary schools.

One of us discussed the choice of Lovell School with a group of parents of students with Down syndrome, who were visiting the school for one day a week in the summer term prior to joining the school in the following September. Their children had attended their local primary schools but inclusion at secondary school is less common in Letham. All of them had visited a variety of secondary schools and they reported that some schools felt unable to cope, while others said that they would give it a try but had reservations. Consequently, they were relieved to find out about the established provision at Lovell. As one mother argued:

> Dean has a right to go to the local school. He loses his friends by coming here . . . We could fight but they will become the guinea pigs again . . . We decided that his happiness was best.

The school hopes to be oversubscribed in general, but already regards itself as oversubscribed for students with Statements. It applies a quota of four students categorised as having 'severe learning difficulties' in each year, a practice of dubious legality. Parents of six such students applied for their children to attend Lovell in the following year. Students who experience the most severe communication and mobility difficulties were not accepted at the school. The teacher who transferred from the special school believes these students could be part of the school, with other students coming to join them in the resource base rather than them moving to mainstream lessons. However, she felt that 'this would need a lot of facilities and building changes' which would not be funded by the LEA.

There are no students in wheelchairs in the school even though there have been in the past. In fact the school, on two storeys in a number of unconnected buildings, does not have lifts to the first floors where all the science laboratories are located. This means, too, that the first floor rooms are not available for community use by wheelchair users or for disabled schoolworkers.

Students are sometime excluded from the school on disciplinary grounds. In Lovell an increase in rates of disciplinary exclusion seems to be associated with a new behaviour policy called 'positive behaviour' (described later in the chapter). An exclusion unit had been set up in the school a couple of weeks before our first visit. In a six months period there had been six permanent disciplinary exclusions and thirteen for five days or less.

Organisational responses to diversity

When we first visited the school it was just beginning to emerge from the vortex following the big bang of reorganisation. It was still attempting to unite diverse groups of staff, from middle and upper and special schools, and a wide variety of students.

Staff were assigned to subject departments, and departments were grouped into faculties. The school was also sub-divided into a Lower School (Years 7, 8 and 9), an Upper School (Years 10 and 11) and a Sixth Form. These divisions, as well as departments and faculties, had their own heads and there were also heads of year. This structure enabled teachers to concentrate on those particular age groups for which they had most experience and to see some possibility of advancement. It also represented a common division within English secondary schools between 'pastoral' and curriculum responsibilities.

The pastoral care hierarchy consisting of form tutors, year heads, faculty heads, and one of the three deputy heads of the school, is responsible for the welfare of students, and some students confirmed they might seek out these people when they wanted to talk over a problem. However, much of the work of pastoral care staff relates to control and discipline, checking attendance and responding to breaches of school and classroom rules. The distinction between pastoral and curricular structures is particularly significant in trying to understand the way schools encourage and discourage the participation of students. Difficulties in learning are seen to be the responsibility of a 'special needs' department, while difficulties in behaviour are primarily viewed as matters of indiscipline and to require the intervention of the pastoral hierarchy.

The department of special educational needs is led by what the school, following the Code of Practice, calls its special educational needs coordinator. She has overall responsibility for organising support for students categorised as having special educational needs or learning difficulties. She manages the work of $1^1/2$ specialist teachers for students categorised as having severe learning difficulties, a specialist teacher for students with visual impairment, a teacher offering general learning support and eight non-teaching assistants. The teachers for students categorised as having severe learning difficulties and with visual impairments have their own teaching bases to which students are withdrawn for varying amounts of time.

The fact that large numbers of non-teaching assistants were employed to support the learning of students with Statements in classrooms is itself a response to a squeeze on school finances. This use of non-teacher support has been criticised recently by government inspectors, particularly at secondary level (Ofsted 1996b), but it has grown in popularity with the devolution of budgets to schools. A school can employ about three learning support assistants for the price of one teacher. However, in our experience, the low pay reflects the employment market rather than the qualifications and expertise of the people involved.

The presence of a sizeable group of non-teaching staff poses a significant challenge to the inclusive intentions of a school in addition to the variety of students. In an L-shaped staffroom the teacher assistants monopolise the short spur as a relatively isolated group, and this tends to be used, too, by the specialist teachers, thus perpetuating a degree of separation between special and mainstream staff.

The school responds to the diversity of students by classifying them, grouping them, differentiating their curricula and supporting them. We have gathered a list of such practices at the school, or 'organisational responses to diversity', in Figure 16.1. The more we have visited the school the longer the list has grown. These structures are partly inherited from the history of education in England, partly prescribed through government legislation, partly absorbed from the prevailing culture and partly created by the school. Such responses provide and reinforce a framework for ascribing value to students and thus become ways in themselves of encouraging the inclusion or exclusion of students. The categorisation of students as having special needs is only one element of these processes.

The responses to diversity vary, then, in the extent to which they are taken for granted as natural features of schools. For example, groupings according to age are less often contested in secondary schools than attainment groups, although they are no less exclusive. A re-examination of age grouping may provide a source of ideas about inclusion in schools, particularly the ways in which differences in age can become a resource for learning and support. Some responses to diversity may push students to greater participation while others may be excluding and reduce participation.

We have listed separately responses to students by category, age, attainment, and behaviour but these all interact. Age carries expectations about changes in attainment and behaviour and the responses to special needs are related to differences in student attainment. However, students with the lowest attainments are not treated simply as an additional set but are located outside of the setting system, and perhaps outside of 'normality' by virtue of their category of 'severe learning difficulties'.

Responding by category

A traditional official category system was in evidence in the school, with students labelled according to their perceived severity of 'need', as mainstream,

Figure 16.1 Organisational responses to diversity

By category
'Special need' or disability
- mainstream (without 'special needs')
- learning difficulty/'special needs' without a Statement
- 'special needs' with a Statement
        Down syndrome
        moderate learning difficulty
        severe learning difficulty
        emotional and behavioural difficulty
        blind
        partially sighted

Class, race, gender?

By age
- grouping according to year
- distinct curricula for different ages, 11–14, 14–16, 16+
- greater freedom of choice 14+ , 16+
- change in teacher student relationships for 16+ curriculum

By attainment
- within class
        worksheets
        group work
        homework
        topic work
        in-class support
- between groups
        attainment sets
        severe learning difficulties curriculum
        visual disability curriculum
        group reading instruction
        individual reading instruction
        level and options Years 10/11 and 12/13
        special tutorials in preparation for 16+ examinations

By behaviour
- merit awards
- detention
- academic remove
- lower sets
- Year 8 special group
- parent referral (unofficial exclusion)
- exclusion, fixed and permanent

By interest
- options choices in GCSE
- a second foreign language
- project work
- PE options

Using diversity as a resource for learning?

learning difficulty or 'special need without a Statement', and 'special need with a Statement'. Within this last group there were a number of sub-groups representing both formal and informal category systems. Students with Down syndrome seemed to form their own group. One blind student summarised a prevalent attitude to these students in the school by differentiating between two students as 'special needs–Down' and 'special needs–not Down'.

Despite the fact that the attainments of students with Down syndrome straddled the moderate and severe learning difficulties categories when they arrived at the school, they were treated organisationally as if they all came within the severe learning difficulties sub-department at the school. Thus, in being included within the school they seemed to be subject to a prejudice that, in general, has been weakening over the last twenty years (see Booth 1985). The coordinator for severe learning difficulties is aware of this anomaly and thinks of herself as working with students 'who are less independent, who need to be taught how to be independent':

> The actual name is wrong, because there's a few of them that haven't got severe learning difficulties . . . it's the kind of support that they need really, to have someone like me checking up on them . . .

She also mentioned the care that needed to be taken about the way special provision was created in the school:

> When we first came . . . our base was called the link room, because it was a link between a special and a mainstream school. But then, as time went on, you know what pupils are – [they started talking about] the missing link type of thing, so you've got to be very careful of what label you give students really.

During the time we were at the school we did not observe any insults aimed at categorised students. There was some use of the word 'thick' as an insult or as self-deprecation, for example, when one student greeted one of us with a 'good afternoon' then realising it was morning, added 'I'm thick, me'. Other forms of informal categorisation were clearly in operation with varying effects on the students. Some teachers did refer to the desirability of middle-class students for the well-being and success of the school but we found little evidence either from the teachers or students we interviewed that this affected classroom responses. Reactions to class as well as gender and race may require more subtle investigation than we have employed up to now. Students told us that there was no racism or sexism in the school, though a bullying survey in the school, carried out by one of the teachers, had revealed considerable levels of racist and sexist name calling.

The model of support that arises from the categorisation of students as having special educational needs distinguishes between ordinary or 'normal' diversity and special or 'abnormal' diversity. It depends first on the school identifying specific individuals and groups of students who are deemed to be in need of something other than the standard provision that is made for most students in ordinary classrooms (McIntyre 1993). The school then targets additional resources at such students in order to create forms of provision which are 'additional or supplementary' (DES 1978, par. 3.45) to its standard mainstream provision. This has a number of consequences: the educational and social experiences of 'special' students, the intended beneficiaries of additional provision, may be markedly different from those of their peers; additional high-level resource is provided for a relatively small number of students, leaving little or nothing for those students whose difficulties are not categorised; the special needs work has no obvious means of engaging with and developing ordinary classrooms to become responsive to diversity. Resources are thus deployed predominantly in setting up alternatives to the ordinary classroom rather than in enriching and enhancing standard provision. The responsibilities of the learning support coordinator for special provision consume most of her time and energy, and appear to prevent her and others in the department from working with subject-teacher colleagues to develop curricula and teaching approaches for all students. As we have suggested, there is an established tradition elsewhere of linking learning support to curriculum development (Gains and McNicholas 1979; Booth, Potts and Swann 1987; Dyson and Gains 1995).

Responding to age

Most schools attempt to cut down student diversity by grouping students according to age; age carries expectations of increasing attainment and maturity. In the English state system, students are very rarely allowed to advance a year or to be retained for an extra year, and hence beliefs about the importance of keeping age-cohorts together generally override any desire to keep students of similar attainment together. In response to the age of its students Richard Lovell is organised into a Lower School (Years 7–9), an Upper School (Years 10 and 11) and a Sixth Form (Years 12 and 13). In each of these phases, the curriculum is organised somewhat differently. The amount of subject choice is increased from zero in Lower School, to a large compulsory core plus limited choice in Upper School, and a large degree of choice in the Sixth Form. Each of these three phases has its own head, together with a team of teachers who take some specific responsibility for students in that phase. The Sixth Form also has its own geographical base, with an exclusive social area, set of teaching rooms and privileged access to the Library for its students. The Sixth Formers also have greater social privileges and a more relaxed relationship with staff. As one student put it, 'lower down the school the teachers talk at you, but in the Sixth Form they talk to you'.

Responding to attainment

Within this age-based structure, the school operates a complex system for grouping its students according to attainment. Within any particular class, teachers are meant to respond to differences in the attainment of students by differentiating the curriculum and drawing on the available resources in terms of curriculum materials, adult helpers and other students. The more practice is developed to support successful mixed attainment teaching, the less pressure there will be to sort students into attainment groups. We discuss our observations of classroom practice below. When we first visited the school the headteacher thought that the extent of classroom responses to student differences was a particular weakness of the school, arguing that 'the actual level of differentiation which is being done within the classroom is woeful'.

Students begin their career at Lovell in 'mixed attainment' groups for registration and tutor period, and continue to be allocated to pastoral groups on this basis. However, as they move through the year groups, they become much more likely to be divided into attainment 'sets'. Different departments choose to 'set' to different degrees but in general, setting increases as students progress through the lower school. In the Sixth Form guided course choice replaces the setting system but effectively results in teaching groups similarly based on attainment.

Although a large amount of support is given to students categorised as having special needs in mixed attainment groups and in sets, a substantial amount of withdrawal teaching also occurs. Individual and group reading instruction for up to four out of the thirty-two weekly periods is provided for students in the learning difficulties room, and additional instruction is given in the severe learning difficulties and visual disability bases. The time that students categorised as having severe learning difficulties spend in their base varies from none to most of the week. The visual disability base is used very selectively for brailling and computer skills.

Students who are approaching their GCSE (16+) examinations and are thought to be capable of achieving high grades are now offered lunchtime 'tutorials'. This is a direct response to the examination league tables and the concern about the popularity of the school. The lunchtime tutorial development is paralleled in respect of low-attaining students. Prior to the introduction of the National Curriculum in 1988, many secondary schools operated some alternative form of curriculum for students in their final years of schooling who were not projected to do well in public examinations. The tight prescription of a common curriculum made such alternatives more difficult to sustain, though Richard Lovell managed to retain some remnant of the alternative curriculum in the form of a scheme of extended work placements. However, the revised National Curriculum (DfE 1994) creates a degree of flexibility in respect of older students, allowing them to follow vocational options in place of traditional academic subjects. Lovell is now seeking to take advantage of this flexibility by developing a more thorough-going alternative curriculum for low-attaining students, though the precise shape of this alternative is not yet clear.

While, clearly, high-attaining students were more valued in some respects, we were impressed and moved by the eloquent support for the comprehensive ideal from the thirty teachers that we interviewed. This was just after it was revealed that the labour politician Harriet Harman was sending her son to a grammar school, and there was a sense of betrayal that she could have ignored the sensitivities of comprehensive school teachers in this way. All the teachers to whom we spoke said that it was effort and engagement they found rewarding rather than high attainment. We are cautious, too, in making assumptions about the excluding or including effects of particular practices. The language of setting, 'upper and lower', 'top and bottom', implies differences in status, and there is no doubt that lower sets contain students who are seen as difficult in behaviour as well as those low in attainment. However, many students told us that they valued having work at the 'right' level. Whether they would have preferred mixed attainment sets which responded successfully to the attainment of all students is a question that could not emerge from their experience. Equally, providing a learning support assistant in a classroom to help a student did enable many students to participate in lessons that would otherwise have been inaccessible, but at times it also reduced their interaction with other students and the amount of direct contact with class teachers. We discuss this further below.

Responding to behaviour

Following reorganisation, there was a widespread feeling amongst staff that the numbers of students in the school with 'difficult behaviour' had increased. There was also dissatisfaction with the 'disempowering' effects of the disciplinary system in place, on classroom teachers. Often, students did not attend detentions for bad behaviour, and frequently, class teachers sought support in managing students from senior colleagues.

As a result, the school has adopted a system known as 'positive behaviour', which originated in the USA and which a working party of staff had seen in operation in another school. The system consists of a set of classroom rules placed prominently in every classroom (Figure 16.2). There are cumulative rewards and punishments called 'consequences' for adhering to the rules and breaking them. Rewards consist of credits, certificates and prizes. Punishments start with a name on the board, which can then have a tick by it, leading to detention with a head of faculty (known as getting a 'faculty'), to exclusion within the school and then exclusion from the school. Exclusion within the school, for part of a day, as a result of the behaviour policy, takes place in the 'academic remove', a name derived from the traditions of the British private school system and an in-joke therefore for the teachers.

Figure 16.2 Classroom rules

1	Arrive on time to lessons and enter the room quietly
2	Remain in your place unless asked to move
3	Come to lessons properly equipped
4	Listen to and follow instructions the first time they are given
5	Allow work to go ahead without interruption

In Year 8, there was a further group of students whose behaviour was seen as exceptionally difficult who were gathered together for half their timetable and taught by a single teacher. There was also a system of informal exclusion known as 'parent referral' whereby a student could be sent home with a letter to parents. Formal exclusion in accordance with procedures laid down in law could be fixed-term, though for no more than five days on any one occasion, or permanent. Formal exclusion carries with it a right of appeal for parents. There was a preponderance of boys in all forms of disciplinary exclusion.

Following the introduction of the new behaviour policy, official and unofficial exclusions had risen. There seemed to be widespread acceptance of the policy by the staff and new student entrants to the school but the older the students the more sceptical they were about its value.

The school have also introduced a 'no blame' bullying policy whereby bullies are encouraged to empathise with their victim without threat of punishment. This creates an anomaly. Bullying may involve offences far more serious and disruptive of participation in school life than the breaches of the classroom code that lead to disciplinary exclusion.

Responding to student interests

In the Lower School there are relatively few opportunities for the curriculum to be guided by the interests of students, though they can opt to continue with a second foreign language. In the Upper School there are limited opportunities to make choices of courses and within the relative small project component of the 14–16 curriculum. Far greater choice operates in the Sixth Form. Physical education, liked by the vast majority of students we talked to, allows for a considerable amount of choice of activity by students throughout the school. It also happens to be a well resourced area of the curriculum. Its facilities shared with the community, including a swimming pool, have recently been refurbished.

Diversity as a resource for learning?

Apart from a few examples of groupwork discussed above, we did not see many examples where the diversity of students was seen as a resource for supporting inclusion rather than as a 'problem' to be minimised. Students made it clear to us, informally, that they saw the wide range of students at the school as of positive benefit to all students. However, the diversity of students remained a largely untapped resource that might be drawn on in an unlimited number of ways in mentoring, peer tutoring, collaborative groupwork, problem solving, geography, creative writing, drama and so on.

A changing system

It is evident that this organisational complexity is evolving. Sometimes this is in response to external opportunities (as in the case of the review of the National Curriculum, removing its influence from 14–16 year olds); sometimes it is a response to external pressures (as in the case of lunchtime counselling); sometimes it is in response to internal pressures (as in the case of the Year 8 'special group'). Whatever factors are involved, however, it is striking that they seem always to move the school towards organisational differentiation rather than organisational homogeneity. To this extent at least, Richard Lovell is behaving in the way Skrtic (1991a and b) describes schools responding to diversity – that is, by creating an increasing number of organisational sub-units to deal with students who are perceived as atypical. In Richard Lovell's case it may be that, as the reorganisation becomes a more distant memory, some stability will be found which will enable the school to reverse this trend and consider how it might strengthen its *common* systems and structures.

The learning support coordinator and the deputy head in charge of the curriculum are considering a variety of models of learning support. Also, there has been a suggestion from department staff that learning support assistants might be assigned to subject departments rather than the special needs department, which would allow for staff with particular subject interests to be recruited, and for the notion of learning and curriculum support to become a greater responsibility of subject teachers. On the other hand, the school continues in other areas of its work to generate forms of provision which are 'additional or supplementary' to its standard provision, and which are targeted at specific groups and individuals.

Observing participation in classrooms

We observed classroom practice in the school and the extent to which teachers employ methods that might be seen as part of a pedagogy for inclusion (see Udvari-Solner and Thousand 1996). We looked at differences in participation of the same students in different lessons and the way they were supported by learning support assistants and learning support teachers.

We found few examples of ways in which support for participation was seen to require a reflection in the curriculum for all students of a diversity of cultures, sexualities, backgrounds and lifestyles. For example, two teachers commented that they had difficulty in teaching about the history of Islam, a topic the school has selected as the one non-European aspect of history in the 11–14 year curriculum. One teacher elaborated: 'it's different when they are learning about their own culture but they don't like learning about other cultures'. This was said during a lesson on medieval castles, which may be part of English folklore, but were created in societies very remote from the experience of these students. The teacher also suggested that the students had no difficulty learning about Roman Britain. Now, the students may have had difficulty with learning about Islam for a whole variety of reasons which may have had more to do with the materials available for teaching it, or the way it appears in what one teacher described as the 'patchwork' curriculum for history. But the presence a few miles from the school of large Asian communities might have suggested ways of making the topic less remote as well as people who might provide expertise in supporting the teaching of it.

We also reflected on the occasions when 'other cultures' were drawn upon in the formal and informal curriculum. There were the hidden examples, such as Arabic numbers and Roman alphabet, references to Australian soap operas, and an informal group working on origami. The lunchtime 'pop choir' sang American songs. Recipes in the 'food technology' lesson had included pasta and coleslaw. The children learnt French and German. We could only speculate, therefore, about what made some other cultures 'other' to some people in the school.

A house style?

Although across the school we observed a diversity of approach from teachers, there was evidence of a 'house style'. Typically, the teacher introduced a lesson, making use of a textbook or worksheet or questions on the board, then students would be set individual tasks. Some students were allowed to do less because of their perceived difficulties; others, expected to complete a task quickly, were asked to carry out extension activities. A number of teachers speculated that the existence of a house style may have arisen in response to the school's turbulent recent history with a 'low-risk' style of teaching emerging as teachers took on unfamiliar age-groups.

Encouraging and reducing participation

A high level of participation from students was associated with teachers who were purposeful, enthusiastic, clear in their directions and instructions and made efforts to link lesson activities to the students' experience. So, for example, in a geography lesson the teacher began a series of lessons about the USA by getting the class to brainstorm what they already knew, mainly, it seemed, as a result of watching American films and television programmes. The contributions of all students were valued equally. For example, a boy with Down syndrome responded, 'they have yellow taxis'. Similarly, in a 'bottom set' French lesson the teacher used cinema posters and film titles to build her lesson around the students' knowledge.

The reviewing of learning affected the maintenance of participation during a lesson. Most teachers started the lesson by reminding the class of what they had studied on previous occasions. Where teachers failed to set up the lessons so that the task was clear and failed to notice and intervene if participation flagged, it was common to see students looking uninterested or substituting their own curriculum of social talk with their classmates. Furthermore, in these classrooms even when students were seen to be getting on with their own work there was a lack of purpose which sometimes led to disciplinary incidents as the teacher attempted to gain control over the direction of the lesson.

Less emphasis was placed on end of lesson reviews. The school behaviour policy recommends that a register of pupil attendance is taken at the conclusion of each lesson as rewards and punishments are confirmed. Some teachers find that this emphasis on administration and behaviour towards the end of a lesson distracts from effective teaching. Where end of lesson reviews did occur they appeared to facilitate the engagement of the students right up to the lesson end. In an English lesson, for example, five minutes before the lesson finished the teacher announced, 'Pens down, I want to see if we can bring this to an end.' Each child was then asked to read aloud a 'headline' from their writing using an appropriate tone of voice, which resulted in several humorous contributions.

Some teachers used specific techniques at various stages of the lesson to encourage engagement with the content. This might involve occasional breaks during an activity for the teacher to remind the class of purposes and deadlines. In one English lesson the teacher invited students to read aloud from their writing, using these examples as a basis for reiterating requirements or illustrating alternative possibilities. One student in a 'bottom set' mathematics lesson suggested the way teachers divided their attention between students affected the degree of their participation. He remarked that 'in some subjects the teachers only give attention to the brainy ones – it's not fair. Like in maths Miss helps us all. There needs to be some attention to those who are struggling.'

The deliberate use of group work and collaborative learning strategies between students as they carried out their tasks was not common in the lessons we observed, although some subjects such as PE used it more than others. As we have argued, encouraging students to be a resource for each other's learning is one way to increase the classroom teaching resources. Planned group work also provides an opportunity for students experiencing difficulties to participate, at least in part of the lesson, without close adult supervision. We did observe some very good collaborative work: in a history lesson, for example, one student worked with Mary who is blind and together they discussed, designed and built a 'Lego' medieval castle. In an English lesson a student opted on his own initiative to work alongside and assist two students experiencing difficulties. There was also a considerable amount of informal 'working' together of students in an unofficial curriculum to do with their social lives or enmities or hobbies. We observed students swapping football cards and teaching each other origami.

Occasionally, 'throw away' remarks by teachers appeared to suggest that a low level of participation was anticipated. So, for example, a geography teacher appeared to have targeted one boy as somebody who was unlikely to make much of a contribution: 'Grant, homework, I assume you didn't do it – you never do, despite letters home to your mum.' Similarly, an English teacher on calling the class register remarked, 'Amazingly we have Shula here.'

The apparent low level of challenge in some lessons may be a device used in order to negotiate compliant behaviour. One science lesson consisted almost entirely of students copying diagrams and writing from the black-board. There was an impression that the teacher might lose control at any moment and that the copying tasks were a way of maintaining order by requiring student actions of a form that was low in demand. One student remarked of another teacher: 'she's the best teacher in the school, she never gives us much homework.'

Variations in participation between lessons

The differences in working climate and student participation were striking when the same students were observed during a series of lessons throughout a day. In a Year 9 'bottom set' science lesson, Shula and her two friends completed little or nothing of the lesson in the fifty minute period, preferring to pass the time in quiet social conversation. When addressed directly by the teacher Shula was either dismissive or openly scornful of his overtures, albeit without being rude enough to gain a disciplinary response.

In the following lesson Shula again found herself in a bottom set, this time for maths. Here, tasks were individualised in that students proceeded at their own pace through a series of worksheet tasks. This lesson was characterised by a reasonable level of engagement in the sense of writing and drawing in exercise books, but much less evidence of engagement with the meaning of the content of these tasks. In this way Shula was observed to conduct herself in much the same way as her classmates.

However, in French Shula sat in the front row, appearing to be very alert and regularly raising her hand to answer questions. Indeed, her whole manner throughout this lesson was that of somebody highly motivated to learn. The lesson was led by teacher who insisted on the active participation of all members of the class in a lesson that consisted almost entirely of teacher directed conversations.

During another series of lessons a boy named Michael displayed equal switches in his degree of participation. In an art lesson he was in trouble early on, caught up in name-calling between a group of boys and angered when, according to him, one boy suggested his mother was a prostitute. As a result of this incident Michael was required to work alone, while later the teacher took him outside for 'a talking to'. The next stage of the lesson involved students gathering around the teacher while she explained how to build up a cardboard cut-out face with papier-mâché. Michael, still agitated, was told to concentrate, to which he replied in a matter of fact way that clearly annoyed the teacher, 'how can I be expected to concentrate?' At this point he was threatened with academic remove. In fact he remained in the lesson and at the end was given a detention form to take to the faculty head.

At the start of the next lesson, German, Michael was still bubbling, and asked his teacher if the language assistant (a German national), who was leading discussion groups in an adjacent room, was living in a house of her own or staying with people during her time in England. This was treated as a rude remark by his teacher and so subsequently, despite usually having his hand up first, Michael was repeatedly overlooked when the assistant came to choose the next group to work with her. After the third rejection he muttered 'Oh f— it' and then remembered the observer who was sitting nearby making notes. The observer reassured him, explaining that he was not there to check up on him but could see that he was upset. When finally he was chosen for the conversation group he went off and returned happily, mouthing the words of the German song they had been learning.

English followed. Michael had reserved a seat for the observer, next to him. The lesson involved a class story which students took it in turn to read. Michael was chosen to read early on and was praised for his contribution. He commented on how much he enjoyed this subject and felt he was good at it. The teacher said she did not feel challenged by him and saw him as a valuable member of the group.

Supporting participation

As we have seen, notions of learning support at Richard Lovell are directed at adapting and giving access to the curriculum for categorised students, rather than making the content and organisation of lessons more inclusive of all students. We saw many examples where assistants flexibly and imaginatively encouraged the involvement of students. But their presence may reduce the challenges posed by classroom activities. For example, the assistant may hold the paper for a student with a physical disability, write the words for a student experiencing learning difficulties, and so on. The continual availability of adult support can limit participation in the lesson and emphasise task completion rather than understanding. Carol, a student with Down syndrome, was observed in a series of lessons. Given the level of support she received, the tasks she was set were always completed, although it seemed that some of these held little meaning for her. In one art lesson two students with Statements completed the tasks of the lesson even though they were both absent because the learning support assistant did the work for them. Meanwhile there was another group of students in the same lesson who had no support and spent most of the lesson talking.

The constant presence of an assistant may be socially reassuring for a student and we saw examples of how this can facilitate interactions between classmates. On the other hand, however, we saw instances where the assistant was a barrier between a student and the rest of the class. This was particularly the case where assistants elected to group students together in order to provide support. This tended to encourage these students to talk to and seek help from the assistant rather than their classmates or, indeed, the teacher. As a result, it was evident in some classes that teachers spent little time interacting with students seen as having special needs and would more often address their remarks to the assistant. Thus the presence of an assistant, acting as an intermediary in communication and as a supporter in carrying out the required tasks, may reduce the responsibility felt by the class teacher for supported students and any long-term adaptations of lessons to facilitate their participation. The participation in the informal social curriculum of students with Statements was limited, too, by the close supervision by support assistants.

Support assistants working with students said to have severe learning difficulties typically sit with an individual or a couple of students in a lesson. After the teacher's introduction to the lesson the student works on specially prepared materials related to the overall themes being studied. Often these materials are prepared by the assistants, many of whom feel that they have become skilled in this type of work. The amount of teacher involvement in these preparations varies considerably and assistants refer to difficulties that this can create. So, for example, on one occasion an assistant was observed leaving the early part of a lesson in order to photocopy a science worksheet she had quickly prepared for two students as a result of reading the class textbook. This had happened, she explained, because the teacher had not been able to say beforehand what the content of her lesson would be. Another teacher commented about this issue of pre-lesson planning. He explained that he felt that the presence in his classes of children who required adapted materials meant that he could not be so flexible about his planning. He sometimes felt frustrated at the constraints this placed on his capacity to change tack in response to unexpected occurrences in the lesson.

The approaches used to support students with visual impairments takes a different form. According to specialist teachers for students with visual disabilities, considerable emphasis is placed on encouraging the students to be independent. Mary, for example, who had optic nerve damage from birth, is said to be 'educationally blind' but can detect outlines and colours. In six months the level of classroom support had dropped from ninety per cent to fifty per cent, and Mary told us that the support staff want her to be completely independent within a year. She uses a stick to negotiate her way around the school. In class she works in Braille and appears to take part fully. She is often enthusiastic, frequently answering questions or reading aloud to the whole class. She carries her Brailler from room to room, although sometimes other students volunteer to help. Sometimes, she notes, other students complain that her use of the Brailler rocks the desk, making it difficult for them to do their work neatly. Walking around the school with her, it is clear that she feels confident about her presence there and is accepted by other students, many of whom greet her as she passes by. Faced with crowded spaces in the recreation areas she proceeds forcefully, sometimes brushing through groups of students who are in her way. Another Year 7 student, Dean, is said to present far more difficulties than Mary. He previously had congenital cataracts which were removed and lenses implanted. In the school records he is said to have difficulties concentrating on his work and interacting with peers. Support aims to improve his persistence, his confidence to work independently and the extent of positive interactions with classmates. During and between lessons Dean spends a lot of time with Grant, a boy who is reported to have learning difficulties. Usually they sit together at the front of the class and on some occasions they are supported by a teacher or an assistant. It was noticeable that in some lessons both of them experienced difficulties with written material.

The support teacher suggests that part of Dean's problem is that staff may underestimate the extent of his visual difficulties. Noting that he wears glasses, they may assume that his vision is satisfactory and that he should, therefore, be subject to the same demands as other students. His mother, who has a similar condition although more severe, is very pleased with the way Dean has settled into the school. She is particularly positive about the direct access she has to the specialist staff and the form teacher when she has a problem. Frequently she speaks to one or other of them on the telephone.

Withdrawal and resource base teaching

As we have noted, a number of groups were taken out of lessons for special teaching. This included a Year 8 group of 'difficult' students and 'academic remove', as well as students involved in group reading lessons. Considerable use was made of the severe learning difficulties base where some students were present at most times in the day and where, commonly, activities in basic number and reading skills were carried out, in much the same way as they would be in a special school. At other times such categorised students engaged in an activity together outside the base. One of us observed a PE group, where five boys with Down syndrome shared a PE lesson. In this situation there was no close supervision and particularly in the changing room, there was a far greater level of informal banter than was observed in other lessons. Other students in a similar situation also have a lark and a laugh, but they also have greater opportunities for informal social exchange during other lessons. The amount of chat before and during this PE lesson raised questions about how more opportunities for the development of spoken language might be provided elsewhere in the curriculum.

Separating learning and behaviour support

We encountered a couple of striking examples of the effects of the responses to difficulties in behaviour and learning in distinct ways. In the case of Michael described earlier, it seemed that it was the chance presence of one of us observing in the classroom and talking to him calmly that prevented him from moving further along the list of negative consequences in the behaviour policy. In our interviews, another student on the point of being excluded made a plea that having a helper by his side who would talk quietly to him rather than shout at him might help him to control his temper and enable him to continue at the school.

Concluding remarks

A commitment to inclusive education involves working towards an ideal in which schools include all students from their neighbourhood and have a mutually sustaining relationship with their local communities. In the English context, when this goal is given the name 'comprehensive community education' it is associated with a political affiliation on the left of centre. The fostering of local community based education, on the Norwegian model, would involve the repeal of legislation which encourages parents to choose schools outside their neighbourhood, fosters competition between schools, and permits schools to select students on the basis of their attainment.

The study of inclusive education, of the interplay of including and excluding processes, is inevitably shaped by its national and local culture and politics. The political context of inclusive education was evident in Richard Lovell as we examined the balance between inclusive and exclusive responses to diversity and how these are changing.

Besides being influenced by the core beliefs of teachers at the school about comprehensive education and by changing political pressures, the approach to participation is heavily influenced by the way students are categorised as having special needs and teachers and assistants are employed to support them. This individual model of difficulties can distract attention from the task of further developing curricula and teaching approaches more evidently responsive to the differences between all students. If a specific policy is not introduced to increase the capacity of classroom teachers to respond to diverse groups then political pressures are likely to lead to increased setting and withdrawal teaching as well as greater disciplinary exclusion. The lack of connection between learning support and behaviour policies was a notable feature of this, as many other schools, and means that avenues of support may be ignored, and contradictory pressures for inclusion and exclusion may be exerted on the same students.

We identified many ways in which the school organised its response to the diversity of its students. The fact that many, such as age, are common to almost all schools, does not make them any the less significant as ways of reducing diversity in groups, or as requiring examination and international comparison, not least in the way in which mixed age groups can become a resource for learning. Further, Richard Lovell has its own particular set of expectations and theories about the relationship between age and maturity and these have a considerable impact on teaching and learning relationships. The nature and basis of student groupings is at the very heart of discussions of inclusion in education and requires urgent re-examination.

An inspector calls

As we completed our initial series of visits to Richard Lovell High, the impact of the wider political context was becoming even more strikingly evident. The school faced its Ofsted inspection a few months later. As we shared our impressions with senior staff we were aware that the worrying implications of a negative inspection report were in the forefront of their minds as we spoke. How far would the headteacher's anxieties about lack of classroom differentiation be confirmed? Would consideration be given to the students' home backgrounds when evaluating the school's academic record? The head suggested that attitudes in favour of greater selection in the school were hardening, with a consequent effect on the participation of categorised students:

> Next year, for Year 7 we're going for pure mixed ability in each of the ten tutor groups. Into Year 8 we have recognised that there is a need to do more setting than we've done previously, certainly in maths, science, technology, modern language and possibly English.

> *There is now going to be a pressure to go back to small groups of youngsters with learning difficulties, to teach them because it's the more cost effective way.* And I think ultimately both the youngsters and the school will be the losers from that. I think we gain a great

deal from having a blind child within a classroom, or having a Down's syndrome child within a classroom. I think just the human process is so important within the school dynamic and to start to get clusters of kids in the hut in the yard business, *I think we'll start to go back to that.*

As far as our integration programme is concerned, sadly, I think there's going to be increasing pressure as class sizes get larger and budgets get shot, so we have to retract again and set up remedial groups to have youngsters out for more time in their bases.

These views were expressed at a time when the officers of the Local Authority were considering plans for total inclusion, which to them meant the setting up of centralised resource bases for students grouped by category of special need in mainstream schools in zones of the city; or the further creation of what we have called mainstream special schools.

However, despite the fears of some members of staff, the Ofsted inspectors gave the school a glowing report, and described it as an 'outstanding example of inclusive education'. Whether this will encourage the forces behind inclusive practice in the school, or whether a continuing competitive system will fuel greater selection will be revealed in the coming years.

Acknowledgement

This study was supported by research grants from The Open University and the Universities of Cambridge and Newcastle. We are grateful for the instructive comments on an earlier draft of this chapter from Kristine Black-Hawkins.

17

ENGLAND RESPONSE: WE WONDER IF WE'RE FOOLING OURSELVES

In the English case-study, which we wrote with Alan Dyson, we set out to examine the contradictory pressures experienced by the staff in one school, who try to 'include and value students in a competitive climate which creates social pressures to devalue and exclude students'. The account treats inclusion and exclusion as political concepts linking them to policies of selection within and between schools.

We claim that we 'look at how the participation of all students is affected by the policies and practices of the school'. We list and discuss the ways students are included in or excluded from physical and conceptual groupings within the school by setting out the 'organisational responses to diversity'. Within this list, we include the responses of the school to the threat of disorder and so, in this respect there is a link between our chapter and the Australian study.

In re-examining the study we feel that we must try to be as critical of our own offering as we are of the contributions of others. It is in this spirit that we have returned, in the title of the response to our study, to the self-reflection that headed Linda Ware's chapter. How successful are we at escaping from a perspective of the education system viewed through the lens of special education or disability? Given all the possible ways of examining the issues of inclusion and exclusion within a school, how far does our choice of approach reflect the professional bases we have inherited, that others define as falling within special needs education? We will return to these questions when we look at the representation of voices and the nature of the perspectives in the chapter.

How does the national context explain and constrain practice?

We argue that an exploration of the national political, economic, cultural and legislative contexts and their history, as well as the particular history of the school, is essential to understanding the processes of inclusion and exclusion in the school. We attempt to point out, directly, the ways Richard Lovell is

226

influenced by them. The fact that our account of these processes is longer than that in other chapters may be taken to imply that England is idiosyncratic in this respect. We think that such an interpretation is both true and false.

The period from the middle 1980s in England was characterised by a massive increase in central government control of education. In the 1970s, most teachers and head teachers thought of education law as lurking in the background: they had a vague idea of it, but did not see it as having a major effect on their day-to-day work. Even in the early 1980s people spoke of the 1981 Education Act as 'enabling legislation'. An official in central government who had responsibility for over-seeing the passage of the Act told one of us that he was sure it would have a major impact on practice but could not identify in which direction this would be. Apart from the fact that a law which is compatible with two opposing shifts in educational policy has little force, it seemed at the time that such a law was a contradiction in terms. In the late 1990s, however, minute by minute, teachers' lives in England are affected by legislation requiring a detailed National Curriculum, examination league tables and regular, publicised school inspections. These laws, as well as the economic changes that have occurred alongside them, have a very direct effect on the nature of inclusionary and exclusionary pressures, or selection of students within and between schools.

Similar laws may have had a stronger influence than is stated for some of the other countries represented in this book, particularly in New Zealand. However, we are sure that there are very significant cultural pressures operating within all the countries covered in this book which if made more explicit would suggest a far greater determination by context in all the studies. The cultural context of inclusion and exclusion is more elusive than political and legislative changes and we feel that we could have written more about such facets of English life. This would have made our account even longer, but we are aware that, as our study develops in the future, we will need to look in more depth at the cultures specific to Richard Lovell, those that the students and staff bring into the school, and those that act on the school from outside.

Of course, there are many similarities between all schools in all the studies. In seeing schools as broadly similar it may seem unnecessary to draw attention to the common framework for understanding inclusion and exclusion that this creates. Our list of 'organisational responses to diversity' was meant to draw attention to both the similarities *and differences* in structures within schools. These structures are partly inherited from the history of education in England, partly prescribed through government legislation, partly absorbed from the prevailing culture and partly created by the school. Such groupings provide and reinforce a framework for ascribing value to students and thus become ways in themselves of encouraging the inclusion or exclusion of students.

Thus it is evident within our account that Lovell is involved in sorting and grouping students on the basis of their perceived 'general ability' and attainment. The relationship of these school processes to expectations of earnings within the labour market is part of our knowledge of how schools function within societies. Such features of schooling have been made quite explicit in England. Some years ago an adviser to the Secretary of State was quoted as saying 'Perfectly normal children . . . had better learn from the earliest possible age *to come to terms with their own capabilities*' (Times Educational Supplement 18 September 1987, our emphasis). The language that teachers used to describe students at Richard Lovell is evidence of the penetration of such sorting mechanisms into the school. So, for example, the teacher who is to lose some of her special school children as a result of their transfer to the mainstream, refers to the taking away of 'the cream'. Similarly, there is reference to fears of Lovell school losing its 'top end', which is assumed to mean the children of the 'aspirational middle classes'.

The use of categories is a further case in point. In our comments on previous chapters we have considered the assumptions and practices of categorisation as part of the authors' perspective. In our account we referred to such categories as part of the context which constrains the inclusion and exclusion of students. It is part of the framework which needs to be re-examined if the approach to teaching and learning is to be revised within a school.

We tried to set policies and practices to do with special education, including the inclusion of categorised students within the mainstream, within the context of educational policies as a whole. A failure to do this distorts the interpretation of such policy. Thus an apparent, albeit limited, presumption in one section of the 1993 Education Act, of the inclusion of categorised students within mainstream schools, has to be understood alongside the excluding pressures generated within other sections of the same law. Equally, we argue that even this tentative presumption of inclusion is undermined by the 'selective notion that educational difficulties in schools can be resolved by identifying and responding to a large group of students defined as having special educational needs', which 'dominates all levels of policy making, and thinking and practice in schools'. Such selective thinking within special educational policy reinforces the selective pressures of educational policy as a whole. Thus, despite talk of greater integration, more and more students are coming to be regarded as being in some senses disabled and unable to respond to usual teaching arrangements. A similar trend has been noted in other countries (e.g. Fulcher 1989). In this way policies set up to facilitate integration may lead to even greater numbers of students being excluded (Ainscow 1991).

In looking at the political pressures in education we might have taken a broader sweep. For the study of inclusion and exclusion in education should be related to inclusion and exclusion in society. The rapid rise in youth unemployment in the 1980s which has continued in the 1990s, particularly amongst boys, represents a particularly virulent form of social exclusion and is paralleled by increasing disparities of wealth in England. We mentioned the similar

228

political directions in New Zealand with the questioning and dismantling of the welfare state and it is clear that other countries face comparable challenges as represented, for example, in Milner's (1994) account of the policy choices facing the Nordic countries.

Voices and perspectives on inclusion and exclusion

Voices of students, staff and parents are evident in the account to varying degrees but it is the impressions and interpretations of the three authors that predominate. We tried to strike a balance between several purposes of the account; to accurately reflect practice in a particular school, to use the stimulus of our engagement with the school to reflect on our own ideas about inclusion and exclusion, and to generate a way of examining these processes within their contexts.

We have interviewed many teachers, learning support assistants and students and in subsequent accounts of the school we will let them speak for themselves to a far greater extent (for example, Ainscow *et al.* 1996). This will however be of little solace to those who would have liked to hear more of what these participants had to say in the account presented here. We have acted here by and large as privileged external observers, feeding back our reports to the school, respecting and responding to comments but taking responsibility ourselves for the content of the study. However, we have also been seen by the school as contributing to the development of the inclusion policies of the school and there has therefore been an element of action research in the work.

There are a range of perspectives represented in the chapter. Some staff have continued to see our concern with inclusion and exclusion as primarily to do with categorised students. This is hardly surprising given the role of the support staff and the nature of support structures created in the school, as well as our backgrounds. A simplified reading of the account might emphasise a conflict between a largely deficit view of learning difficulties, present in official government policy and incorporated into the school, and our attempts to broaden our exploration of barriers to learning. Yet, such tensions were also apparent in discussions between staff and in our observations of classroom practice. It was striking how the task of responding to students categorised as having special needs was often regarded as being essentially about the preparation of alternative materials, whereas, in practice, the level of participation in classrooms was higher where the teacher adjusted the overall process of the lesson, particularly by utilising group work.

We did not set out clearly our reasons for rejecting other perspectives: we felt that this was the task of the responses to the case-studies and the final chapter of the book, and did not wish to distract other contributors from their own interpretations. In our critique of some other chapters we draw attention to the fact that they examine only sections of the processes of inclusion and exclusion in schools because of their focus on disabled students or students categorised by their low attainment. We argue that you cannot understand the barriers to the participation and learning of such categorised students, and how they might be overcome, without looking more broadly at the inclusionary and exclusionary pressures affecting all students both inside and beyond the school. We have suggested, for example, that such a broader view is more evident in what some of the teachers say in the New Zealand study than in the way that study is directed by its authors.

Writing a decade ago, one of us argued for links to be drawn between diverse efforts to overcome exclusionary pressures within the curriculum:

> There is a current vogue for seeing initiatives about learning diffi-
> culties, and others concerned with the removal of racism and sexism
> from the curriculum, as separate from one another. Yet a support
> teacher who encounters a black girl having difficulty swallowing a
> dose of white male history needs to make a single curriculum adap-
> tation; the curriculum should be made appropriate for that pupil.
>
> Booth 1987, p. 4

Our attempts to examine all processes of inclusion and exclusion within a school and to set them in context of the pressures on the education system as a whole produced a long and, perhaps, cumbersome study which even then may have conveyed a sense of incompleteness. In places, too, it lacks depth and detail. We recognise, with hindsight, that we could have applied our per-spective to our study differently. Like Julie Allan, for example, we might have selected for comparison the educational experience of a small number of students within the school, subject to different constellations of inclusionary and exclusionary processes.

A concentration on categorised students and the processes of exclusion that affect them distracts us from seeing the lack of participation of other students or understanding it, and we provided examples of the way this happened in Richard Lovell. When it is represented as the channel through which educational problems are resolved, special education can obscure those features of schools and the education system which would enable failure, lack of participation and disaffection to be productively addressed.

In our report of classroom practice, too, there is an evident concern with teaching and learning processes affecting all students. The range of features of practice examined in our 'organisational responses to diversity' illustrate a concern with participation, and ascriptions of value, across the school as well as providing indications of the way notions of inclusion and exclusion can be given specific meaning by specifying what students are included in or excluded from.

We pointed out how some forms of selection into groups, such as age, may be taken for granted and seen as natural, while others are taken as unnatural.

What is taken for granted and what is contested differs from chapter to chapter as we saw in the New Zealand study where Reading Recovery was seen to involve an everyday withdrawal.

We indicated the way responses in the school to perceived difficulties in behaviour and learning were distinct, and largely uncoordinated. This is a feature of many schools and it can prove very resistant to change. A preoccupation with the maintenance of order is a well known and understandable feature of school life but it can drive the development of contradictory policies on student participation. At times this contradiction may be apparent in the reaction by different members of staff to the same student. According to our perspective, in a school that wishes to minimise exclusion a concern with 'increasing participation in the cultures and curricula of the school' has to inform every contact with students, including 'disciplinary' actions.

However, it is clear to us that our study could have made far greater use of a range of starting points for uncovering barriers to participation. The fall in the availability of traditionally male forms of employment has affected the attitudes to education of boys in schools. It may be part of the explanation for the increasing disparity between the attainments of boys and girls in terms of examination success at 16 years old (Cooper 1989; Abraham 1995). Where setting by attainment occurs in schools, lower sets usually contain an over-preponderance of boys, and Richard Lovell is no exception. In the case of students categorised as having difficulties or special needs, boys are always in the majority, as indicated in several of the chapters. However, while the issue of gender crops up in all the chapters in one form or another, it is not a central issue in any of them. Looking at why many more boys than girls are vulnerable to exclusion and appear to have difficulties in participating in education must form a major part of any full investigation of inclusion and exclusion in a school. It is a deficiency of our study that it is given so little mention there. Such a lack, as well as the limited attention given to other major issues of class, race and sexuality, may lead the reader to question our claim to be concerned with all barriers to the participation and learning of students.

18

MAKING COMPARISONS: DRAWING CONCLUSIONS

We have presented case-studies of schools in eight countries set in their national and local contexts in order to illuminate differences in perspective on inclusion and exclusion. We provided an individual analysis of each chapter in which we examined the extent to which school and national contexts were related, drew attention to and contested the assumptions of the authors and the perspectives revealed in the texts.

In this final chapter, we review what the studies and our responses reveal about the nature and significance of perspectives, about the possibilities for redefining a field of 'special education' as the study of inclusion and exclusion, and conclude by commenting on the implications of our work on this book for the development of comparative research in this field.

In chapter 1 we set out our concerns about the way much of the existing comparative research in special education ignores the relationships between policy, practice and culture. Indeed, frequently, research in any one country underplays the significance of differences of view about issues of inclusion and exclusion, and the variation in interpretation of practice between and within groups of parents, teachers, other professionals and academics. Where such differences are recognised they may be seen as reflecting differences in amounts of knowledge, to be resolved by research evidence, rather than as evidence of more fundamental clashes of interest underpinned by moral and political positions and philosophies. In reflecting a national perspective, academics and researchers may treat their own country as a monoculture.

We explored the meaning of 'perspective' as a complex interplay between understandings of reality and value systems. We deliberately set out to construct a method for exploring inclusion and exclusion which would reveal, rather than obscure, differences of perspective between and within countries. In fact, the perspectives of the researchers themselves proved to have a deep shaping effect on the ways in which they carried out and reported what started off as a common task.

As we have pointed out, we did not attempt the development of a pedagogy for inclusion through this book, though we recognise the significance and potential of such a task, and the contribution made to it by some of the chapters. We argue that pedagogies cannot be selected and borrowed from a culturally-neutral peg. They are inseparable from the conceptions of and responses to student diversity within organisations, cultures and policies. In those chapters that most clearly discuss pedagogies for inclusion, the development of inclusive practice is seen to be closely related to the creation of an inclusive culture and philosophy. This echoes work which shows how the establishment of collaborative practices arises most effectively in classrooms with a collaborative culture (Hart 1992).

The nature and significance of perspectives

We do not see the book as discovering differences of perspective, but argue that in demonstrating the significance of such differences we make them harder to ignore in future research. The failure to recognise and discuss such differences has served as a major barrier to communication about this area. It is a denial of the obvious that can only be accounted for by the operation of powerful ideological and personal forces. We relate these to dominant traditions of research, which see the fruits of research endeavour in terms of decontextualised generalisations. Such traditions are reinforced by the globalisation of communication about research in journals and conferences. In these fora subtle differences of meaning of concepts, policies and practices are hidden by the use of an apparently shared language to conceptualise and discuss education. Consequently, instead of the results of educational research being about real schools in real cities and villages, schools become artefacts of international academic and research communities.

In our commentaries we drew attention to the nature of the perspectives of the different authors, the participants in the schools they studied and those of the policy makers who set the framework for practice within schools. In this section we concentrate on some of the key differences of *researcher* perspective that are evident in the texts. In this way we provide an overall map that can be used to reflect upon and engage with the significance of perspectives for further research in this area.

In Figure 18.1 we re-present our list of dimensions on which perspectives on inclusion and exclusion differ. We included that list in chapter 1 as a scaffold to help the reader to develop a critique of the case-studies. As we have indicated, we brought some of these dimensions to this study from the start. However, our intensive engagement with the texts of our colleagues enabled us to develop our list. We think of this as conceptual refinement prompted by empirical engagement with the texts. We do not claim that our list is exhaustive but present it as one way of starting to formulate differences in perspective. However, we would hope that our demonstration of some of the positions that can be taken about the nature and investigation of 'inclusion' and 'exclusion' will help to encourage others to make perspectives explicit and avoid a unidimensional view.

Figure 18.1 Dimensions of difference in perspectives on inclusion and exclusion

Definitions
1   Are inclusion and exclusion seen as unending processes or as states of being inside or outside the mainstream, or of being either 'fully' or not included?
2   Are some exclusions taken for granted and only some examined and contested?
3   Are inclusion and exclusion seen as separate processes, affecting different groups of students, or are they seen as necessarily linked?
4   Are inclusion and exclusion applied to a limited group of categorised students or are they applied to all students whose participation in mainstream cultures, curricula and communities might be enhanced?

Responding to diversity
5   Are some students seen as 'other', as 'them' rather than 'us'?
6   Are difficulties in learning or disabilities attributed to defects or impairments in students or seen as arising in relationships between students and their social and physical environment?
7   Is the response to difficulties experienced by students seen only as individual and technical or as also a matter of values and philosophies, policies, structures and curricula, affecting all students?
8   Is diversity celebrated as a resource to be valued or seen as a problem to be overcome?
9   Is participation within a local mainstream school seen as a right or as dependent on professional judgement?
10 Is there an emphasis on a common curriculum for all or on special curricula for some?

Recognising differences of perspective
11 Are inclusion and exclusion in school connected to wider social and political processes?
12 Are the concepts used to discuss inclusion and exclusion seen as universal or as embedded within a social and cultural context that makes translation complex and hazardous?
13 Are approaches to inclusion and exclusion seen as common within a country amounting to a national perspective or as reflecting particular perspectives, voices and interests?
14 Are differences in perspective on inclusion and exclusion among and between staff and students explored or ignored?
15 Are the differing voices within groups of researchers revealed or obscured?
16 Are forms of presentation and research method seen as part of the approach to inclusion and exclusion or as distinct from it?

We have grouped the dimensions together under three themes, defining terms, responding to diversity and recognising the significance of perspectives. We see the dimensions under each theme as interactive. For example, the way inclusion and exclusion are defined radically affects the way student difficulties are conceived and the interventions that are made to prevent or reduce them. Our third theme is the least transparent. It is about how far authors recognise and represent differences of perspective in their case-studies. This includes a willingness to see the processes of inclusion and exclusion and perspectives on them as influenced by national and local contexts. The dimensions in this third theme, it seems to us, have a particular significance, for they form the basis for successful communication about comparative research in this area. Without relating research to its context researchers fail to convey sufficient reality for others to build on their findings.

As we noted in Chapter 1, perspectives may be highly complex – interweaving strands of experience, knowledge and beliefs. Furthermore, there may be inconsistencies within the perspectives of any one individual and, of course, these may change over time. Consequently, the idea of mapping perspectives is fraught, particularly if such a typology is used to characterise the positions of individuals. By and large, perspectives act as guiding assumptions of authors, which may remain implicit or even unrecognised. Yet we know from discussions with contributors that, for some, the process of carrying out the research challenged and modified their views.

Defining terms

We were a little surprised by the limited attention given to defining terms in some chapters, especially given the extensive discussion of subtleties of meaning and issues of translation that occurred during the process of developing the chapters. Even where definitions of inclusion and exclusion are included in chapters, this does not end the need for clarification. In the England chapter we define inclusion using notions of 'participation', 'culture', 'curriculum', 'community', 'mainstream' and 'neighbourhood'. These are themselves complicated concepts, though we suspect that they can be given meaning in most countries. Such a definition, even with its limited specificity, begins to narrow down the answer to the questions 'included in what?', 'excluded from what?'.

We had also thought that the idea that inclusion and exclusion should principally be viewed as unlimited processes (**dimension 1**) had been broadly accepted, since it permits an examination of the fine detail of increasing student participation, the pressures that actively stifle student involvement, produce disaffection or are the precursors to ejection from the mainstream. Yet, for example, Linda Ware in her introduction, conceives of both mainstreaming and inclusion as states. She defines the first 'as attendance in a special class', and the second as involvement in 'the regular class'. This persistence in seeing inclusion as a fixed state, or as a number of fixed states may help to explain why it has become prevalent to make a firm distinction between integration and mainstreaming on the one hand and inclusion on the other, in an effort to signal a more ambitious aspiration. It is certainly the case that many students transferring into the mainstream from special schools continue to be given a broadly separate education and fail to shed their special label. Often, they do not transform into 'mainstream students', as Julie Allan illustrates. The disappointment that inclusion has not proceeded as far as a particular author might like may then be blamed on the restriction of the concept. However, through her exploration of the Theater Issues class, Linda Ware clearly reveals that she sees inclusion in practice as an unending process. Such inconsistency is common in the perspectives of all of us.

Jeff Bailey refers to inclusion only as 'full' inclusion, and Keith Ballard and Trevor MacDonald talk of their school as 'inclusive', implying that others can be designated simply as 'non-inclusive'. In the Norwegian chapter there is extensive discussion of definitions, and the notion of inclusion as an *active* process informs the observation of classrooms and playground, yet we learn that Berg is 'on the way towards achieving inclusiveness' as if this is a realisable goal. Yet, of course, it is sometimes pertinent to write of inclusion and exclusion as states, for example in answering the question: who is included in and who is excluded from the student community of a school?

Processes of inclusion and exclusion can be taken for granted in at least two ways (**dimension 2**). One of these was revealed quite strikingly during a visit to English secondary schools by a South African visitor. She was shocked by the frequency of setting – at how often students were placed in teaching groups according to attainment. However, she defended the South African practice of making students resit a year if they failed to make the grade, a practice evident in the chapters in this book on the Netherlands and the US. We suspect that it is common in England not to see grouping by attainment as involving exclusion, and even less common to challenge grouping according to age. Several of the chapters refer to schools that select students on the basis of their religion. This represents an under-explored form of exclusion in education, as we have suggested when discussing the Ireland chapter.

The Ireland chapter exemplifies another aspect of taken-for-granted exclusion. There are a group of students who are not part of the education system at all in Ireland, which is the only country in our sample not to have passed an educability law to entitle all children to education. But several other chapters assume that only some students can be candidates for the mainstream, and this is enshrined in the 'together to school again' policy in the Netherlands. Such a view is most powerfully challenged through Linda Ware's account of Josh, but also by the discussion of the right to belong evident in several other chapters.

In examining groupings we have to be clear on the difference in significance between voluntary and compulsory exclusion, both for the system that creates it and for the people that it affects. Compulsory exclusion, however, can have both a legal and an economic basis. A refusal to provide the assistance to support the education of disabled students in the mainstream, for example, can amount to compulsory segregation, even though the law may in theory give such students the right to mainstream attendance. Such a system is described in both the Netherlands and Ireland.

Linking the processes of inclusion and exclusion (**dimension 3**) can emphasise the active nature of processes required to sustain inclusion. If we see a lack of participation as actively caused by exclusionary pressures, then inclusion has to combat them and depends on the balance of competing forces being in its favour. Further, the linking of inclusion and exclusion allows us to ask who is subject to exclusionary pressures and thereby broadens our concern to the inclusion and participation of all these students.

We had hoped to make this link a unifying theoretical strand of the case-studies. From our perspective, the chapters can be read as concerned with the processes of both inclusion and exclusion. One might argue that, conceptually, it is impossible to consider a concept without implying something about its opposite. However, direct references to the link between inclusionary and exclusionary pressures are not common in the case-studies apart from the England chapter, and we feel that a more overt comparative examination of the processes of inclusion and exclusion is still to be attempted.

Commonly in England the notion of exclusion is reserved, officially, to describe the event of disciplinary exclusion from school and the notion of inclusion is usually thought to be concerned with students categorised according to disability or special need. Very little consideration is given to other groups vulnerable to exclusion, such as traveller students or pregnant students (Booth 1996). If such divisions are unchallenged, the academics and researchers who concern themselves with different groups of students fail to communicate and the theoretical understanding of exclusion from school is distorted.

Most of the chapters are primarily concerned with the inclusion or exclusion of students categorised as disabled or as being special because they are perceived as 'abnormally' low in attainment or difficult to control (**dimension 4**). They are thus located quite firmly within a traditional field of special education, however much the authors might wish to distance themselves from it. In our comments on the New Zealand chapter we questioned the conceptual clarity of replacing a traditional special education approach with the advocacy of the rights to inclusion of disabled students, a position apparently adopted in England by Oliver (1995).

Jeff Bailey goes furthest in suggesting that inclusion for all cannot occur without some assigning of students to special education categories. Yet, the limits of such an approach are revealed by brief observation of the way that barriers to participation and learning arise in classrooms for a much wider group of students than those categorised. Further, we have argued that the attempt to treat the difficulties that arise for students in schools as if they can be resolved by addressing the education of a limited group of categorised students is counterproductive, in deflecting attention from the possibilities of improving learning opportunities for all. On our definition of inclusion as 'the process of increasing the participation of students in the mainstream', it can make no sense to restrict our concern only to the inclusion of some of those students vulnerable to exclusionary pressures. Such a perception arises, we suspect, because of the persistence of an association of inclusion with the step of getting students out of special schools into the mainstream. Once such students are in the mainstream their inclusion can be seen to become part of the much broader task of promoting student participation. Thus, when in the mainstream, they become part of the diversity of mainstream students, not a special category of 'integrated students' as Roger Slee reports from one Australian school (Slee 1996), and is evident in some of our case-studies.

Responding to diversity

We do not suggest that it makes any sense to attempt to avoid all forms of categorisation, and agree with Jeff Bailey that not all categorisation involves negative labelling. A focus on categorised students can be part of an attempt to enhance the participation of a particular group or advocate their rights. The recognition of the particular support some disabled students need is an essential part of a response to diversity that accepts and celebrates difference.

Nevertheless, in describing the learning characteristics of students, several chapters categorise some students as 'having learning difficulties' or as 'having special needs' or assign them to categories such as 'educable mentally retarded' or 'mild mental handicap'. Such categorisations can be seen to divide students into the 'normal' (like us) and the 'less than normal' (not like us), as acknowledged in the Norway chapter (**dimension 5**). As one test of the inclusiveness of our language we might consider whether the people described in our studies would be happy with the way we describe them.

An illuminating episode occurred during the seminar to shape the development of the case-studies that may allow us to reflect on the extent to which students categorised as having learning difficulties or as having special needs are also placed in a special category of humanity. One of our collaborators asked whether there were many schools like Richard Lovell in England. We suspected that the questioner was asking whether there were other secondary schools which included a sizeable population of students categorised as having severe learning difficulties, a group excluded from the education system in Ireland. However, in order to emphasise our perspective of being concerned with all students in the school and to challenge the assumptions of the questioner, one of us answered: 'there are many schools which include students of these ages in England'. If for the purpose of discussing inclusion and exclusion, categorised students are seen as part of the diversity of students, should their presence be seen as the defining feature of a school? The answer created a pause of incomprehension and some careful clarification was about to begin, when an observer present interrupted: 'come on, you know it's the only one like that'.

In fact, there are at least five secondary schools in England that could be considered to be 'mainstream special schools', with a relatively large number of students categorised as having severe learning difficulties and many more who include one or a few students so categorised. We accept that such information is of interest. But we were concerned to promote discussion of why the presence of such students should be seen as the defining feature of Richard Lovell, whether our concern with the participation of all students could penetrate the screen of such a perception, and whether such a view ultimately involved regarding such students as other than 'us'. We have considered this example several times and are concerned that the point we are making may be elusive. Nevertheless, we feel that it captures the essence of the shift in perspective that we are trying to make in our own thinking about the field.

The assigning of students to diagnostic categories, often as a precursor to allocating them to different settings for treatment, most evident in the chapters from the Netherlands and Australia but also in several other case-studies, is part of the medicalisation of educational difficulties often called the 'medical model', though this caricatures the variety of approaches to understanding disease within medicine. According to such a model, student difficulties arise because of student deficits or impairments (**dimension 6**). Such thinking is frequently challenged in relation to disabled students. An alternative, social model of disability is well-rehearsed, if less commonly applied in practice than one might suppose. It is not a feature of education legislation in England, for example. According to such a model, as is now well known, the failure of a disabled student to gain access to a school or a curriculum is not caused by the student's impairment, but by the failure of the educational system to make appropriate adaptations. Disability is then seen to be created by such failure in the systems and fabric of society.

A social view of difficulties in learning is less discussed, even by proponents of a social model of disability. On such a view learning difficulties are not something students have, but arise in a relationship between students and tasks and the resources available to support learning. The difficulties in learning experienced by students can be understood and responded to in the same way as the difficulties in learning experienced by teachers. Therefore, the insights that we have about our own learning can be applied to the understanding of the learning of students. Equally, the insights we gain in understanding the learning of some students, for example those traditionally designated as the ones with learning difficulties, can be applied to the learning of other students not so designated. Susan Hart has argued that students with learning difficulties or special needs should be replaced by the notion of students whose learning 'gives cause for concern' (Hart 1996, p. 10). We suggest that an emphasis on the social nature of difficulties in learning and disabilities can be signalled by the concept of 'students who experience barriers to learning'.

Intervention in response to difficulties might be seen, then, to involve the identification and removal of barriers to learning, rather than diagnosing and treating the defects of students. However, the physical image conveyed by a barrier, like the notion of student defect, might suggest that difficulties should be addressed, primarily, through interventions of a technical if not individual nature (**dimension 7**). The chapters of this book take a wide variety of complex positions on the degree to which school difficulties should be responded to in these ways or require a change in school values, cultures and philosophies as well as changes in policies, school organisational structures and curricula affecting all students.

The focus on student difficulties within the traditional special education enterprise, with its attempts to create homogeneous groups for special treatment, conceives of diversity as a problem to be overcome rather than a cause for celebration (**dimension 8**). Our examination of 'organisational responses to diversity' in the England chapter revealed an emphasis on diversity as problematic. Yet, if we recognise and welcome diversity we open up the possibility of using diversity as a resource for learning.

In many classrooms the principal aspect of diversity that is recognised is the distinction between a single teacher, assumed to be relatively mature and knowledgeable and a group of students seen as uniformly immature and ignorant. However, there is an immense resource available to assist learning that is present by virtue of the difference between students; differences of age and maturity, of knowledge, attainment and experience, of skills and personal qualities. It is a luxury of developed nations that they can fail to utilise such a resource. We argue, and the point is echoed through the examples in some chapters, that the utilisation of such a resource is a defining feature of our perspective on inclusion.

The acceptance that students have a right to attend a neighbourhood mainstream school, which, it should be acknowledged, they may not wish to exercise, is an assumption or assertion of some chapters (**dimension 9**). It can be seen as part of a broader view that students should have the same educational opportunities irrespective of race, class, gender, sexuality, cultural background, disability or attainment. The acceptance of such a view, radically alters the idea of what is important research in this field, much of which continues to attempt to determine where students identified as having difficulties are most effectively educated (see Hegarty 1993). The acceptance of a student's right to belong in the mainstream does not rule out occasions when rights conflict and may be resolved by exclusion. This can happen, for example, if a participant in education is so violent that it infringes the right to a safe education of others.

Kari and Marit illustrate the Norwegian connection between the 'right to belong' and the 'right to learn'. They define the latter as 'every child has to be given equal opportunities to develop their abilities', which might be seen as being promoted by 'right to be educated' or 'educability' law. There is another notion of rights in relation to learning illustrated in some chapters, notably New Zealand and England, which emphasise an entitlement to a common, national curriculum. Certainly, we could order chapters according to their degree of focus on providing special curricula for some students or on a common but flexible curriculum for all students (**dimension 10**).

Recognising the significance of perspectives

We have given considerable prominence to what we see as the significance of national and regional policies and legislation, as well as cultural histories, in providing a framework for the local understanding of inclusion and exclusion. We argue that an understanding of what is observed in schools is severely limited without such knowledge of context about another country or one's own. We asked others, and set out ourselves, to address what an international audience needs to know about national and local policies and cultures, and school structures, cultures and curricula to make sense of the processes of inclusion and exclusion within a school. For example, how far can we understand inclusion without knowing about grouping policies and their legal regulation, or without establishing the significance of 'community' in particular cultures, or cultural attitudes to disability or travellers? We feel that researchers in this area have frequently ignored an obligation to interrelate macro and micro determinants of practice.

We saw the case-studies as cases of 'a school in a local region in a country'. We prompted authors to give more detail of context, but this did little to reduce the differences in the quantity of discussion in the case-studies of national contexts (**dimension 11**). In some chapters the context is interpreted almost exclusively as being about special education legislation and policies on the inclusion of categorised students, rather than inclusionary and exclusionary pressures within the education system and society more generally. Chapters also differ in their attention to other aspects of context. The particular history of the school and the influence this has on inclusionary and exclusionary processes is addressed in the New Zealand, Norwegian and England case-studies but only marginally in others.

The case-studies provide a firm basis for developing a view of national perspectives as constrained by a framework of national policies, histories and cultures but always constructed from a plurality of contrasting and conflicting strands. It is to be hoped that researchers will no longer represent an official view, gleaned from government policy documents, often displaying inconsistencies and problems of conceptualisation, as the national view of inclusion and exclusion.

The use of special education categories to depict groups of students particularly reveals the degree to which authors recognise the variation in perspectives within and between countries (**dimension 12**). Academics are still willing to present papers to international audiences with titles which take for granted that local terms, such as 'emotional and behavioural difficulty', have international currency. As we argued in response to Jeff Bailey, even where an 'international definition' is said to have been given by the American Psychiatric Association, a claim which itself implies a view of national dominance rather than international collaboration, categories such as Attention Deficit Hyperactivity Disorder cannot but be given local meaning and prevalence.

Categories which have particular meanings in one locality can be seen as 'first order concepts', which require explanation for people without the cultural knowledge that lies behind their use. Using words that are less context-bound can be termed 'second order concepts'. This challenge to the taken for granted nature of categorisation can be seen as a basic requirement for academic study in this area. Notions of community, participation, neighbourhood, inclusion and exclusion, normality or 'them' and 'us', disability, categorisation, the assigning of value according to attainment and behaviour, are all ideas which can be given meanings in a variety of countries and through which local first order concepts can be interpreted in order to be understood in different cultures (see Booth 1995).

We have detected suggestions from some authors that national policies are more coherent than our analysis of the texts reveals them to be. However, most chapters do reveal differences of perspective within countries (**dimension 13**) and there is little attempt within them to present a single national perspective on all aspects of inclusion and exclusion. Yet, the degree of representation of a diversity of voices as well as the selection of voices that are featured, differs considerably between case-studies. In the England case-study, for example, we articulated deep political conflicts about the degree of selectivity that should structure the education system, although the different voices of participants in the school are muted (**dimension 14**). We have questioned whether the inclusion of frequently submerged voices, like those of school students, in a text in which they are surrounded by the discourse of professional academics, makes their message more or less likely to be heard.

In the Irish study the national differences of view are given a small amount of space, but the chapter itself is constructed around the differences in view of the researchers (**dimension 15**). We feel that such differences should be revealed more frequently. How can academics develop and defend a point of view constructed from an amalgamation of perspectives?

The chapters are relatively uniform in their presentation styles except for the US chapter, which presents contrasting 'academic' and 'narrative' dis-

courses (**dimension 16**). We contested the characterisation of the convention-
ally academic discourse as 'non-narrative' and argued that the less
academically conventional style might actually be the more academic. We
hope that Linda Ware's chapter will point the way towards a greater diversity
of presentation styles, and that our structuring of this book contributes in a
small way to this process, in the footsteps of the break with the traditional
construction of textbooks in Jenny Corbett's 'Badmouthing' (Corbett 1996).
Linda, Keith Ballard and Trevor MacDonald go furthest in trying to make
their research approach inclusive of the subjects of their research, though
only some of the participants in the schools were chosen as research partners.
Others were committed to research methods that distanced them from the
people they studied and could be seen, thereby, to marginalise them further.

Are some perspectives more equal than others?

Clearly, we have not adopted a relativistic position that all perspectives are of
equal value, and in this respect we embrace but do not unequivocally celebrate diversity. The adoption of particular perspectives and a critique of
other perspectives is apparent in our analysis of the case-studies and our discussion of dimensions along which perspectives may differ in this chapter.
Since perspectives are 'ways of viewing connected to values', they express
commitments to particular directions for the development of practice and
necessarily presume a critique of other positions. We do not equally favour all
directions for the development of practice or value equally all responses to
difference.

There are further respects in which we see some perspectives as less attractive than others. We argue that academic debate is furthered when writers
make their views and assumptions explicit and explore them self-critically and
avoid inconsistency. The more views of inclusion and exclusion are articulated and avoid contradiction, the better they can be connected to a coherent
programme for the development of policy and practice.

Finally, and of critical significance, the holders of some perspectives do not
recognise the possibility of other perspectives. Thus, some proponents of a
deficit view of educational difficulties may see their view not as a perspective
involving a value position but as a scientific truth unconstructed by its context. Inevitably, discussions with those who recognise differences in
perspective are more productive than with those who do not.

Redefining the field?

We argue that a field of special education can be redefined, in part at least,
using the concepts of inclusion and exclusion. Students placed in special
education categories are some of those who have been subject to exclusionary
pressures in schools, and their categorisation itself has often contributed to

the process of exclusion. The attempt to engage such students in curricula appropriate to their interests and attainments and foster their participation with others can be seen as fostering their mainstream inclusion. For us, however, a *redefinition* requires us to go further than to change words, to merely relabel traditional special education with the phrase 'inclusive education'. It involves detaching a concern with inclusion and exclusion from a particular history of special education, concerned with the identification and remediation of student deficits and defects. It requires that we see students with disabilities and those who experience difficulties in learning as part of the diversity of the student population, subject to a wide variety of inclusionary and exclusionary pressures. It means that we have to resist a division between 'us' and 'them', the normal and abnormal students and the use of the euphemistic categories, such as 'learners with SEN', which obscure such a practice.

From our perspective, then, a redefinition of the field in terms of inclusion and exclusion requires a shift from seeing inclusion as about individual special educational planning and special pleading for individual students, to the development of a pedagogy of inclusion and a commitment to the rights of all to belong. It leads us to have a concern with all exclusionary pressures and all students whose participation in mainstream cultures, curricula and communities can be enhanced; with policies and curricular for diversity. Such a redefinition can be seen as one of the possible set of perspectives represented in the case-studies.

The traditional special education enterprise that educational difficulties can be resolved primarily by identifying and treating student deficits can be seen as a failed experiment or fantasy. The retention of this view prevents questions being asked about the prevention of difficulties, the removal of barriers to learning and the improvement of teaching and learning relationships. In its concentration on the difficulties of individuals, it leads us to overlook, and therefore prevents us from responding appropriately to, the common barriers to learning of groups of students; for example, the glaring over-representation of boys, black students and disadvantaged students among those who are seen to experience difficulties in school or are subject to exclusionary pressures (see Booth 1995; Epstein 1997; Nixon *et al.* 1997; Potts 1997; Riddell 1996; Warren 1997; Sewell 1997). The failure to examine gender issues, in particular, has been a clear feature of the case-studies in this book. It can be argued sensibly, for example, from the empirical evidence, that responses to difficulties in learning should be as much concerned with the way schools can contribute to the construction of masculinities as with direct responses to differences in attainment.

In redefining our field in terms of inclusion and exclusion, our work has evident connections with disciplines outside of education: for example, geographers, too, work on the occupation of space and exclusion from it (Sibley 1995; Massey 1995), and other social scientists on social exclusion connected to poverty and racism (Brown and Crompton 1994; Miles and Thranhardt 1995) or on the notions of social justice which underpin a concern for students vulnerable to exclusion (Christensen 1997). In understanding the processes of teaching and learning and the history of developments, we look to a mainstream experience of working with diverse groups rather than confining ourselves to the contribution to this history of people calling themselves special educators (see Clark *et al.* 1997; Hart 1996). We believe that our examination of organisational responses to diversity starts an examination of the way groupings and categorisations in a school structure the processes of inclusion and exclusion. This more systematic structural analysis can be extended to comparative studies of legislation, education systems, policies and cultures.

Yet, we remain uncertain how far an incorporation of special education into a new field of inclusion and exclusion in education will proceed with those who have established their careers within a field of 'special education'. Professionals and academics who make their living from a particular way of ordering reality do not take readily to seeing their territory reapportioned and may make all sorts of contortions to display a readiness to change while avoiding a shift of position (see Booth 1997).

The case-studies that emerged for this book show how some researchers made a straightforward translation of our interest in processes of inclusion and exclusion into a traditional special educational concern with students categorised according to a medical, defect model. They also reveal the continuing power of positivist thinking in research. This is shown, overtly, through the use of methods aimed at producing context-free generalisations applied to a case-study task designed to reveal the dependence of the meaning of policies and practices on the contexts in which they arise. It also persists in the assumption in some of the other studies that local definitions and categories have international currency.

We recognise the difficulties of producing studies in a changing field. In discussing the England case-study we indicated that a commitment to looking at all processes of inclusion and exclusion made it difficult to limit the length of the study. Nevertheless, whatever the difficulties in setting up studies in a redefined field, we believe that the connection of special education to the mainstream of academic research through the concepts of inclusion and exclusion is a clear consequence and benefit of the exploration of perspectives in this book.

Planning future research

Research that recognises the diversity of perspectives within and between countries, and makes its assumptions about perspectives explicit, offers the best basis for the future study of the processes of inclusion and exclusion. It is research which acknowledges the hazardous nature of communication and the painstaking attention that we need to give to issues of translation when we learn about practice in other countries. This does not mean we should give up but we should remain aware, as Andrews pointed out when cautioning herself about her research in a country where her familiarity with the language was very limited: 'how difficult it is to understand another, even if they are of the same gender, class, nationality, sexual orientation, and all the other categories a good professor of sociology would alert her students to' (Andrews 1995, p. 47). Much comparative research echoes the caricature of the English abroad who, faced with someone who does not speak their language, believe they will communicate effectively by speaking more slowly and turning up the volume.

We are at the beginning of an exploration of the subtle differences of the meaning of the processes and practices of inclusion and exclusion between different countries. We are particularly concerned to build comparative studies that are inclusive of countries more economically and culturally disparate than those that are part of this study. We link this to a wish to return from our advocacy of perspectives, to research studies more carefully targeted at promoting change in policy and practice.

We hope our study will encourage more research that recognises the complexity and plurality of perspectives, voices and interests and the need for researchers to make them explicit. This might include studies which explode the myth of researcher consensus and develop more creative forms of presentation. Notions of what constitutes inclusive research should be re-examined so that they encourage research partnerships which more commonly include those with the least power in the system, particularly students in schools.

The examination of the nature of perspectives permits an understanding of the way research in this field has been constrained by a particular history of special education, dominated by a particular medical and psychological view of why students experience difficulties in schools, and how they might be resolved. We suggest that a perspective which fully utilises the fertility of the concepts of 'inclusion' and 'exclusion' allows a break from such a history and the creation of a new one.

BIBLIOGRAPHY

Abberley, P. (1987) 'The concept of oppression and the development of a social theory of disability', *Disability, Handicap and Society*, 2(1), 5–19.

Abraham, J. (1995) *Divide and School: gender and class dynamics in comprehensive education*, London: Falmer.

Adviesraad voor het Basisonderwijs (1990) *Opmaat tot samenspel (The start of inclusion)*, Zeist: ARBO.

Ainscow, M. (1991) (ed.) *Effective Schools for All*, London: Fulton.

Ainscow, M. (1995a) 'Education for all: making it happen', *Support for Learning* 10(4), 147–157.

Ainscow, M. (1995b) 'Special needs through school improvement; school improvement through special needs', in Clark, C., Dyson, A. and Millward, A. (eds) *Towards Inclusive Schools?* London: Fulton.

Ainscow, M., Booth, T. and Dyson, A. (1996) 'Inclusion and Exclusion; listening to some hidden voices', Paper presented at the 3rd International Research Colloquium on Inclusive Education, Auckland, New Zealand.

Alban-Metcalfe, J. (1996) 'Country briefing: special education in England', *European Journal of Special Needs Education*, 11(1), 144–149.

Allan, J. (1994) 'Integration in the United Kingdom' in Riddell, S. and Brown, S. (eds) *Special Educational Needs Policy in the 1990s; Warnock in the market place*, London: Routledge.

Allan, J., Brown, S. and Riddell, S. (1995) 'Students with special educational needs in mainstream and special schools in Scotland', Final report to the Scottish Office Education Department, University of Stirling.

American Psychiatric Association (1987) *Diagnostic and Statistical Manual of Mental Disorders (3rd edn revised)*, Washington, DC: American Psychiatric Association.

American Psychiatric Association (1994) *Diagnostic and Statistical Manual of Mental Disorders (4th edn)*, Washington DC: American Psychiatric Association.

Anderson, E. (1973) *The Disabled Schoolchild: A Study of Integration in Primary Schools*, London: Methuen.

Andrews, M. (1995) 'A monoglot abroad: working through problems of translation', *Oral History*, Autumn 1995, 47–50.

Apple, M. (1982) *Knowledge and Power*, New York: Routledge.

Armstrong, D. (1995) *Power and Partnership in Education*, London: Routledge.

Armstrong, D. and Galloway, D. (1992) 'On being a client: conflicting perspectives on assessment', in Booth, T., Swann, W., Masterton, M. and Potts, P. (eds) *Policies for Diversity in Education*, London: Routledge.

Armstrong, F. J. (1995) 'Appellation Controllée: mixing and sorting in the French education system', in Potts, P., Armstrong, F. J. and Masterton M. (eds) *Equality and Diversity in Education 2: national and international contexts*, London: Routledge.

Bailey, J. G. (1978) 'The development and evaluation of a simulation course in mainstreaming', unpublished doctoral dissertation, University of Cincinnati.

Bailey, J. G. and Curtis, S. (1996) 'Parental management of children with ADHD' in Rice, D. and Bailey J. (eds) *ADHD: Medical, Psychological and Educational Perspectives*, Sydney: AASE.

Baker, M. J. and Salon, R. S. (1986). 'Setting free the captives: the power of community integration in liberating institutional adults from the bonds of the past' *Journal of the Association for Persons with Severe Handicaps*, 11, 176–181.

Ballard, K. (1991) 'An ecological analysis of progress toward non-restrictive environments in New Zealand' in Ashman, A. F. (ed.) 'Current themes in integration', *The Exceptional Child Monograph*, 2, 23–36). St Lucia: Fred and Eleanor Schonell Special Education Research Centre.

Ballard, K. (1995) 'Inclusion, paradigms, power and participation' in Clark C., Dyson A. and Millward A. (eds) *Towards Inclusive Schools?* London: Fulton.

Ballard, K. (1996) 'Inclusive education in New Zealand: culture, context and ideology', *Cambridge Journal of Education* 26(1), 33–46.

Barkley, R. A. (1988) 'The effects of methylphenidate on the interactions of preschool ADHD children with their mothers', *Journal of the American Academy of Child and Adolescent*, 27(3), 336–341.

Barton, L., Ballard, K., and Fulcher, G. (1992) 'Disability and the necessity for a sociopolitical perspective', *Monograph #51 of The International Exchange of Experts and Information in Rehabilitation*, (pp. 1–13). New Hampshire: University of New Hampshire Press.

Beegle, G., Counts, J., Ware, L. and Gee, K. (1995) *'Evaluation report for Supported Education in Kansas (SEIK)'*, Kansas: Statewide Severe Disabilities Systems Change Project.

Benn, C. and Chitty, C. (1996) *Thirty Years On: Is Comprehensive Education Alive and Well or Struggling to Survive?* London: Fulton.

Bhabha, H. (1994) *The Location of Culture*, London: Routledge.

Biklen, D. (1985) *Achieving the Complete School: Strategies for Effective Mainstreaming* New York: Teachers College Press.

Biklen, D. (1988) 'The myth of clinical judgement', *Journal of Social Issues*, 44(1), 127–140.

Bishop, R. (1994) 'Initiating empowering research?' *New Zealand Journal of Educational Studies*, 29(1), 175–188.

Blyth, E. and Milner, J. (eds) (1996) *Exclusion from School*, London: Routledge.

Bogdan, R. and Taylor, S. (1992) 'The social construction of humanness: relationships with severely disabled children', in Ferguson, D., Ferguson, D.L. and Taylor, S. (eds) *Interpreting Disability*, New York: Teacher's College Press.

Bond, M. H. (1991) *Beyond the Chinese Face*, Hong Kong: Oxford University Press.

Booth, T. (1983) 'Integrating special education', in Booth, T. and Potts, P. (eds) *Integrating Special Education*, Oxford: Blackwell.

Booth, T. (1985) 'Labels and their consequences', in Lane, D. and Stratford, B. (eds) *Current Approaches to Down's Syndrome*, London: Harper Row.

Booth, T. (1987) Preface to Booth, T., Potts, P. and Swann, W. (eds) *Curricula for All: preventing difficulties in learning*, Oxford: Blackwell.

Booth, T. (1988) 'Challenging conceptions of integration' in Barton, L. (ed.) *The Politics of Special Educational Needs*, London: Falmer.

Booth T. (1994) 'Continua or chimera?', *British Journal of Special Education*, 21(1), 21–24.

Booth, T. (1995) 'Mapping inclusion and exclusion: concepts for all?', in Clark, C., Dyson, A. and Millward, A. (eds) *Towards Inclusive Schools?* London: David Fulton.

Booth, T. (1996a) 'A perspective on inclusion from England', *Cambridge Journal of Education*, 26(1), 87–99.

Booth, T. (1996b) 'Stories of exclusion; natural and unnatural selection', in Blyth, E. and Milner, J. (eds) *Exclusion from School*, London: Routledge.

Booth, T. (1998) 'From special education to inclusion and exclusion: can we redefine the field?', in Haug, P. and Tøssebro, J. *Theoretical Perspectives on Special Education*, Kristiansan: Norwegian Academic Press.

Booth, T. and Jones, A. (1987) 'Extending primary practice', in Booth,T., Potts, P. and Swann, W. (eds) *Curricula for All, Preventing Difficulties in Learning*, Oxford: Blackwell.

Booth, T., Potts, P. and Swann, W. (eds) (1987) *Curricula for All, Preventing Difficulties in Learning*, Oxford: Blackwell.

Brown, C. (1995) Personal communication, 14.10.95.

Brown, P. and Crompton R. (1994) *Economic Restructuring and Social Exclusion*, London: UCL Press.

Brown, S. (1994) 'Multiple policy innovations: the impact on special educational needs provision', *British Journal of Special Education*, 3(3), 97–100.

Buhrmester, D., Whalen, C. K., Henker, B. and MacDonald, V. (1992) 'Prosocial behavior in hyperactive boys: effects of stimulant medication and comparison with normal boys', *Journal of Abnormal Child Psychology*, 20(1), 103–121.

Carnoy, M. and Levin, H. M. (1985) *Schooling and Work in the Democratic State*, Stanford: Stanford University Press.

Centraal Bureau voor de Statistiek (1993) *Statistiek van het basisonderwijs, het speciaal onderwijs en het voortgezet speciaal onderwijs 1992/1993 (Statistics of primary education, special education and secondary special education)*, Heerlen: CBS.

Christensen, C. (1997) 'Competing notions of social justice and contradictions in special education reform', *The Journal of Special Education*, 31(2), 181–198.

Clark, C., Dyson, A. and Millward, A. (eds) (1995) *Towards Inclusive Schools?* London: Fulton.

Clark, C., Dyson, A., Millward, A. and Skidmore, D. (1995) 'Dialectical analysis, special needs and school organisations', in Clark, C., Dyson, A. and Millward, A. (eds) *Towards Inclusive Schools?* London: Fulton.

Clark, C., Dyson, A., Millward, A. and Skidmore, D. (1997) *New Directions in Special Needs*, London: Cassell.

Clay, M. (1991) *Becoming Literate: the construction of inner control.* Auckland: Heinemann.

Codd, J. (1993) 'Managerialism, market liberalism and the move to self-managing schools in New Zealand', in Smyth, J. (ed.) *A Socially Critical View of the Self-Managing School*, London: Falmer.

Commissie Leerlinggebonden Financiering in het Speciaal Onderwijs (1995) *Een steun in de rug. Leerlinggebonden financiering in het primair onderwijs (Financing special needs in primary education)*, Den Haag: SDU.

Cooper, M. (1989) 'The youth unemployment "crisis" of the 1980s: how two comprehensive schools have responded', *Evaluation and Research in Education*, 3(2), 81–88.

Corbett, J. (1996) *Badmouthing; The Language of Special Needs*, London: Falmer.

Corker, M. (1993) 'Integration and deaf people: the policy and power of enabling environments' in Swain, J., Finkelstein, V., French, S. and Oliver, M. (eds) *Disabling Barriers – Enabling Environments*, London: Sage Publications/Open University.

Cornett-Ruiz, S. and Hendricks, B. (1993) 'Effects of labeling and ADHD behaviors on peer and teacher judgments', *Journal of Educational Research*, 86(6), 349–355.

Cotter, R. B. (1988) 'Effects of Ritalin on reading', *Academic Therapy*, 23(5), 461–468.

Cotter, R. B. and Werner, P. H. (1987) 'Ritalin update: implications for reading teachers', *Reading Psychology*, 8(3), 179–187.

Crabtree, C. and Whitaker, J. (1995) *How Independent Are the 'Independent' Special Needs Tribunals?* Bolton: Bolton Institute of Higher Education.

Csapo, M. (1986) 'Zimbabwe: emerging problems of education and special education', *International Journal of Special Education*, 1(2), 141–160.

Csapo, M. (1987) 'Special education in Sub-Saharan Africa', *International Journal of Special Education* 2(1), 41–67.

Debenham, C., and Trotter, S. (1992) 'Welcome to Newham! Defining services to parents', in Booth, T., Swann, W., Masterton, M. and Potts, P. (eds) *Policies for Diversity in Education*, London: Routledge.

Delamont, S. (1992) *Fieldwork in Educational Settings: Methods, Pitfalls and Perspectives*, London: Falmer.

den Boer, K. (1990) 'Country briefing: special education in the Netherlands', *European Journal of Special Needs Education* 5(2), 136–150.

Department of Education and Science (1970) *The Education (Handicapped Children) Act*, London: HMSO.

Department of Education and Science (1978) *Special Educational Needs: Report of the Committee of Enquiry into the Education of Handicapped Children and Young People (The Warnock Report)*, London: HMSO.

Department of Education and Science (1981) *The Education Act*, London: HMSO.

Department for Education (1986) *The Education Act*, London: HMSO.

Department for Education (1988) *The Education Reform Act*, London: HMSO.

Department for Education (1993) *The Education Act*, London: HMSO.

Department for Education (1994) *Code of Practice on the Identification and Assessment of Children With Special Educational Needs*, London: HMSO.

Department for Education and Employment (1996a) *Statistics in Schools*, London: HMSO.

Department for Education and Employment (1996b) *The Education Act*, London: HMSO.

Department of Employment (1995) *The Disability Discrimination Act*, London: HMSO.

Disabled Persons Assembly (New Zealand) (1987) *Submission on the Amendment to the Education Act*, Wellington: DPA.

Disabled Persons Assembly (New Zealand) (1994) *Policy Documents*, Wellington: DPA.

250

Dixon, J. (1994) 'Doing ordinary things – is it possible?' In Ballard, K. (ed.) *Disability, Family, Whanau and Society* (pp. 71–92), Palmerston North: Dunmore Press.

Dunn, L. (1968) 'Special education for the mildly retarded – is much of it justifiable?', *Exceptional Children* 35(1), 5–22.

Dyson, A. and Gains, C. (eds) (1995) Special Issue on the Special Needs Co-ordinator, *Support for Learning*.

Epstein, D. (1997) 'Cultures of schooling/cultures of sexuality', *International Journal of Inclusive Education*, 1(1), 37–53.

Evans, P. (ed.) (1993) Special Issue on Integration, *European Journal of Special Needs Education*, London: Routledge.

Ferguson, D. L. (1994) 'Is communication really the point? Some thoughts on interventions and membership', *Mental Retardation*, 32(1), 7–18.

Ferguson, D. L. (1995) 'The real challenge of inclusion: confessions of a 'rabid inclusionist', *Phi Delta Kappan*, 77(4), 281–287.

Fetterman, D. M. (1994) 'Empowerment evaluation', *Evaluation Practice*, 15(1), 1–15.

Fetterman, D. M. (1996) 'Empowerment evaluation: an introduction to theory and practice', in Fetterman, D. M., Kaftarian, S. J. and Wandersman, A. (eds) *Empowerment Evaluation: Knowledge and Tools for Self-Assessment and Accountability*, (pp. 3–46), Thousand Oaks, California: Sage Publications.

Finlay, F., Boyd, M., Hallahan, M., and Kennedy, M. (1994) 'Integration: pipe dream or reality?' *Reach*, 7(2), 85–88.

Fuchs, D. (ed.) (1995) Special Section on Special Education, *Phi Delta Kappan*, 76(7).

Fulcher, G. (1989) *Disabling Policies? A Comparative Approach to Education Policy and Disability*. London: Falmer.

Fuller, B. and Clarke, P. (1994) 'Raising school effects while ignoring culture? Local conditions and the influence of classroom tools, rules and pedagogy', *Review of Education Research* 64(1), 119–157.

Gains, C. W. and McNicholas, J. A. (eds) (1979) *Remedial Education: Guidelines for the Future*, London: Longman.

Garfinkel, B. D., Brown, W. A., Klee, S. H. and Braden, W. (1986) 'Neuroendocrine and cognitive responses to amphetamine in adolescents with a history of Attention Deficit Disorder', *Journal of the American Academy of Child Psychiatry*, 25(4), 503–508.

Garfinkel, H. (1967) *Studies in Ethnomethodology*, Englewood Cliffs, New Jersey: Prentice Hall.

Gerber, M. M. (1994) 'Postmodernism in special education', *The Journal of Special Education*, 28(3), 368–378.

Gilbert, G. and Hart, M. (1990) *Towards Integration: Special needs in an ordinary school*, London: Kogan Page.

Giroux, H. (1981) *Ideology, Culture and the Process of Schooling*, London: Falmer.

Goody, C. (1992) 'Fools and heretics, parents' views of professionals', in Booth, T., Swann, W., Masterton, M. and Potts, P. (eds) *Policies for Diversity in Education*, London: Routledge.

Gray, J. (1995) 'Labour's struggle to avoid class war', the *Guardian*, 10 August, 1995.

Hart, S. (1992) 'Collaborative classrooms', in Booth, T., Swann, W., Masterton, M. and Potts, P. (eds) *Learning for All: curricula for diversity in education*, London: Routledge.

Hart, S. (1996) *Beyond Special Needs: enhancing children's learning through innovative thinking*, London: Paul Chapman.

Hegarty, S. (1993) 'Reviewing the literature on integration', *European Journal of Special Needs Education*, 8(3), 197–200.

Helgeland, I. (1992) 'Special Education in Norway', in *European Journal of Special Needs Education*, 7(2), 169–183.

Heshusius, L. (1994). 'Freeing ourselves from objectivity: managing subjectivity or turning toward a participatory consciousness?' *Educational Researcher*, 23(3), 15–22.

Houtveen, A.A.M. (1994) *Onderwijs op maat in het basisonderwijs (Adaptive instruction in primary education)*, Utrecht: ISOR.

Hutton, W. (1995) *The State We're In*, London: Jonathan Cape.

Interagency Group (1991) *Inclusive Education for All: Report of the interagency visit to Sweden, Denmark and Canada, October–November 1990*, Wellington: New Zealand Society for the Intellectually Handicapped (Inc.), New Zealand Crippled Children's Society, Royal New Zealand Foundation for the Blind, Special Education Service.

Ireland (1965) *Report of the Commission of Inquiry on Mental Handicap*, Dublin: Stationery Office.

Ireland (1971) *Report of the Primary Education Review Body*, Dublin: Stationery Office.

Ireland (1977) *Department of Education Circular to Managerial Authorities and Principal Teachers of National Schools*, 23/77, Dublin: Stationery Office.

Ireland (1990a) *Needs and Abilities: A Policy Document for the Intellectually Disabled*, Dublin: Stationery Office.

Ireland (1990b) *Report of the Primary Education Review Body*, Dublin: Stationery Office.

Ireland (1992) *Education for a Changing World*: Green Paper on Education, Dublin: Stationery Office.

Ireland (1993) *Report of the Special Education Review Committee*, Dublin: Stationery Office.

Ireland (1994a) *Census 91. Volume 1. Population classified by area*, Dublin: Central Statistics Office.

Ireland (1994b) *Department of Education: Statistical Report 1992–1993*, Dublin: Stationery Office.

Ireland (1995) *Charting our Education Future*: White Paper on Education, Dublin: Stationery Office.

Irish National Teachers' Organisation (INTO) (1993) *Accommodating Difference: an INTO policy document on the integration of children with disabilities into mainstream national schools*, Dublin: INTO.

Kavanagh, A. (1993) *Secondary Education in Ireland: Aspects of a Changing Paradigm*, Dublin: The Patrician Brothers.

Kelsey, J. (1993) *Rolling Back the State: Privatisation of Power in Aotearoa/New Zealand*. Wellington: Bridget Williams Books.

Kisanji, J. (1993) 'Special education in Africa', in Mittler, P., Brouillette, R. and Harris, D. (eds) (1993) *World Yearbook of Education: Special Needs Education*, London: Kogan Page.

Kozleski, E. B. (1995), 'Inclusionary practices and the culture of school.' Paper presented at the *Annual Meeting of the Association of Persons with Severe Handicaps (TASH)*, San Francisco, California.

Kyle, J. (1993) 'Integration of deaf students', *European Journal of Special Needs Education* 8(3), 201–220.

Ladd, P. (1991) 'Making plans for Nigel: the erosion of identity by mainstreaming' in Taylor, G. and Bishop, J. (eds) *Being Deaf: The Experience of Deafness*, Milton Keynes: The Open University.

Lane, H. (1995) 'Constructions of deafness', *Disability and Society*, 10(2), 171–189.

Levine, M. (1979) 'Some observations on the integration of handicapped children in British primary schools' in Meisels, S. J. (ed) *Special Education and Development*, Baltimore: University Park Press.

Lockheed, M. E. and Levin, H.M. (1993) 'Creating effective schools', in Levin H.M. and Lockheed, M. E. (eds) *Effective Schools in Developing Countries*, London: Falmer.

Lynas, W. (1986) *Integrating the Handicapped Into Ordinary Schools: A Study of Hearing-impaired Pupils*, London: Croom Helm.

McGee, P. (1990) 'Special education in Ireland', *European Journal of Special Needs Education*, 5, 48–64.

McIntyre, D. (1993) 'Special needs and standard provision', in Dyson, A. and Gains, C. (eds) *Rethinking Special Needs in Mainstream Schools: Towards the Year 2000*, London: David Fulton.

Mackinnon, D., Statham, J. and Hales, M. (1996) *Education in the UK: facts and figures*, London: Hodder and Stoughton.

Marks, G. (1994) 'Armed now with hope: the construction of the subjectivity of students within integration', *Disability and Society* 9(1), 71–84.

Massey, D. (1995) *Space, Place and Gender*, Oxford: Polity.

Mazurek, K. and Winzer, M. A. (eds) (1994) *Comparative Studies in Special Education*, Washington DC: Gallaudet University Press.

Meijer, C.J.W. (1994) 'The Netherlands', in Meijer, C.J.W., Pijl, S.J. and Hegarty, S. (eds) *New Perspectives in Special Education*, London: Routledge.

Meijer, C.J.W. (1995) *Halverwege, van startwet naar streefbeeld (Halfway: from the intentions to the aims of inclusion)*, De Lier: ABC.

Meijer, C.J.W., Meijnen, G.W. and Scheerens, J. (1993) *Over wegen, schatten en sturen (Estimating and regulating: the inclusion policy)*, De Lier: ABC.

Meijer, C.J.W., Pijl, S. J. and Hegarty, S. (eds) (1994) *New Perspectives in Special Education*, London: Routledge.

Miles, M. and Miles, C. (1993) 'Education and disability in cross-cultural perspective: Pakistan', in Peters, S. J. (ed.) (1993) *Education and Disability in Cross-Cultural Perspective*, New York: Garland.

Miles, R. and Thranhardt, D. (eds) (1995) *Migration and European Integration: the dynamics of inclusion and exclusion*, London: Pinter.

Milich, R., Carlson, C. L., Pelham, W. E. and Licht, B. G. (1991) 'Effects of methylphenidate on the persistence of ADHD boys following failure experiences', *Journal of Abnormal Child Psychology*, 19(5), 519–536.

Milner, H. (1994) *Social Democracy and Rational Choice; The Scandinavian Experience and Beyond*, London: Routledge.

Ministry of Education (Holland) (1985) *Wet op het Basisonderwijs (The Primary Education Act)*, Lelystad: Vermande.

Ministry of Education (New Zealand) (1989) *The Education Act*, Wellington: Ministry of Education.

Ministry of Education (1995a) *Education in New Zealand*, Wellington: Ministry of Education.

Ministry of Education (1995b) *Full attendance of special needs students: Circular 1995/07 to Chairpersons of Boards of Trustees and School Principals*, 6 April, Wellington: Ministry of Education.

Ministry of Education (1995c) *Special Education Policy Guidelines*, Wellington: Ministry of Education.

Ministry of Education (New Zealand) (1996a) *Special Education Guidelines*, Wellington: Ministry of Education.

Ministry of Education (New Zealand) (1996b) *Special Education 2000*, Wellington: Ministry of Education.

Ministry of Education, Research and Church Affairs (1987) *Curriculum Guidelines for Compulsory Education in Norway*, Oslo: Aschehoug.

Ministry of Education, Research and Church Affairs (1994) *Core Curriculum for Primary, Secondary and Adult Education in Norway*, Oslo, Aschehoug.

Ministry of Education, Research and Church Affairs (1995a) *Opplæring i et flerkulturelt Norge*, NOU 1995: 12.

Ministry of Education, Research and Church Affairs (1995b) St. meld. nr. 29 (1994–95) *Om prinsipper og retningslinjer for 10-årig grunnskole – ny læreplan*, Oslo: Aschehoug.

Mitchell, D. and Ryba, K. (1994). *Students with Education Support Needs: review of criteria for admission to special education facilities and for the allocation of discretionary resources*, Hamilton: School of Education, University of Waikato.

Mittler, P. (1979) *People Not Patients*, London: Methuen.

Mittler, P. (1993) 'Childhood disability: a global challenge', in Mittler, P., Brouillette, R. and Harris, D. (eds) *World Yearbook of Education: Special Needs Education*, London: Kogan Page.

Mittler, P. (1995) 'Special needs education: an international perspective', *British Journal of Special Education*, 22(3), 105–108.

Mittler, P., Brouillette, R. and Harris, D. (eds) (1993) *World Yearbook of Education: Special Needs Education*, London: Kogan Page.

Moen, V. and Øie, A. (1994) *Kartlegging av undervisning for barn og unge med særskilte behov i grunnskolen og i den videregående skolen*, Volda: Møreforsking, Rapport nr. 9403.

Mordal, K.N. and Strømstad, M. (1995) *'How to realize suitably adapted education in one school for all?'* Paper presented at the 4th International Special Education Congress, Birmingham.

Morris, J. (1992) 'Personal and political: a feminist perspective on researching physical disability', *Disability, Handicap and Society*, 7(2), 157–166.

Morrison, T. (1993) *The Nobel Lecture in Literature*, New York: Knopf.

National Curriculum Council (1989) *A Curriculum For All – Special Needs in the National Curriculum*, York: NCC.

National Education Association (1990) *Academic Tracking (report of the NEA Executive Committee Subcommittee on Academic Tracking)*, Washington DC: National Education Association.

New Zealand Educational Institute (1991) *Special Circular 1991/17: Report on Special Education*, Wellington: NZEI.

Niland, N.M.C. (1993) 'Integration in multi-grade schools: how teachers cope', Thesis submitted in partial fulfilment of requirements for the inservice B.Ed. degree. Dublin: St. Patrick's College.

Nilsen, S. (1993) 'Undervisningstilpasning i grunnskolen – fra intensioner til praksis', doktorgradsavhandkling, Universitetet i Oslo, Oslo: Institut for Spesialpedagogikk.

Nixon, J., Martin, J., McKeown, P. and Ranson, S. (1997) 'Confronting "failure": towards a pedagogy of recognition', *International Journal of Inclusive Education*, 1(2), 121–142.

Nordahl, T. and Overland, T. (1992a) *Individuelt læreplanarbeid*, Oslo: Ad Notan Gyldendal.

Nordahl, T. and Overland, T. (1992b) *Participation or Social Isolation? A Study of Integration and Social Participation in the Primary School*, Oslo: The Royal Ministry of Church, Education and Research.

Norwich, B. (1994) *Segregation and Inclusion: English LEA statistics 1988–92*, Bristol: Centre for Studies on Inclusive Education.

Oakes, J. (1985) *Keeping Track: How Schools Structure Inequality*, New Haven, Conn.: Yale University Press.

Oakes, J. (1990) *Multiplying Inequalities: The Effects of Race, Social Class, and Tracking on Opportunities to Learn Mathematics and Science*, Santa Monica: Rand.

Oakes, J., Gamaron, A. and Page, R. N. (1992) 'Curriculum differentiation: opportunities, outcomes, and meanings', in Jackson, P. W. (ed.) *Handbook of Research on Curriculum*, Washington DC: American Educational Research Association.

Oakes, J. and Guiton, G. (1995) 'Matchmaking: the dynamics of high school tracking decisions', *American Educational Research Journal*, 32(1), 3–33.

O'Buachalla, S. (1988) *Education Policy in Twentieth Century Ireland*, Dublin: Wolfhound Press.

O'Connell, T. (1987) 'Attitudes to integration', *Reach*, 1(2), 51–57.

Office for Standards in Education (1995) *Pupil Referral Units; The First Twelve Inspections*, London: Ofsted.

Office for Standards in Education (1996a) *Reporting on Particularly Good or Poor Teaching: The Code of Practice*, London: Ofsted.

Office for Standards in Education (1996b) *Promoting Achievement, for Pupils with Special Educational Needs in Mainstream Schools*, London: Ofsted.

O' Hanlon, C. (1993) *Special Education Integration in Europe*, London: Fulton.

O' Hanlon, C. (ed.) (1995) *Inclusive Education in Europe*, London: Fulton.

Okyere, B.A. (1994) 'Special Education in Ghana', *International Journal of Special Education* 9(1), 13–18.

Oliver, M. (1988) 'The social and political context of educational policy: the case of special needs', in Barton, L. (ed.) *The Politics of Special Educational Needs*, London: Falmer.

Oliver, M. (1990) *The Politics of Disablement*, Basingstoke: Macmillan.

Oliver, M. (1992) 'Changing the social relations of research production?' *Disability, Handicap and Society*, 7(2), 101–4.

Oliver, M. (1995) 'Does special education have a role to play in the twenty-first century?' *Reach*, 8(2), 67–76.

O'Mahony, P. (1992) 'While we await the report', *Reach*, 6(1), 5–9.

Organisation for Economic Cooperation and Development (1991) *Review of National Policies for Education: Ireland*, Paris: OECD.

Organisation for Economic Cooperation and Development (1995) *Integrating Students with Special Needs into Mainstream Schools*, Paris: OECD.

Page, R. N. (1991) *Lower Track Classrooms: A Curricular and Cultural Perspective*, New York: Teachers College Press.

Pelham, W. E., Milich, R., Cummings, E. M. and Murphy, D. A. (1991) 'Effects of background anger, provocation, and methylphenidate on emotional arousal and aggressive responding in Attention Deficit Hyperactivity Disordered boys with and without concurrent aggressiveness', *Journal of Abnormal Child Psychology*, 19(4), 407–426.

Pelham, W. E., Vodde Hamilton, M., Murphy, D. A. and Greenstein, J. (1991) 'The effects of methylphenidate on ADHD adolescents in recreational, peer group, and classroom settings. Special Issue: Child Psychopharmacology', *Journal of Clinical Child Psychology*, 20(3), 293–300.

Peters, S. J. (ed.) (1993) *Education and Disability in Cross-Cultural Perspective*, London: Garland.

Peters, S. J. (1995) 'Disabling baggage: changing the education research terrain', in Clough, P. and Barton, L. (eds) *Making Difficulties: Research and the Construction of SEN*, London: Paul Chapman.

Pijl, S. J. and Meijer, C.J.W. (1991) 'Does integration count for much? An analysis of the practices of integration in eight countries', *European Journal of Special Needs Education* 3(2), 63–73.

Pijl, S.J., Meijer, C.J.W., and Hegarty, S. (eds) (1997) *Inclusive Education: A Global Agenda*, London: Routledge.

Pijl, Y.J. and Pijl, S.J. (1995) 'Ontwikkelingen in de deelname aan het (voortgezet) spe-ciaal onderwijs (Developments in the number of students attending primary and secondary special education)', *Pedagogische Studiën* 72(2), 102–113.

Plattel, R. (1994) *De variabele groep (The part-time Special Group)*, Marum/Groningen: De Springplank/RGAB.

Polkinghorne, D. E. (1988) *Narrative Knowing and the Human Sciences*, Albany: University of New York Press.

Potts, P. (1997) 'Gender and membership of the mainstream', *International Journal of Inclusive Education*, 1(2), 175–188.

Psychological Society of Ireland (1994) *Response to the Report of the Review Committee on Special Education*, Dublin: Irish Psychological Society.

Pugach, M.C. (1995) 'On the failure of imagination in inclusive schooling', *Journal of Special Education* 22(3), 105–108.

Reezigt, G.J. (1993) *Effecten van differentiatie op de basisschool (The effectiveness of grouping procedures in primary education)*, Groningen: GION.

Reezigt, G.J. and Knuver, A.W.M. (1995) 'Zittenblijven in het basisonderwijs (Grade retention in primary education)', *Pedagogische Studiën* 72(2), 114–133.

Reid, R., Maag, J. W., Vasa, S. F. and Wright, G. (1994) 'Who are the children with Attention Deficit Hyperactivity Disorder? A school-based survey', *Journal of Special Education*, 28(2), 117–137.

Reynolds, M. C., Wang, M. C. and Walberg, H. J. (1987) 'The necessary restructuring of special and general education', *Exceptional Children*, 53, 391–398.

Rice, D. N. and Bailey, J. G. (1996) *ADHD: Medical, Psychological and Educational Perspectives*, Sydney: AASE.

Riddell, S. (1996) 'Gender and special educational needs', in Lloyd, G. (ed.), *Knitting Progress Unsatisfactory: Gender and Special Issues in Education*, Edinburgh: Moray House.

Rieser, R. and Mason, M. (eds) (1990) *Disability: Equality in the Classroom, A Human Rights Issue*, London: Inner London Education Authority.

Roach, V. (1995) 'Supporting inclusion: beyond the rhetoric', *Phi Delta Kappan*, 77(4), 295–299.

Rosenbaum, J. E. (1976) *Making Inequality: The Hidden Curriculum of High School Tracking*, New York: Wiley.

Rothbard, G. (1990) 'Going Dutch! A perspective on the Dutch system of special education', *European Journal of Special Needs Education* 5(3), 221–230.

Royal Ministry of Church, Education and Research (1987) *Curriculum Guidelines for Compulsory Education in Norway*, Oslo: Aschehoug.

Sabatino, D. A. and Vance, H. B. (1994) 'Is the diagnosis of attention deficit/hyperactivity disorders meaningful?' *Psychology in the Schools*, 31(3), 188–196.

Sarason, S. B. and Doris, J. (1982) 'Public policy and the handicapped: the case of mainstreaming', in Lieberman, A. and McLaughlin, M. (eds), *Eighty-first Yearbook of the National Society for the Study of Education*, Chicago: NSSE.

Schaffer, E.C. and Nesselrodt, P.S. (1992) 'The development and testing of the Special Strategies Observation System', Paper presented at the annual meeting of the American Educational Research Association, San Francisco.

Scheepstra, A.J.M. and Pijl, S.J. (1995) *Leerlingen met Down's syndroom in de basisschool (Pupils with Down syndrome in primary education)*, Groningen: GION.

Schnorr, Roberta F. (1990) 'Peter? He comes and goes: First Graders' Perspective on a Part-Time Mainstream Student', in *JASH* 15(4), 231–240.

Schrag, P. and Divoky, D. (1975) *The Myth of the Hyperactive Child*, New York: Pantheon Books.

Scottish Office (1995) *The Parents' Charter in Scotland*, Edinburgh: HMSO.

Sewell, T. (1997) *'Black Masculinities and Schooling'*, Stoke: Trentham Books.

Sibley, D. (1995) *Geographies of Exclusion: Society and Difference in the West*, London: Routledge.

Simon, B. (1991) *Education and the Social Order 1940–1990*, London: Lawrence and Wishart.

Simon, B. (1997) 'The Tory Bill', *Forum*, 39(1), 4–6.

Skrtic, T. (1986) 'The crisis in special education knowledge: a perspective on perspectives', *Focus on Exceptional Children*, 18(7), 1–16.

Skrtic, T. M. (1987) 'An organizational analysis of special education reform', *Counterpoint*, 8(2), 15–19.

Skrtic, T. M. (1988) 'The organizational context of special education', in Meyen, E. L. and Skrtic, T. M. (eds), *Exceptional Children and Youth: An Introduction*, Denver: Love Publishing.

Skrtic, T. (1991a) *Behind Special Education: A Critical Analysis of Professional Culture and School Organization*, Denver: Love Publishing.

Skrtic, T. (1991b) 'The special education paradox: equity as the way to excellence', *Harvard Educational Review*, 61(2), 148–206.

Skrtic, T. M. (1995) *Disability and Democracy: Reconstructing [Special] Education for Postmodernity*, New York: Teachers College Press.

Slee, R. (1995) 'Inclusive education: from policy to school implementation', in Clark, C., Dyson, A. and Millward, A. (eds) *Towards Inclusive Schools?* London: Fulton.

Slee, R. (1996). 'Inclusive schooling in Australia? Not yet', *Cambridge Journal Of Education,* 26(1), 9–32.

Solum, E. (1991) *Normalisering. Grunnlag og mål for omsorg*, Oslo: Ad Notam.

Sonntag, E. (1994) 'Women of action: caring at home for a daughter or son with an intellectual disability', in Ballard, K. (ed.), *Disability, Family, Whanau and Society*, Palmerston North: Dunmore Press.

Strauss, A. A. and Lehtinen, L. E. (1947) *Psychopathology and Education of the Brain-injured Child*, New York: Grune and Stratton.

Stubbs, S. (1995) 'The Lesotho National Integrated Education Programme: A Case Study of Implementation', M.Ed. Thesis, University of Cambridge.

Sullivan, M. (1991) 'From personal tragedy to social oppression: The medical model and social theories of disability', *New Zealand Journal of Industrial Relations*, 16, 255–272.

Swan, G. (1994) 'Australia', in Mazurek, K. and Winzer, M. W. (eds), *Comparative Studies in Special Education*, Washington: Gallaudet University Press.

Taylor, S. (1988) 'Caught in the continuum: a critical analysis of the principle of the least restrictive environment', *Journal of the Association for Persons with Severe Handicaps*, 13(1), 41–53.

Thomson, D. (1991) *Selfish Generations? The Ageing of New Zealand's Welfare State*, Wellington: Bridget Williams Books.

Thousand, J. S. and Villa, R. A. (1995) 'Inclusion: alive and well in the Green Mountain State', *Phi Delta Kappan*, 77(4), 288–291.

Times Education Supplement, April 12th 1996, 'Sackings stay on Labour's agenda.'

Tomlinson, S. (1993) 'The multi-cultural task group: the group that never was', in King, A. and Reiss, M. (eds) *The Multicultural Dimension of the National Curriculum*, London: Falmer.

Udvari-Solner, A. and Thousand, J. (1995) 'Effective organisation, instructional and curricular practices in inclusive schools and classrooms', in Clark, C., Dyson, A. and Millward, A. (eds) *Towards Inclusive Schools*, London: Fulton.

UNESCO (1995) *Review of the Present Situation in Special Needs Education*, Paris: UNESCO.

United States Department of Education (1990) 'To Assure the Free Appropriate Public Education of All Children with Disabilities', *Twelfth Annual Report to Congress on the Implementation of the Individuals with Disabilities Education Act*, Washington: US Government Printing Office.

United States Department of Education (1995) 'To Assure the Free Appropriate Public Education of All Children with Disabilities', *Seventeenth Annual Report to Congress on the Implementation of the Individuals with Disabilities Education Act*, Washington: US Government Printing Office.

Van der Werf, M.P.C., Nitert, E.H.M., and Reezigt, G.J. (1994) *Effectieve en minder effectieve basisscholen voor allochtone leerlingen (Effective and less effective primary schools for ethnic minority pupils)*, Groningen: GION.

Van Rijswijk, C.M. and Kool, E. (1995) *Overgangsvormen tussen regulier en speciaal onderwijs (Transitional provisions between regular and special education)*, De Lier: ABC.

Veenman, S.A.M., Lem, P., Voeten, M., Winkelmolen, G. and Lassche, H. (1986) *Onderwijs in combinatieklassen (Instruction in mixed-age classrooms)*, Den Haag: SVO.

Vislie, L. (1995) 'Integration policies, school reforms and the organisation of schooling for handicapped pupils in western societies', in Clark, C., Dyson, A. and Millward, A. (eds) *Towards Inclusive Schools?* London: Fulton.

Wade, B. and Moore, M. (1992) *Patterns of Educational Integration; international perspectives on mainstreaming children with special educational needs*, Wallingford: Triangle Books.

Ward, J. (1993) 'Special education in Australia and New Zealand', in Mittler, P., Brouillette, R. and Harris, D. (eds) *World Yearbook of Education: Special Needs Education*, London: Kogan Page.

Ware, L. (1994a) 'Innovative instructional practices: a naturalistic study of the structural and cultural conditions of change' (unpublished doctoral dissertation), Lawrence: University of Kansas.

Ware, L. (1994b) 'Intentions, purposes, and emotions among teachers in the process of change', Paper presented at the Annual Meeting of American Evaluation Association, New Orleans: Louisiana.

Ware, L. (1994c) 'Opening windows of opportunity: the challenge of implementing change', in Thornton, C. and Bley, N. (eds) *Windows of Opportunity: Mathematics for Children with Special Needs*, Reston, Virginia: National Council of Teachers of Mathematics.

Ware, L. (1995a) 'The aftermath of the articulate debate: the invention of inclusive education', in Clark, C., Dyson, A. and Millward, A. (eds) *Towards Inclusive Schools?* London: Fulton.

Ware, L. (1995b) 'Preliminary findings on inclusion in Longview', *Evaluation Report for Supported Education in Kansas (SEIK): Statewide Severe Disabilities Systems Change Project*, Lawrence: Kansas.

Ware, L. (1995c) 'Reconstructing welfare policy: voice and empowerment in evaluation research', Paper presented at Evaluation '95, Vancouver: British Columbia.

Ware, L. and Gee, K. (1995) 'Listening to teenagers: what they're saying about what's happening in their schools', Paper presented at the Annual Meeting of the Association for Severe Handicaps (TASH), San Francisco, California.

Warren, S. (1997) 'Who do they think they are? An investigation into the construction of masculinities in a primary classroom', *International Journal of Inclusive Education*, 1(2), 207–232.

Wearmouth, J. (1996) 'Registering special needs; for what purpose?' *Support for Learning*, 11(2), 118–122.

Weatherley, R. and Lipsky, M. (1977) 'Street level bureaucrats and institutional innovation: implementing special education reform', *Harvard Educational Review*, 47(2), 171–197.

Whalen, C. K., Henker, B., Buhrmester, D. and Hinshaw, S. P. (1989) 'Does stimulant medication improve the peer status of hyperactive children?' *Journal of Consulting and Clinical Psychology*, 57(4), 545–549.

Wiesinger, R. (1986) 'Disabled persons in the Third world: changing situation and changing perspectives for the future', *International Journal of Special Education* 1(1), 21–34.

Wilczenski, F. L. (1992) 'Measuring attitudes toward inclusive education', *Psychology in the Schools*, 29(4), 306–312.

Will, M. (1986) 'Educating children with learning problems: a shared responsibility', *Exceptional Children*, 53(5), 411–416.

Williams, P. (1993) 'Integration of students with moderate learning difficulties', *European Journal of Special Needs Education* 8(3), 136–150.

Wilson, B. J. and Schmits, D. W. (1978) 'What's new in ability grouping?', *Phi Delta Kappan*, 59, 535–536.

de Wit-Gosker, T. (1995) *'Can I get compasses now?'* Enschede: Association for Integration of People with Down's Syndrome.

Zigmond, N., Jenkins, J., Fuchs, L., Deno, S., Fuchs, D., Baker, J., Jenkins, L. and Coutino, M. (1995) 'Special education in restructured schools: findings from three multi-year studies', *Phi Delta Kappan*, 76(7), 531–540.

NAME INDEX

SUBJECT INDEX

ability *see* attainment
abnormality *see* normality
acceptance: of behaviour 181, 188, 201;
   of disability 181; of diversity 78, 93–4,
   98, 109, 120, 142, 188–9, 238–40, 243;
   of learning difficulties 181; peer
   172–3, 175, 179; social 59–63
activities of daily living programme
   110
adaptive education 19, 101–19, 121, 125,
   138, 143, 147, 239; attitudes to
   108–10; *see also* individual education
   plans *and* special educational needs
age groupings *see* segregation
Americans with Disabilities Act 21
appraisal, self 180
aspiration, school 204
assimilationist model 65, 67
attainment: discrimination 99, 218, 240,
   242; and exclusion 2, 186, 194; and
   gender 231; grouping by 44, 198,
   209–10, 213–14, 228, 236, 241; low 2,
   5, 230, 237; mixed teaching 197, 203;
   pressures 193; *see also* learning
   difficulties *and* selection, academic
attendance, pupil 198, 206, 208, 218
Attention Deficit Hyperactivity
   Disorder (ADHD) 19, 110, 121,
   171–85; coping with 183; definition of
   189, 190, 242; diagnosis of 176–7, 190;
   gender bias 183; and inclusion 181–4;
   medication for 172–3, 175, 180, 183,
   190–92; *see also* medical model
Australia 8, 19, 171–85, 186–92, 226, 238
Austria 7
autonomy, of schools *see* power

behaviour: acceptance of 181, 188, 201;
   consequences of 214; deviation 2, 4;

difficulties 3, 27, 104, 115–16, 131,
   140, 208, 214–15, 242; discrimination
   242; policy 208, 214–15, 224, 231;
   reasons for 234; and segregation 201,
   210; support 223
Belgium 144
belonging: rights *see* rights; sense of 116;
   see also social acceptance
brain: damage 27, 171, 172, 189;
   dysfunction 171, 172, 189
buddy system *see* support, peer
bullying 215

case-studies 11, 17; Australia 176–82;
   critical commentary 16–18, 20, 43–9,
   63–7, 95–100, 118–22, 143–8, 165–70,
   186–92, 194, 226–31, 243;
   development 12; editing 12–13;
   England 193–225; feedback 12;
   interviews 9, 129; Ireland 152–62;
   language accessibility 12;
   methodology 28–9, 71–2, 108–10,
   128–30, 147–8, 175–6, 195–6;
   Netherlands 123–42; New Zealand
   75–80, 84–7; Norway 101–17;
   presentation 12, 242, 243; reporting
   29–40; revision 12–13; Scotland
   52–60; staff input 11; structure 12;
   theatre arts 29–40, 43; USA 29–40; *see
   also* comparative research
catchment areas: and community 196,
   206; and special needs 206
categorisation 4, 9, 19, 48, 97, 100, 104,
   147, 166, 171, 186, 188–9, 193, 200,
   207, 209–12, 228–30, 238, 239, 242–3,
   245; defining 242; and support
   funding 54, 64, 96, 123, 126, 130, 160,
   162, 168, 172; *see also* labelling *and*
   segregation

264